DAIM ZAINUDDIN
MALAYSIA'S REVOLUTIONARY AND TROUBLESHOOTER

T0158245

DAIM ZAINUDDIN

MALAYSIA'S REVOLUTIONARY
AND TROUBLESHOOTER

Michael Backman

First published in Thailand in 2018 by
River Books Co., Ltd
396 Maharaj Road, Tatien,
Bangkok 10200 Thailand
Tel. (66) 2 225-4963, 2 225-0139, 2 622-1900
Fax: (66) 2 225-3861
Email: order@riverbooksbk.com
www.riverbooksbk.com

Editor Narisa Chakrabongse
Production Paisarn Piemmettawat
Design Ruetairat Nanta

ISBN 978 616 7339 95 5

Printed and bound in Thailand by Bangkok Printing Co., Ltd.

CONTENTS

PROLOGUE

I first started to write this book around 2000. Daim fascinated me. He was a well-known politician. He was rich. He was Malay. And so therefore he must be corrupt, or so went conventional wisdom – particularly in Malaysia where rumours and gossip have always had wider currency than research and fact. I knew that Daim had been one of Malaysia's most highly accomplished technocratic ministers ever. Twice, he had pulled Malaysia from the brink of economic disaster – once in 1985-86 and again in 1998. Such real achievement doesn't normally go hand-in-hand with the sort of maleficence that Daim seemed to be accused of. The other thing I knew about Daim was that he was already a very wealthy man before he went into politics. So his was not the usual Southeast Asian trajectory whereby a man goes into politics to *get* rich. Instead, it seemed to me he went into politics because he *was* rich and that he might have some know-how to offer.

Conventional wisdom and the facts seemed far apart when it came to Daim, so herein lay a good reason to write this book I thought. It seemed to me that the innuendo surrounding Daim's business accomplishments were linked to his ethnicity. It was as if the only way a Malay could get rich was if he was corrupt. I wondered if the attacks on Daim were a form of racism by and large? Sadly many of the attacks came from other Malays. So perhaps many Malays believed that the only way for a Malay to get rich was through improper means.

I commenced the book, and Daim even consented to a series of interviews, but then I became involved in other projects, I moved to London, and then Daim himself left parliament in 2004. I decided to put the manuscript away, to be worked on 'later'.

'Later' took some time to arrive. For a number of years, the manuscript slipped my mind. But then one day the lawyers for a newspaper in which a column of mine had been published contacted me. The column was about Malaysia and contained a brief mention of Daim. They said that Daim's wife had been in touch and that she wanted to sue the author for what had been said. It was ironic – I didn't consider the remark defamatory, and furthermore, I was sitting on a manuscript that I felt gave a refreshingly accurate view of Daim and his accomplishments. Daim's wife and I ended up meeting at my office in London, and my interest in the manuscript was rekindled. I asked if Daim would consent to being interviewed again. It turned out that he would – so I was able to add to, and update, the manuscript. It seemed timely to, because by 2014-2016, the issue of corruption and economic management in Malaysia had again come to the fore. So this is how this book evolved. It is a celebration of not a perfect Malay, but a successful Malay. Because now, more than ever, young Malays need a role model, and it is time that all the lazy innuendo, all the rehashing of hearsay dressed up as journalism, is stripped away to reveal the true nature one of the Malay world's most important figures of the second half of the twentieth century.

Michael Backman
London, 2018

I

MALAYSIA'S IBN BATTUTA

There was a time when Malays were known across much of the world as confident, successful traders and seafarers. Malay was an important common language or *lingua franca* from the coastal regions of southern Africa to parts of southern China and of course right across Southeast Asia. Sultans on the Malay Peninsula, and their ministers, signed trade agreements with their counterparts in India and elsewhere. The Malays were entrepreneurial and outward looking. How could they not be? The Hajj – one of the five pillars of Islam – required the Malays, as with all Muslims, to be travelers: they were required to visit Mecca at least once. And with Hajj routes came knowledge, curiosity and commerce. So how is it then that today, the Malays seem more inward looking, more pre-occupied with ticking boxes than pushing boundaries, more interested in arguing amongst themselves over imported differences over religious doctrine, and more content with fighting over the pieces of the economic pie than expanding that pie, unlike their sixteenth-century counterparts?

Why should Malaysia be beset by corruption scandals today and be so seemingly self-absorbed in arguments that seem to go around and around, while the rest of the world develops, progresses and achieves? Why so much bitterness and suspicion from a people once so famous for their collegiate ways and hospitality? Why must it be assumed, even among Malays themselves, that any wealthy Malay must have become that way through improper means; that only rarely is credit paid when it is due; and that the political system now seems more about tearing down past luminaries in order to make today's ones appear brighter? The Malays today seem a race adrift and in need of some heroes. They are in need of leadership – leadership that inspires and unites, rather than leadership that defines itself by who can be made to submit to it and what it can take. When an emperor has no clothes, it is not clothes that a country needs but a new emperor. And when it comes to defining the job description for a new emperor it is important to look back to see what worked and what didn't. Former prime minister Mahathir Mohamad and his ablest finance minister Daim Zainuddin were among the most extraordinary leaders the Malays have had. They were not perfect, not by any stretch, but what is undeniable is that the welfare and the future of the Malays was always at the heart of their policy making. It is Daim who is the focus of this book.

Why write this book? The reason is simple. Tun Daim Zainuddin steered Malaysia out of two economic disasters that threatened to devastate the Malaysian economy. These could have had dire social and political consequences given

Malaysia's racial mix. And yet he is a greatly misunderstood politician. He has probably been Malaysia's single greatest policy strategist. But his reward has been to attract an extraordinary level of innuendo. He has been, if much of what circulates anonymously on the Internet is to be believed, one of Malaysia's most corrupt politicians. His wealth is the only evidence that is proffered for this, as if the only way a Malay could be so successful is through corruption and by abusing his position. The truth is that unlike many politicians in Malaysia, Daim was wealthy long before he went into politics. But the innuendo is not surprising surmises Daim, when, despite Malaysia's many professional and incorruptible civil servants, the only Malays that many non-Malays ever have to deal with face-to-face – Malay police and Malay local council administrators who are responsible for small approvals – all too often are corrupt, giving the erroneous impression that all Malays are corrupt.

Perceptions of Daim as an abuser of power and the like are so entrenched that among many his malfeasance has become conventional wisdom, not requiring substantiation, despite his achievements and his personal integrity. How has this happened?

I have come to know Daim over some years after having spent many hours with him in Malaysia and in London, some of which has included travelling with him. He is well read, well travelled, and highly intelligent. Apart from his slight physical stature, the first thing one notices when meeting him in person are his intense, dark eyes. They are the eyes of a thinker.

His is curious and outward looking. He despairs that young Malays seem to be retreating from their seafaring, trading traditions and are becoming more insular when the world about them grows more global and intertwined. 'The first word of God was *Iqra* – Read, ' he told Malay business students at a speech to a university. 'Read also for pleasure, widen your horizon, do not be a person who is encyclopaedic about his business and who knows nothing about the world around him. Nurture an intellectual curiosity about everything around you.'[1]

I am sympathetic to Daim. He is certainly worthy of considerable respect for all his achievements and his obvious intelligence. But do not expect a hagiography. I do not agree with all that Daim has done. I do not agree with some of his approaches. And I certainly do not agree with his opinions on some matters. But Daim presents an attractive subject matter for a book – the gap between the public's understanding of him and the reality is just so immense. This means there is a job to be done for a writer keen on righting wrongs.

The paradox of Daim was best summed up by *Finance Asia* magazine, when it said of him that he 'is at one and the same time one of the most gifted financiers to emerge this century, and a deeply troubling individual for many Malaysians'.[2] Daim knows that he is controversial, but he is unrepentant. He is largely

---

1   Daim, Z., 'Managing business: My personal experience', speech to business students at Universiti Utara Malaysia (UUM), published in March 1995.

2   'Financiers of the century: Daim Zainuddin', *Finance Asia*, December 1999/January 2000.

indifferent to it and occasionally at times seems to have reveled in it. Only in later life perhaps has he come to wish that his actions might have been better explained at the time; that there had been greater transparency, if only to avoid some of the mistruths about him that have become conventional wisdom.

When he was at the height of his political power, almost every Malaysian had an opinion about him. But whether positive or negative, they almost invariably were strongly held. The paradox of this is that the man himself not so much shuns publicity (some Malaysians referred to him as 'Mr Diam' – *diam* means 'quiet' in Malay) as has a cavalier indifference to it. Also, tact is not one of Daim's defining characteristics. And only rarely does he bother to defend himself or explain his actions when criticised. By and large, he seems to adopt a 'couldn't care less' attitude to his detractors, which has tended to infuriate them even more. Others have taken his silence as confirmation that this or that rumour or allegation must be true.

There is one thing on which most informed Malaysians do agree, however. Daim was instrumental in pulling Malaysia out of the 1985-86 recession during his term as finance minister from 1984 to 1991. His success was such that in 1998, when Malaysia faced an even bigger crisis as it was swept up in the Asian financial crisis, he was once again drafted into the finance portfolio. In response to both crises, Daim's panaceas attracted a great deal of criticism. During his first tenure as finance minister, Daim made many dramatic and sometimes unpopular reforms. By and large, though, he did what was needed, even if it sometimes meant flying in the face of the sensitivities of his political colleagues. Government cost cutting and the removal of privileges from some quarters caused much disquiet, particularly within the main ruling party, the United Malays National Organisation (UMNO), but at the end of the process the Malaysian economy emerged restructured and back on its growth trajectory. And during his second stint as finance minister, he oversaw the introduction of currency and capital controls, a move that was greeted with controversy around the world. Daim is self-effacing about his role in both crises. He told me in mid-2000 that his main responsibility had been 'to tighten a few screws' and then to let the economy take care of itself. Of course, his role was much greater than that. The truth is that he threw the economic rule book out the window. And he and Malaysia have seemed to have gotten away with it.

Daim is well known as a politician. But the term cheapens his contribution. Politicians the world over do not enjoy a good reputation. In reality, in public life Daim was a policy strategist, and given the context – what he had to work with in Malaysia, both parliamentary colleagues and an electorate well versed on patronage politics but not so on economics – he was brilliant. He was able to steer a largely economic illiterate cabinet into taking or at least agreeing to the correct economic policy prescriptions at critical junctures in Malaysia's development.

His reappointment as finance minister in 1998 during the Asian economic crisis has impressive parallels. 'One is reminded of a similar "call-back for duty" in the aftermath of the 1969 racial strife when Tun Dr Ismail offered to come back from retirement to help put the nation back to stability as Minister for Home Affairs,' according to two Malay observers.[3] Tun Dr Ismail was seen as someone who stood for the rule of law above any particular race and the respect he commanded from all quarters helped to calm Malaysia in the wake of the rioting.

Daim has a similar respect for the rule of law. One position that he has not held but which he dearly would love to have had was Attorney General – so, he says, he could commence corruption proceedings against many in public life whom he feels should have been charged. For many Malaysians fed on a rich diet of gossip and innuendo but starved of substantiation, this will come as a surprise.

Why has Daim attracted such innuendo? Why do rumours persist of corruption on a grand scale when even evidence of *any* corruption has never been forthcoming? Daim admits that the fault is partly his. 'I never bothered to refute these sorts of stories', he told me. 'I didn't bother because I never thought anyone would believe them'. It was, he can see now, a mistake.

Daim is rich. And there is a presumption that a Malay must only have become rich through improper means. It is a galling paradox particularly for Daim's family. (Daim has been married three times, and has had children with each wife.) No-one questions the wealth of Malaysians who happen to be ethnically Chinese. But if you are Malay then that is a different matter. The most important consideration in this regard is that Daim was already very wealthy when he went into politics. He had made his fortune in property. Early on, he had taken on a local Chinese partner but not so that he could pass any concessions and land grants immediately over to the partner. He and his partner were equals and as Daim said to me in London in 2015, 'I needed to learn everything about business that I could – and I learned it from him. He was very important to me.' One figure is that by the time Daim went into Parliament, he was already worth around $250 million. Agreeing on the value of real estate that has not been sold is always difficult and so determining the wealth of most people with many assets is difficult but Daim does not take issue with the order of magnitude of the sum. Clearly Daim did not enter politics to become wealthy. He already was.

Daim is typically labelled enigmatic. It is an appropriate description. In public particularly, he is a man of few words and is not comfortable boasting of his feats. To a degree, this is a problem shared by the rest of the Malaysian government. Under Dr Mahathir it had been in a hurry to achieve, but along the way it found insufficient time to fully explain what it was doing and why. 'We are so busy governing that we don't leave enough time for explaining the polices', Dato' Jamaludin Jarjis, the Parliamentary member for Rompin and head of the Back Benchers' Club, said to me in December 2000. I put the proposition that Malaysia has had a habit of under-selling itself to Kuala Lumpur Stock Exchange (KLSE) chairman Mohammed Azlan Hashim. He agreed. 'Yes! This is our biggest weakness. We need to explain our actions more fully and carefully,' he said.

---

3   Noor, I., & M. Azaham, *The Malays Par Excellence…Warts and All*, Pelanduk, 2000.

Having government ministers who are conversant in business is a plus for any government in any country. A cabinet drawn only on former civil servants, academics or career politicians is dangerous for sound economic policy. It is also the case that being a smaller, developing country, Malaysia, like other such countries has had a talent shortage. It means that capable and talented people inevitably must have several roles, leading to potential conflicts of interest. Typically, the conflicts are very real. The problem has been more acute for Malaysia where public administration largely has been in the hands of the Malays, meaning that the talent pool that can be drawn upon is even smaller.

For the gossips and the shallow thinkers, Daim's involvement in business has been proof alone of wrongdoing. But for those who have themselves had to deal with policy making at the national level, a first-hand knowledge of business is an enormous attribute in a finance minister. Singapore's founding prime minister Lee Kuan Yew described Daim in his semi-autobiography *From Third World to First: Singapore and the Asian Economic Boom*, as having 'a quick mind, is good at figures and decisive, and has been successful in business before he became finance minister.'[4] For Lee, Daim initiated economic policies that drove Malaysia forwards. He was also 'a shrew deal maker who honoured his agreements.' These attributes were a function of his business experience.

Tunku Razaleigh Hamzah, Daim's predecessor as finance minister, had a similar view of the usefulness of Daim's business past. In 1998, in a note sent to Daim for his sixtieth birthday Razaleigh said 'his successful foray into the business world prepared him for a political career that gave him star status to a supporting role [to that of prime minister Mahathir].' It was a view that Razaleigh repeated when I later visited him at his Kuala Lumpur home. He made it clear that he and Daim had often disagreed on policy and process but that Daim's business experience had been a tremendous asset when it came to his later role as finance minister.

But perhaps the most forceful advocate of this view was Shaukat Aziz, who served as Pakistan's prime minister from 2004 to 2007, and the finance minister from 1999 to 2007. Aziz had formerly been a senior executive with Citibank for many years, and so had the unique perspective of having dealt with finance ministers who did not have hands-on business experience as well as having been in business himself. He told me in London in 2015 that 'Daim had his pulse on the real economy. Many ministers sit in their offices and implement IMF reforms and so on but they are not close to the real economy. They are not close to real businesses in the way that Daim was. You can have finance ministers who are excellent theoretical economists in a World Bank sense but they simply do not understand the real economy; how real business people think and what problems they face...Daim was very good on business, very good on understanding the economy, and very good at understanding the macro environment. It is very unusual to have all three.'

---

4   Lee, K.Y., *From Third World to First: Singapore and the Asian Economic Boom*, Harper Collins, 2011, p. 249.

When I first arrived in Malaysia to start work on my research for this book back in 2000, a friend of mine told me with much certainty that, right in the middle of the economic crisis that had just passed, Daim had boarded a flight out of Malaysia with six bags of cash. He had bought two first class seats – one for himself and one for the bags of cash. How did she know this? A friend had 'told her'. I was about to relay the story to Daim to gauge his reaction during one of our meetings later that year, but I didn't have to. Instead, he told me his version! *The Times* of London, he said, had reported that he had left Malaysia aboard his own jet with the six bags of cash. 'Can you believe that! *The Times* said that! *The Times* actually said that!' He was more incredulous than hurt. But what can you expect from a Murdoch newspaper? he added. Clearly, the story was ridiculous. 'Why didn't you just do a telegraphic transfer like everyone else?' I jokingly asked Daim. He simply shook his head with an air of resignation.

At a conference that I attended in Jakarta in 2000, I chatted with two of Daim's own parliamentary colleagues who were visiting – both of whom were members of the ruling coalition. I mentioned that I was considering writing a book on Daim. One of them immediately relayed to me a story that involved Daim's alleged misdeeds in awarding government contracts. The story was rather extravagant and fanciful, even by Malaysian standards, so I asked him whether he was aware of any evidence that would support the story. He wasn't. Then why tell the story, I asked, particularly if it concerns one of one's colleagues? If this is what some of Daim's own colleagues are prepared to believe I thought to myself, then the claims from the opposition must be even more extravagant. And indeed, they were.

An essay entitled 'Who is the real Daim?', which appeared on a *Reformasi* website, 'Justice for Anwar', in 1998, suggested that Daim's wealth was once as high as M$65 billion, although was now significantly lower. It went on to say that Daim had demanded big 'fees' when negotiating contracts with two Japanese banks. Additionally, it alleged that during the economic crisis, Mahathir had asked Daim for help in propping up the ringgit and Daim had lost '$1 billion' trying to do just that. The *Reformasi* website became home to many absurd and extreme claims, and this was one of them.

When I read to Daim some of this website's more extravagant claims and asked him to comment, his reaction was genuine laughter, albeit tinged with some disappointment that the site had alleged that his wealth was now down to a third of what it claimed it once was. 'I can't be a very good businessman if I'm down to just a third,' he quipped. He had met the chairman of only one of the two Japanese banks mentioned, and the chairman had later sent him a collection of press clippings and certainly 'no money', he laughed. After examining the document, Daim recognised it as having started out as one of the many poison pen letters (*surat terbang*) that circulate among Malaysians, although it had since been added to and embellished.

Where did the public relations go wrong? Daim believes now that his acquisition of United Malayan Banking Corporation (UMBC) in 1984 was the point when the problems started. Already a successful businessman, he had long been interested in banking and desired a banking license. Licenses were rarely handed out and so the only way to obtain one was to acquire an existing bank. An opportunity arose. As will be discussed in a later chapter, the owners of UMBC needed to sell and Daim saw his chance. He applied to acquire the bank but the regulatory approvals process took almost one-and-a-half years. By the time he was appointed finance minister in July 1984, the approvals process for his family to acquire the bank still had not been completed. But in his first week as minister, the file relating to the approval finally reached the finance minister's office from the Treasury. Daim was appalled. The final stage of the process required the finance minister to sign off on the sale, which meant that Daim was in the awkward position of having to sign off on his own acquisition of a bank. Daim sent the file back to the Treasury pointing out that he could not possibly deal with it since it related to his own private businesses. Instead, the approval was referred to the cabinet (without Daim) which approved the sale.

In 1986, the Cabinet decided that ministers should sell their shares to avoid conflict-of-interest accusations, Daim duly complied. Mahathir particularly was keen that UMBC should stay in Bumiputera (Malay) hands, as was UMNO, and so it was decided that Pernas, a government agency, should buy the stake.

But with hindsight, Daim now feels that how the UMBC transactions were handled was an enormous tactical error: the process behind it was inadequately explained. It looked as if one of Daim's first acts as finance minister was to help himself to a bank, and later, to sell it to a government agency. And certainly, in later years that is how his political enemies sought to portray it. The process had, in fact, been transparent, but not to outsiders. And as a consequence, Daim was portrayed as having abused his power. It is at that point, Daim feels, that the rot set in. 'Why didn't you fully counteract the rumours?' I asked him several years later London. 'Because it never occurred to me that anyone would believe them,' he said. He was wrong. It was made worse because much of the criticism came from within UMNO particularly during the party's internal strife in 1987. This was particularly galling for Daim because it was UMNO that wanted the bank to stay in Malay hands and he was asked to buy it for that reason.

Daim was also a great believer in affirmative action for the Malays. For the sake of national peace and thus prosperity, Daim believed it was essential to break the nexus between business success and Chineseness; that if someone was successful and prosperous it should no longer be assumed automatically that that individual must be Chinese.

Malays were assumed to be uninterested in business, lazy even. The truth is they had, over the decades, been frozen out. The private sector had become dominated by the Chinese who not unreasonably preferred to hire other Chinese, and to starve off the competition. Winstedt (1947, p, 137-138) perfectly encapsulates the problem:

'The prime difficulty of the Malay today is how to acquire capital to apply to industry. A government scholarship can qualify him to be a civil servant, doctor, lawyer. If he wants to enter commerce, he finds that Chinese and Indians reserve employment for their own races. .....A Kelantan Malay tried to start a firm for the purchase of rice from his own countrymen, whereupon the Chinese hauliers raised the hire of lorries for this interloper so that he could not compete with Chinese buyers. A Malay cooperative society attempted to sell copra direct to Singapore, but as the only carriers were a Chinese shipping line, the first cargo was left on the jetty and the next arrived short in weight, wily sailors having pushed part of it overboard.'

These are not the observations of a Malay, but an Englishman – a *mat salleh* – writing in the 1940s. The problem was so entrenched that by the 1970s, little had changed.

The presumed disinterest in business of the Malays had become a self-fulfilling prophecy. Any business acumen that the Malays might have had was lost, not having had the opportunities to learn business by doing business. Daim has observed that by the 1970s, far too often when a Malay was allocated some land or some permit, rarely did he (for it was almost always a he) develop it and build on it, but instead would sell it on as soon as possible for a quick profit, usually to a local Chinese or an Indian, thereby defeating the intention of the allocation.

Herein lays the rationale for Daim's interest in affirmative action policies. But not the sort of passive affirmative action of share allocations to Malay cooperatives that had been tried and shown to be ineffectual. Instead, Daim, as finance minister, pioneered a much more direct approach whereby promising young Malays were entrusted with real businesses so that a critical mass of Malay business people would quickly develop and foster others. Daim had succeeded in business (and done so long before he entered politics). But he was one of the very few Malays to have done so. Daim's approach of catapulting handpicked young Malays into the upper echelons of business met with some success, some failure, and a lot of controversy. But it changed Malaysia forever.

I asked Daim on a recent visit of his to London, when looking back on his life and all the things he has done, during what period does he remember feeling happiest? He smiled as he allowed his mind's eye to drift back decades. In 1957, he was sailing to London from Malaya to undertake law studies. The trip went via South Africa because of the Suez Crisis. He spent his time wandering around Cape Town. The Apartheid system was oppressive and offensive, but the people, the foods, the natural scenery – all caught Daim's interest. He was intellectually engaged and he developed a life-long fascination for the African continent.

Daim is well-known in Malaysia for his business acumen with almost all the attention focussed on his activities in Malaysia. But what is little appreciated are the successful businesses he has built outside Malaysia. The important word here is 'built'. He has not bought say, a pre-existing hotel in London like so many other Malaysian and Singaporean investors because owning property requires little management acumen. Instead, he established an international banking group, with banks in some of the world's toughest economic terrains. In many instances, he created new banks that previously had not existed, in economies that scarcely had functioning banking systems.

And for the cynical who will say, well, of course Daim accumulated these interests and does business in the developing world because he can pay officials off to get what he wants, Daim is absolutely adamant: he has never paid a bribe for a banking license. He recounts a story when a certain central bank governor asked for money for the final approval for a licence that he was to be given, and Daim contacted the President's office to complain. The central bank governor soon was sacked. But elsewhere, when the demands proved too intractable, he withdrew, preferring to do business elsewhere. 'Once they know you pay', he says, 'the demands will never stop'.

His ICB Banking Group grew to encompass banks in Albania, Djibouti, Malawi, Mozambique, Hungary, the Czeck Republic, Bosnia, Senegal, Tanzania, Zambia, Ghana, Guinea, Bangladesh, Indonesia, and Laos. 'Why these countries?' I asked Daim, and 'why Africa particularly?' 'Because of the time I spent there when I was on my way London to study. I was in South Africa first, but later on I travelled to the other parts. I always wanted to do something there.'

So often in our formative years, our attention is caught by something new, and it is interesting how often these things stay with us. Daim is no different. To many, Daim is the epitome of *homo economicus*: a rational, calculating business-minded operator who ruthlessly seeks out the next profit. He is a good businessman but the reality is that he is also a romantic. 'Do you like to spend time in Africa and do business there because it reminds you of the Malaysia that you knew when you were growing up?' I asked. He thinks a little, smiles, and answers 'Maybe.' But one also gets a sense that he likes business because he likes the game. He enjoys strategizing. And for Daim, that is the link between politics and business. Both, when well played, are like chess games in which your intellectual ability is pitted against that of your opponents. Daim is cool-headed and not reactive. He likes to plot and plan. At school, his grades were not brilliant. Perhaps he has spent his adult life proving to himself, as much as to everyone else, that he is clever after all. And there is a lot of joy in that. Each dollar that you earn, each business that you acquire, is a slap in the face for those in the past who thought you couldn't do it.

In some respects, Daim is like the Malays of old – self-confident but not arrogant, curious, outward looking and good at business. The Malays were well-connected to the *Ummah*, the international community of Muslims not just through shared religious beliefs but because of trade. The Malays were traders, like many Muslims. As mentioned, the requirement to do the Hajj meant that ordinary Muslims worldwide were natural travellers – more so than almost any other group in the world. For them, it was an obligation. And with travel comes knowledge and the opportunity to spot business opportunities across borders.

Trade was a traditional preserve of the Malays. The Malay sultans, rather than being impractical and interested only in pageantry and show, were deeply enmeshed in trade and commerce. '…A chief led his people in commerce as well as in the judicial court and on the battlefield…' according to Winstedt (1947, p. 132). And so the Kedah sultans in the mid-seventeenth century sold copious tin and elephants to Bengal and Coromandel for example. The sultanate in Malacca had become so central to trade that the Portuguese felt obliged to capture it. The traveller Tome Pires who visited Malacca in the early fifteenth century, famously wrote that, 'Whoever is lord of Malacca has his hand on the throat of Venice.' It seems inconceivable today that a tiny Malay kingdom could have had such an impact on Europe. And yet it did, and it was not alone.

It was a golden age for the Malay sultanates. Brunei, Johor, Aru and Patani were among the other successful trade-oriented Malay sultanates. And then there were the other pro-trade, Malay-like sultanates such as Makassar, Bone and Aceh.

These were illustrious courts, well-known entrepots, with literary writings and scholarship; musical performances; lavish textiles, woven with gold; and so on. But the sultanates drew their power from wealth and that wealth was drawn from trade. The prestige, the flourishing of culture and their prosperity was all underwritten by trade and business. The Malays were confident and worldly. They demanded respect from the wider world and they earned it. So where did it all go wrong?

Ibn Battuta, the fourteenth century Moroccan Berber, travelled to Mecca and most of the known Islamic world and beyond, including North and West Africa, Eastern Europe, the Middle East, South Asia, Central Asia, China and even Sumatra and Malacca over a period of thirty years. He dictated on his return to Morocco an account of his extraordinary journeys and the many rulers he met.

In 1345, Ibn Battuta travelled to Samudra Pasai, a sultanate in present day Aceh, in northern Sumatra. He records that he met with the local ruler, Sultan Al-Malik Al-Zahir Jamal-ad-Din, a pious Muslim, and noted that Sumatra was rich in tin, camphor, betel nut, and cloves. He stayed in Samudra Pasai for about two weeks after which he was supplied with a small boat to sail to China.

Along the way, he sailed to Malacca where he met the local ruler and stayed as a guest for three days. The journey to China took him briefly to Vietnam where he records meeting a local princess, after which he finally reached Quanzhou in China's Fujian province.

Ibn Battuta was one of the greatest explorers the world has seen. But he was not European. Nor was he Christian. He was from northern Africa. And he was a Muslim. He did not travel because he wanted to conquer or convert. He travelled because he was curious. He wanted to see the other; to observe for the simple sake of knowledge.

Today, seven-hundred years on, Daim is like a modern Ibn Battuta, something of a loner, both self-absorbed and yet outward looking. Curiosity drove Ibn Battuta east and he reached what today is Malaysia. That same intellectual curiosity drove Daim west, to Africa and beyond, to explore and later to do business. And, of course, travel, foreign education and broad experience overseas generally, meant that Daim was better informed and better equipped to serve Malaysia when called upon to do so. It has been this outward-looking nature and broad experience that has made Daim one of the cleverest and most successful Malays of modern times. Imagine a Malaysia full of Ibn Batutas. It would be the local Chinese who then would be in need of preferment policies.

II

THE REAL DAIM

Daim is inclined to appear shy. His self-effacing demeanor and dislike of self-aggrandisement are in keeping with traditional Malay values. But it means that whilst he has been a prominent Malaysian, few Malaysians really know what he is like.

It is important to understand Daim's character before looking at his actions in Malaysian public life, because it is a man's character that sheds light on his motivations. Misunderstand the character and you risk misunderstanding the motives, and in relation to Daim that seems to be a common mistake that others have made.

Daim is a slight man – not tall and not muscular, but trim and fit looking. He looks as old as he is, but has aged well nonetheless. His face is fine featured and his eyes are bright and hold a constant look that is somewhere between quizzical and analytical. It is hard not to get the impression that he sizes up everyone and every situation. Perhaps he has developed this skill from being in politics – particularly the robust form of politics that is practised in Malaysia, in which there are few friends, just acquaintances and enemies. Or perhaps he has always been like that, which has made him well suited to politics.

One common theme with Daim is that those who know him and have had reason to interact with him closely, either in business or politics, very often have nothing but a very deep respect and liking for him. They enjoy his company and like to tell of the various character traits that they find endearing. All this is in contrast to the many stories that circulate about Daim's alleged ruthlessness or his alleged avariciousness. These stories come from those who do not know Daim well, and who recycle hearsay as a substitute for their own ignorance.

There are many paradoxes to Daim. He is humble, but confident in his abilities. He has been one the greatest champions of the Malays of the modern era and yet speaks English at home and with his family. He is wealthy but unpretentious, has a good sense of humour, but politically can be quite ruthless. He has a 'winner-take-all' approach to his political enemies. (He did concede in conversation with me that former opposition leader Lim Kit Siang, who had lost his parliamentary seat in the 1999 general elections, had been a good performer in Parliament, but then quickly added that the reality was that Parliament wasn't that important anyway and besides, Lim was arrogant.) He is also utterly pragmatic – witness his Thatcherite approach to government spending in 1985-86 as finance minister and contrast it with his Keynesian, high-spending approach in 1997-98. The two approaches are the ideological antithesis of one another, but as far as Daim is concerned they suited the times.

Daim is acutely intelligent. This fact is not lost on many other highly capable political leaders. Lee Kuan Yew, Singapore's founding prime minister, well-known for his razor-sharp intelligence and inability to suffer fools, found in Daim a fellow traveler. Whenever Lee needed to reach the Malaysian hierarchy to talk things through or to get something done, it was usually to Daim that Lee turned. Shaukat Aziz, former senior banker and Pakistan's prime minister, told me in London in 2014 that he found Daim 'shrewd, wise and with a great business sense – he's very smart and very wise…his mindset is merit driven and he opens his arms to anyone with ability.' Aziz had some remarkable achievements turning Pakistan's moribund economy around with free-market reforms and the privatisation of state-owned enterprises. Had he learned anything from Daim's handling of the Malaysian economy that he was able to implement in Pakistan? 'Absolutely', he said.

Laksamana Sukardi, Indonesia's minister for state-owned enterprises from 1999 to 2004, made a similar observation in written answers. He said that whilst he was a minister charged with sorting out many of Indonesia's problems in the wake of the Asian economic crisis of 1997-98, he contacted Daim for some tutelage. 'When I was appointed as minister I contacted Tun Daim to get his advice and to learn from his valuable experiences. I considered Tun as my senior…he helped me in promoting Indonesia's recovery, especially when it came to asset sales and the privatisation of Indonesian state-owned enterprises.'

Mambury Njie, finance minister of Gambia from 2010 to 2012, told me that he had found Daim generous with his experience and practical knowledge to the point where he regarded him as a role model and referred to him as 'uncle'.

Daim has the reputation for saying very little but in actual fact, and as is little appreciated, he can be extraordinarily talkative, particularly on a one-to-one basis. When I was considering writing this book I was warned that Daim was a man of few words, that I could expect only short meetings with him and that he was prone to give one-word answers. Even a close relative of his remarked that she didn't know why I would want to try to write a book on Daim 'because he won't tell you anything!' Indeed, my first impression was that Daim was reluctant to participate. But I soon found that my meetings with him typically went for two hours at a time, he did most of the talking and that he had ideas and opinions on practically everything. Others have found the same. Then Defence Minister and later Prime Minister Dato' Seri Najib Tun Razak said to me at his office in late 2000 that, 'If you engage Daim on a one-to-one basis he can be very charming. In fact, he will do most of the talking.' The private Daim and the public Daim are worlds apart, according to Najib, and this has led to much confusion among those who do not know him well, about just what sort of person he is.

Journalists too have experienced the chatty Daim, but then some have found the opposite. One American journalist who I spoke with in Paris described Daim as 'very impressive and a smart guy'. But then another who is now based in the United States told me that he found him 'distant, uncommunicative and weird'. Bill Mellor, who was then Editor in Chief of *Asia Inc.* magazine told me at his Bangkok office how, when he once went to Kuala Lumpur to interview Daim, he was first instructed to submit his questions to which formal, written answers would be given. That done, Mellor would then be permitted a meeting with Daim but was told that the meeting would be brief, would be more a courtesy call and for photographs than for anything else and that Daim probably wouldn't say much or if he did he could be expected only to give general answers. Instead according to Mellor, after he was ushered into Daim's office, Daim looked up at him and said simply, 'So what do you want to know?' To his surprise, Daim proceeded to give detailed and lengthy answers that were specific to the point of being disarmingly frank.

It is true though that Daim prefers to speak little in more social situations. On each of the occasions that I ate with him and his friends, he said almost nothing, preferring to listen – even if in the presence of close friends. This can have a somewhat dampening effect on table conversation. Because of who he is, everyone is aware of Daim's presence and is hyper-sensitive to his shifts in mood and preferences, so it is difficult when the object of everyone's attention remains seemingly distant and uncommunicative. For those who do not know him, they might reasonably wonder if Daim is in a bad mood. Perhaps he might be, but generally it is simply Daim being Daim.

Daim enjoys irony and a good laugh. At times, he seems almost impish and slightly naughty. He likes to stir people just to see what will happen. Several of the government's more prominent critics were or are employed in Malaysia's universities. During one of our meetings, I asked Daim if he felt that academic freedom had gone too far in Malaysia. How did he feel, for example, when K.S. Jomo, a professor at the Universiti Malaya, routinely criticised the government and yet was employed in a government university with government funds? Daim seemed untroubled by this. In fact, he said that in 1999 he had his secretary call up Jomo to ask him to participate in the government's budget dialogue to help frame the budget for the following year. Jomo agreed and duly turned up at Daim's office with his suggestions for the budget. Daim retold the story with obvious delight. He clearly enjoyed the irony in having a government critic come and offer ideas on how the government should shape its budget.

Daim's unwillingness to suffer fools is famous. Sally Cheong, in her book *Bumiputera Entrepreneurs*, warns: 'When you see him, don't waste his time. Go straight to the point. Don't speak in innuendoes and be as honest as you can. He will forgive the innocent but he cannot stand actors.'[1] It's good advice. Daim's close friend, the late Alex Lee, also said of him: 'Tun prefers a low profile. Behind his tough exterior, he is surprisingly soft-hearted. But he can be hard too when he feels a person does not deserve help ... He is deep, does not talk or reveal much. He is difficult to fathom. That is why he is often misunderstood. Yet when he does speak, it is in a no-nonsense direct style. He does not beat about the bush. For him, white is white and black is black. Like Dr Mahathir, Tun is performance-oriented.'[2]

---

1   S. Cheong, *Bumiputera Entrepreneurs in the KLSE*, CRS, 1996, p. 1.

2   M.S. Cheong and Adibah Amin, *Daim: The Man Behind the Enigma*, Pelanduk Publications, 1995, p. 167.

One should not dilly dally either when he has made a request. National Economic Action Council (NEAC) working group member (the late) Dr Zainal Aznam Yusof said to me of Daim in 2000, 'He is as everyone knows a very impatient man. My experience with him is that if you are given any task by him, you do it immediately – he has very little patience for all the usual excuses such as bureaucracy and so on.' While Daim may not suffer fools, this is not to say that he is uncaring. 'Tun has his heart in the right place', said Universiti Malaya Professor (the late) Mahani Zainal Abidin. It is a view, she said that she shared with her NEAC working group colleague Wan Azmi Wan Hamzah. 'You can appeal to Tun if you think something is not right and he will listen to you', she told me.

Coupled with Daim's impatience is his demand for punctuality. This is unusual in Malaysia where the culture has evolved such that it is routine to keep business colleagues and friends waiting with either no excuse or a cursory blaming it on the traffic. Perhaps Daim learned the habit of punctuality when he was studying in London – the English habit of arriving right on time, neither late nor early, out of respect for the other party – is well known. But it is also a requirement for those who know they need to allocate their time as efficiently as possible.

Ken Kwaku, a former World Bank economist and special advisor to Benjamin Mkapa, president of Tanzania from 1995 to 2005, related to me in 2015 a story whereby an African president had honoured Daim with an invitation to meet. Daim arrived on time and was kept waiting for three hours without explanation. Daim decided to head to the airport so he could continue to his next destination only to discover at the airport that the president had instructed Daim's jet not to leave while he rushed through the traffic with his driver to get to the airport for a meeting in the lounge. The president's reward was a polite but firm lecture from Daim on the value of time. Thereafter, the two became good friends and according to Kwaku, the president became an advocate for punctuality.

What sort of a thinker is Daim? There should be little doubt about his mental ability. 'Tun firstly is highly intelligent and secondly, he is very hard working', said Professor Mahani. 'He remembers every detail – really he has a very good memory', she added. I asked defence minister Najib if he regarded Daim as intelligent. His reply was immediate, firm and unequivocal. 'Yes! He's very intelligent!' But is Daim an original thinker? Dr Zainal Aznam Yusof offered this: 'Daim's strength is not in thinking about the grand things; he is less of a visionary. He's much more of a man who gets things done. He is a man of action. That is where his strength lies'. It was a sentiment echoed by Professor Mahani. 'Tun's main contribution to public life has been to get things done – he has a sense of urgency,' she said. Problem solving and action are Daim's strong points. Nonetheless, as Kuala Lumpur Stock Exchange (KLSE) chairman Azlan Hashim said to me, 'Tun is very receptive to ideas and new alternatives'.

Daim has little interest in form or formality. I watched him disembark from his jet one day in Kuala Lumpur after a flight from northern Malaysia, walk across the tarmac, climb into a nondescript Toyota family van after having loaded up the back, and then drive himself home. There were no security personnel, no accompanying police vehicles, nothing – just Daim. Ignoring the fact that he had just climbed out of his private jet, the rest of the scene seemed terribly ordinary. Daim looked like any other middle-class man who had just returned from a weekend away.

An expatriate businessman who is based in Kuala Lumpur told me how on one occasion he went to watch a badminton match at a public sports arena. He walked down the aisle towards the court to get a better view and sitting alone at the bottom of the steps, not on a chair but on a step, was the country's finance minister who was there, presumably also to get a better view. Daim was apparently oblivious to his surroundings; he was captivated by the match.

Foreign political leaders have noticed the same low-key trait. Stephen Kalonzo Musyoko, vice president of Kenya from 2008 to 2013, told me in reply to written questions that when Daim first visited his office in Kenya, he tried to work out who, among the visiting entourage, was Daim. He singled out one of the visitors whom he thought must be the former Malaysian finance minister but was soon proved wrong. 'The most inconspicuous person in the delegation turned out to be Tun Daim! He was of astonishingly slim build!'

Roberto Ongpin, one of the Philippines' wealthiest businessmen and also that country's trade and investment minister from 1979 to 1986, said of Daim in response to written questions, 'My first impression of him was that he was a very quiet, modest and soft-spoken individual. Over the years that we have known each other, I found him to be a very intelligent and incisive individual, with a great sense of humour.'

The Reverend Dr Makhenkesi Stofile, a prominent African National Congress activist, and then South Africa's minister of sport and recreation from 2004 to 2010, and subsequently, South Africa's ambassador to Germany, said of Daim in 2014 that when he first met Daim he realized from his various titles that he was an important man. 'But when we met, he did not "wear" any of his titles or positions on him. I found him to be a very humble and respectful person.' Stofile said that he found Daim trustworthy and a plain speaker – an attribute he greatly appreciated.

Another prominent African, Ken Kwaku, mentioned earlier, also was taken aback by Daim's self-effacing demeanor compared with the more typical experience of African politicians. Kwaku related this to me in reply to my questions. 'The first thing that struck me about Tun was his simplicity and sense of humour. He was dressed casually in a long-sleeve batik shirt and casual shoes. I was then twenty years in the World Bank and had met many finance ministers particularly on the African continent who wore expensive Savile Row pin-striped suits with Mont Blanc pens and the latest Rolex watch. Wow! What an impression! At a later meeting, Tun proceeded to greet my wife by asking what a beautiful woman like her was doing with a character like me. All this added up to the beginning of a friendship that has lasted the past two decades.'

The unpretentiousness is mirrored in Daim's friends in Malaysia. They are not necessarily the top of the elite of Malaysian society, but rather are people with whom Daim can feel comfortable and relaxed. They are not ostentatious;

they tend to be successful middle-class people with relatively simple tastes and demeanor. In fact, they eschew the ostentation of other wealthy Asians. One or two who I met were somewhat disparaging of what they termed the 'Chanel set' and the 'Versace set' – the two being quite separate categories, apparently, but both evenly despised. They are most commonly seen in Jakarta. These are the Asians 'who are not confident within themselves', I was told.

Whilst a minister, Daim did not travel with a bodyguard or with a large posse of personal staff and minders. In fact, he often travelled with no personal staff. This is in contrast to almost all other ministers and deputy ministers, who like to make their presence known by being surrounded by bodyguards and other staff. Daim finds this bothersome and unnecessarily ostentatious. A lot of the time, he would simply rather travel on his own. In Kuala Lumpur, his ministerial personal staff was limited to just one political secretary.

The relaxed nature of Daim continues at home. He has several houses. One residence, used mostly while he was a minister because of its large entertaining facilities, sits in the hills that overlook Kuala Lumpur and is reached by a narrow and winding road. The house is part of an 11-acre compound that also has a *surau* (small mosque) that is adjacent to the house, a sports complex with a swimming pool, badminton and squash courts, and a separate private museum and art gallery. A wall surrounds the compound, and at the front gates there is a sentry post that is manned by a cheerful Gurkha guard. Daim likes durian and grows durian trees at the back of the compound. He bought the land in 1970 when no one wanted to live in the area and paid just 50 cents a square foot for it. Despite the massive size of the house, there is an air of informality about it. After one late-evening interview session in 2000 with Daim that finished after midnight, we walked to the front of the house to find several friends sitting on the front step in the heat of the night talking and taking cool drinks. I made my way to my car while Daim disappeared down the driveway and into the night to take an evening walk.

Daim's success has brought the expected benefits. In Langkawi, for many years he made frequent use of two adjacent sea-front chalets. The chalets were comfortable rather than opulent – perfect for relaxing and making for an uncomplicated weekend. One of the chalets was for Daim. The other was for his guests. Between the chalets and the sea-front is a thick canopy of tropical trees that occasionally see wild monkeys, tree shrews, hornbills and other animals pass through. Daim has a big collection of cars, including three Rolls-Royces. One he keeps in the garage under his house in Kuala Lumpur. Another was kept in Langkawi, and the third is in London. (Cars are a passion. Motor racing is one of his pastimes, something that ties in with his interest in cars. He has been the patron of the Motor Racing Association of Malaysia.)

But money and power have not changed Daim's personal style. Like most Malays who have made good, he has the almost obligatory accoutrements of wealth and success to prove it – in Daim's case there is the large house, the collection of motor vehicles, a private art collection and a private jet – but beyond this, his tastes remain relatively modest. He is still very much a *kampung* boy made good. He is famous for his modest eating habits, and for his preference for wearing jeans, a T-shirt or batik shirt, and sandals. Only when protocol demands it does he dress more formally. One of the better-known incidents involving Daim and his relaxed sense of dress was when he was refused entry to the Royal Selangor Club because he was wearing slippers. There is nothing special about Daim wearing flips-flops (or slippers as Malaysian call them) – he often does in preference to shoes – but what made the Selangor Club incident amusing was the fact that he had just stepped out of a Rolls-Royce. Daim graciously accepted the refusal ('rules are rules') and had the club's staff tell the person he was meeting for lunch to meet him on the verandah outside where they could dine instead.

Daim's personal frugality is legendary and has been a life-long habit. According to Wan Azmi Wan Hamzah, Daim, 'is always scribbling (and always in pencil) on the backs of used envelopes. I never knew him to use a notepad (nor a pen) while he was at Peremba. And he would rush off to see the PM or whoever always armed with one of those used envelopes – for his talking points as well as fresh note taking.'[3] A close friend of Daim's related how on a visit to Africa, he and Daim were waiting at an airport for their flight to leave. Hungry, they decided to search out the airport restaurant for a bite to eat. All that was available was a set meal that included several courses, but Daim simply wanted some soup and a bread roll. On asking if he could merely have that part of the set meal and what the price would be, he was told that he would still be charged the same as if he was having the entire meal. This seemed unfair to Daim, so he elected to go without, despite his hunger. Such apparent stinginess is common among many first-generation, self-made entrepreneurs. Similar stories have been told about Hong Kong entrepreneur Li Ka Shing and Indonesia's late Liem Sioe Liong. It is probably an ideal quality for a finance minister.

I saw a small but telling example of Daim's frugality on a visit to Langkawi. One evening we went to a simple but good open-air seafood restaurant. The food was tasty and plentiful. At the meal's end, when it was time to leave, the last to leave was Daim as he lingered at the table to fill a half-finished mineral water bottle with the remnants of another bottle so that he could take it with him. The sight was commendably frugal.

The position of women in society is an interest of Daim's, although largely one has a sense that it is for pragmatic reasons. Daim is a strong believer in merit and he wants to see things get done. If the best person for the job is a woman then so be it. And in Daim's view, often the best person for a job will be a woman. In some respects, such a view is not out of keeping with traditional Malay culture in which woman have always had full and often commercial roles.

The Western world generally is greatly ignorant of the role of women in Muslim societies. Whatever happens in the Middle East is deemed to be the sum total of Islamic civilisation. But it is common to see women in senior

---

3   Ibid., p. 175.

management positions in both the civil service and the private sectors of both Malaysia and Indonesia, for example. I asked Daim whilst he was still serving as finance minister if he felt that affirmative action policies to favour women in his own Finance Ministry should be adopted. He couldn't see the point. He pointed out that women already held many senior positions, so there was no need for such policies. And how were the women in his ministry performing? To Daim, the question almost made no sense. As long as an employee was performing and delivering, he had little interest in what sex they were. The fact that many of his senior officers were women seemed unremarkable to him at the time.

But elsewhere, female participation rates have attracted Daim's interest. During a speech in 1994, he lamented Malaysia's then comparatively low female workforce participation rate. At 48%, it was considerably lower than most OECD countries, where the rate was in excess of 60%. '[I]n order to draw this potential pool of human resources into the labour force, the corporate sector will have to provide appropriate facilities as well as be prepared to offer more flexible terms of employment.'[4]

But by 1999, Daim was able to praise the role of Malaysian women in public administration and the country's universities. In higher education, the number of female students at institutions of higher learning was more than 50% of total enrolment. In the professional and managerial category in the public sector, almost 43% were women. There were also several women who served as secretary-generals of ministries, he told Parliament.[5]

On one occasion, as will be discussed later, Daim said to me that in many instances women in Malaysia are more impressive when it comes to business than some of the men. He felt this was the case particularly on the East Coast where many women ran the stalls in the markets and generally looked after the family's finances. And certainly, Malaysia has a prominent Minangkabau minority, a group that is both Muslim and matrilineal whereby it is the daughters who inherit the family's wealth. Finally, Ken Kwaku mentioned to me in 2014 that in Africa, Daim had sponsored the construction of a women's vocational ICT centre in Ghana and in Zanzibar, had supported female political candidates.

What of Daim's religious beliefs? He is a Muslim and he is intensely religious. But he is not a fundamentalist. Indeed, a measure of the degree to which he is serious about his faith is that he is not a fundamentalist. His piety is heartfelt but he feels no need for ostentatious and intrusive displays of adherence.

He prays often. On several occasions when I was due to see him, the meetings were either held up or interrupted because he wished to pray. Said Gambia's Mambury Njie to me about the first time he met Daim, 'I realized that while we were meeting it was time for prayers and I observed that there was a praying mat in his office and he asked us for a few minutes to do his prayers. That move really deepened my respect for a man with a very strong faith.'

---

4   The speech was delivered at the Universiti Teknologi Malaysia on 3 April 1994.

5   Budget 2000 speech given to Parliament by Daim on 29 October 1999.

Daim does not drink alcohol, although this has not always been the case. He says he gave up consuming alcohol in the 1960s. (His wife quipped to me that Daim is physically so slender that it was just as well because any amount of alcohol would affect him!) He stopped smoking cigarettes in the 1980s, and he does not eat pork or bacon. He uses his considerable wealth to support various Islamic activities. He has paid for the construction of at least four mosques in Kedah state. The *surau* on the grounds of his house in Kuala Lumpur that is used for Thursday night prayers each week is also used during the day for a Koranic school for as many as 50 children. There are several classes a day and they, and the Imam who conducts them, are sponsored by Daim. He has been a regular speaker at Islamic conferences and has been involved in the development of Islamic banking in Malaysia.

He has been a leading proponent of the notion that Muslims *should* go into business and they should succeed. 'Some Muslims believe this world is for the non-Muslims – that Muslims should only pray and think of the hereafter. So why go into business and make money? You can't take the money with you when you die. It is a wrong interpretation of the Islamic faith. As long as it is not *haram* and your business practices are not immoral, I cannot see any reason why Muslims cannot pursue a career in business. I think it is possible to be both a businessman and a good Muslim,' he has been quoted as saying.[6]

This attitude of not being ashamed to advance materially despite an adherence to Islam is one that Daim has drawn broader implications from. For Daim, the main task for Muslims is to lift each other out of poverty and misery; to enhance the dignity of the world's Islamic community. This is perhaps more important than fussing over whether this religious rule of that rule is strictly applied to. 'Shall we take the incremental approach, introducing Islamic principles bit by bit, making sure our economic well-being is not jeopardised,' asked Daim rhetorically at the Islamic Development Bank seminar, 'or shall we plunge full scale into an Islamic financial system? Do we want to isolate ourselves from the mainstream of development and from the rest of the non-Muslim world? My own view is that, we have to adopt a practical approach and the system of Islamic financial instruments should recognise these constraints. Otherwise, the ultimate objectives of all our efforts, which is to enhance the dignity of fellow Muslims, may not be realised.'[7] Daim might be pro-Islamic, but he is no extremist. 'It is most unfortunate that in recent years, there has been several deviationist teachings which totally reject material things, the Western world and its institutions, including financial institutions. These teachings have made some inroads, not only in this country but also in some other countries as well. This has to be nipped in the bud.'

At an Islamic Chamber of Commerce meeting in Kuala Lumpur in December 1993, Daim said, 'We are seen as a bunch of turbaned and bearded terrorists covered in a shroud with a gun in the hand ready to shoot at anyone opposing

---

6   S. Cheong, *Bumiputera Entrepreneurs in the KLSE*, CRS, 1996, p. 6.

7   As reprinted in *Daim Speaks his Mind*, op. cit.

our so-called return to fundamentalism: that is the test we are and will be going through … We have to prove to our friends in the West that we are not enemies nor do we want to confirm or affirm the labels and prejudices hurled at us. We seek trade and economic partners based on respect and equality.'[8] Like Daim's economics, his religion is pragmatic and practical. He said to me during our discussions that, in his view, the main reason for retaining the Internal Security Act, which allows detention without trial and, as a consequence, has earned Malaysia much international criticism, was because religious tensions are easily inflamed and the Act allowed religious trouble makers to be quickly apprehended and detained. He is deeply religious, but he is no zealot – it is the zealots who are wrong and confused, for religion should help and not hinder the human condition, he believes.

Daim has had a range of interests outside politics and business. He has always been a sports fanatic – not just as an observer, but as an active participant. He has been very keen on squash and badminton, and in his younger days, football (soccer). He is passionate in his dislike of golf, though, particularly because it takes up too much time. It is unusual for someone in Asia of Daim's stature not only to not play golf but to not even pretend to like it. It is normally assumed that he is a golfer. One Kuala Lumpur businessman who had just bought a controlling stake in a significant listed Malaysian company was described by Singapore's *Business Times* as a 'frequent Daim golf partner'.[9] I asked Daim if this was so. He said that he has never played golf with him and that he doesn't play with anyone. In fact, and as he mentioned to me several times subsequently, not only does he not play golf, but he 'hates' it. He would rather challenge business and political colleagues to a game of badminton. While everyone else, for example, is used to thinking of the Sultan of Brunei as one of the world's richest men, Daim sees him more as one of his preferred badminton partners.

Daim is also interested in the arts. Before he joined the cabinet, he was chairman of the Malaysian National Art Gallery. He has an extensive private collection of paintings and antiques, kept in the private art gallery next to one of his Kuala Lumpur residences. On display in various rooms are paintings by Malaysian artists such as Ibrahim Hussein, Latiff Mohidin and Chang Fee Ming, paintings by other Asian artists, European paintings dating from the 17th century and possibly earlier, textiles, *kendi*, *tempat sirih*, bronze sculptures, carved ivory netsuke from Japan, snuff bottles from China, lacquerware from Burma, and so on.

Charity is another interest of Daim's. He donated his ministerial and parliamentary salary to charity, something he did during both stints as finance minister. He has also established the Yayasan Pok Rafeah, a charitable foundation named after his late mother. There is another foundation, Yayasan Haji Zainuddin, named after his late father. Both are funded by Daim and give scholarships and loans to poor students, and medical assistance and other aid to the poor. They

8   Ibid.

9   'Changing of guard in corporate Malaysia', *Business Times*, 21 August 1999.

also help to finance the construction of mosques and built two residential schools in Aceh after the 2004 tsunami, as well as making substantial donations for schools in Sri Lanka. Other schools were built in Senegal and in Pakistan. A mosque was built for former communists in southern Thailand. Large donations were made to West Africa to help with the Ebola outbreak in 2014. Substantial donations have been made to Hawaii's East-West Center, which was established to promote better relations and understanding among the people and nations of the United States, Asia, and the Pacific through cooperative study, research, and dialogue. Included was a US$1 million donation to fund a leadership program at the Center for Orang Asli and other indigenous Malaysians. (Daim has served on the Center's board of governors.) And a house is funded on an ongoing basis in the UK at Cambridge for use by the Cambridge Malaysian Education and Development Trust.

Daim tends to rise at 6am. Time permitting, he likes to swim for morning exercise (there is a large pool next to his house) and, in the evenings, to take a stroll. He generally does not get to bed until after midnight. Each Sunday he takes a break from this schedule and does not get out of bed until at least midday. As he explains, he 'accumulates sleep', storing it up on Sunday for the rest of the week when there is little time for sleeping. Sunday afternoons, he likes to play badminton. I asked Daim if he ever does simple things in Kuala Lumpur such as visit a shopping centre on a Saturday afternoon or maybe go and drink coffee at Starbucks near Lot 10 at Bukit Bintang? 'Never,' said Daim. Was he afraid of being recognised? 'No one would recognise me,' he laughed. No, it was simply a matter of time. It is understandable. Daim has packed a great deal into his life.

III

THE YOUNG STUDENT

Abdul Daim bin Zainuddin was born on 29 April 1938 at Derga village in the eastern part of Alor Setar, the capital of the northern Malaysian state of Kedah. The family was large – Daim was the youngest of 13 children – though this was typical of Malay families at the time. Daim's grandmother lived in the family household when he was growing up. His main recollection of her is of her returning from fishing – she loved to fish. She would head off to go fishing in the morning and return in the evening in time for evening prayers having missed her lunch. Later, in the evenings, she would gather all the children around and tell them Malay folk stories before they went off to bed. But as with other Malay families, the dominant figure in the household was Daim's father.

Daim describes his relationship with his father, a clerk in the Land Office, as 'very traditional' but also somewhat distant, particularly as there were simply so many other siblings. The relationship was a comfortable one, but his father was very strict and Daim says he had little choice but to be obedient. As is the case in many traditional Malay families, if he wanted something from his father, it was best to first approach his mother. She might then intercede with his father on his behalf. Daim's father believed that a good education was critically important. He did two unusual things that stood Daim and his siblings in good stead for later life: he resigned from his job to oversee the education of his children; and he insisted that they have an English-medium education. The latter was particularly unusual for a Malay family. At the time, most Malay parents were concerned that an English education might damage the religious and cultural identity of their children. The British also preferred that Malay parents send their children to Malay schools, which did not go beyond primary level.

Daim went to the Malay primary school in Seberang Perak, Alor Setar. He was admitted to the Special Malay Class at Sultan Abdul Hamid School in 1949, an English-medium school in Alor Setar. In the meantime, he was asked to attend an interview for the selection of the best student in Kedah state to be sent to the Malay College Kuala Kangsar, a premier school in the state of Perak. At the interview, however, Daim learned that the parents of successful applicants would have to pay the first three months' tuition fees. His parents were not poor, but nor were they wealthy. The fees would have been a burden on the large family, so Daim stayed on at Sultan Abdul Hamid School.

Daim did well enough, although he spent more time playing sports than studying. He readily passed through Standard VI, doing so well that he was offered a double promotion which he turned down, but later, he did not pass all his topics in Standard VII, though he did pass overall. A new rule required that each student must pass every topic to be promoted to the next level, so Daim left Sultan Abdul Hamid School and was eventually accepted into Standard VIII at St Xavier Institution in Georgetown, on Penang Island. For much of his time at St Xavier's, he was the only Malay in his class. The other students were mostly Chinese and some Indians. Fortunately, Daim passed Standard VIII with not too much effort. He seems to have viewed schooling not so much as a way to get an education but as a way to obtain credentials, so he tended to be somewhat economical with his studies. He maintained his passion for sports, though, particularly football, hockey and badminton.

Later Education

After passing the Senior Cambridge Overseas School Certificate examination, Daim took a job as a temporary teacher. The job paid very little, and his parents encouraged him to choose a more lucrative vocation. Daim's father had always wanted him to be a lawyer, so the family sold some of the land it owned to raise the funds for tuition and to give Daim an allowance so that he could be sent to London to study law. Daim's elder brother, too, was sent away – to Australia to study accounting.

Daim arrived in London in the spring of 1957 to take up law at Lincoln's Inn. The Suez Canal was not open, so the journey to Europe took him via southern Africa. The ship stopped in Durban and Cape Town in South Africa. For Daim, it was his first experience of racial prejudice – an interesting observation from someone who had grown up in multi-racial Malaya. Daim's first impression of England was that it was gloomy and cold. The British, he said to me, 'were like the weather, very cold!'

Daim thrived in Europe. Lincoln's Inn, the best known of London's Inns of Court, must have been particularly stimulating. Located near Fleet Street and not far from the River Thames between Waterloo Bridge and Blackfriars Bridge, the calm, dignified legal precinct is packed with history and charm. Oliver Cromwell, poet John Donne and founder of the US State of Pennsylvania, William Penn, are among Lincoln's Inn's most famous alumni.

Many other Malaysians also were in London to study, and for Daim it afforded an opportunity to mix with the children of the Malaysian elite. Some, like Daim, were to become Malaysia's future leaders. Hussein Onn, Tunku Razaleigh, Aishah Ghani, Manan Othman, Michael Chen and Alex Lee were among them. Malaysian ministers used to visit London and they often made themselves available for meetings with the Malaysian students. The then education minister, Razak Hussein, took a keen interest in student affairs. Lee Kuan Yew also visited London as a member of the Singapore delegation for talks with the British government over the status of Singapore and he, too, met with the students.

It must have been a stimulating time to be both Malaysian and a student. Daim's period in London (1957-59) coincided with Malaya (or Malaysia, as it was called from 1963) gaining independence from Britain.

Politics has always interested Daim, but that is not to say that he always considered becoming a politician. Most of Daim's fellow students in London were older than him and were interested in politics, so he was often a party to political discussions during his student days. But according to Daim, 'It never occurred to me that I would one day be a Minister in the Malaysian Government. I was interested in politics but my interest was limited to reading political books and biographies and attending meetings. There was no serious interest in participating beyond that, maybe as a backbencher in the Government, if ever.'[1]

Daim seems to have adopted a rather cavalier attitude to his studies yet again, but the one thing that he really enjoyed was the ability to travel. He travelled around England, to Ireland and through Europe. It was his first time overseas and he made the most of it. What was his favourite place that he visited? Stockholm, in Sweden. The cold-climate architecture of the *Gamla Stan* (the Old Town), which sits on a series of small islands connected by ornate stone bridges, and the palaces of Stockholm, particularly the *Kungliga Slottet* (the Royal Palace), greatly impressed him.

In September of 1957, he sat for two papers, Criminal Law and Roman Law, and passed both. In December he took two more papers, which he also passed. By May 1958, he had passed the necessary five papers to get him into the final, which he passed as well. Once again, Daim admits that he was not so much interested in gaining an education as gaining the necessary pieces of paper to get him to the next step. Daim's study partner for the finals was Hussein Onn, who later became Malaysia's third prime minister. Daim claimed that Hussein was a very diligent student – excessively so. 'He wanted to put in everything...and he was slow in answering exam questions. He never finished more than three out of five questions in any paper.'[2] Daim was called to the English Bar 18 months later at the age of 21.

Post-London

On Daim's return to Malaysia from London in 1959, he joined the Shearn Delamore chambers in Kuala Lumpur, practised there, and then left for Kota Bahru, in the north-eastern state of Kelantan, to join Wan Mustapha, who was legal adviser to the Pan-Malayan Islamic Party (PMIP, or PAS as it is better known today). The link to Mustapha and PMIP was not on account of Daim being a PMIP sympathiser but had more to do with his desire to earn more money and to meet people.

After just one year in Kota Bahru, Daim returned to Kuala Lumpur where he joined the government service. He was posted to Johor Bahru, in the southern Malaysian state of Johor, as a magistrate. Daim described to me his time as a

1   M.S. Cheong and Adibah Amin, *Daim: The Man Behind the Enigma*, Pelanduk Publications, 1995, p. 21.
2   Ibid., p. 10.

magistrate as being initially interesting. But he grew bored after only a short period. He was too low down to deal with particularly interesting or complex cases and had to make do with routine, petty offences, he explained.

Later he was posted to nearby Muar to be the president of the Sessions Court and was then transferred to Ipoh, in Perak state, as deputy public prosecutor. He resigned in 1965 and returned to Kuala Lumpur where he joined law firm Allen & Gledhill. (It was during this period that he had his first taste of political intrigue, which is discussed in Chapter 5.) He resigned after three years and started his own practice. However, he had come to realise that the law was not the road to wealth. He gave it up and went into business a year later.

IV

THE BUSINESSMAN

To succeed, you must show interest in money and in wanting to make money. There must be that strong urge. There is nothing immoral in this urge. If you don't have it, I think you should not go into business. Business is all about making money. You must enjoy making money. If you don't enjoy it, do something else. I would like however, to distinguish between wanting to make money and greed. Do not be greedy. Greed destroys your self respect.[1]

To understand Daim the policy maker, it is necessary to understand what drives him. So, what does drive Daim? The answer is quite simple: business. It is his main passion. And what sort of business does he like best? Property. 'I am really a property man,' he told me, notwithstanding his later success in founding an international chain of banks in some of the world's toughest economies.

Property is his first love in business and is, he believes, what he knows best. He built his considerable wealth on it, he studied urban planning in the United States in the 1970s and his first major public role was to head Peremba, the construction and property arm of the Urban Development Authority. Property has been both a personal and a public interest for Daim. It has a policy aspect, too. Daim saw the state's involvement in property and construction via Peremba as a way to redress the imbalance in Malay, compared with Chinese, ownership of property in Malaysia's cities and major towns.

In many respects, Daim typified Mahathir's image of the modern Malay, who was dynamic in both business and politics and who was self-confident and on a par with those in the Chinese business community. Daim's philosophy on business success is simple, and very much like that of a typical traditional Chinese businessman: 'I study the project, look at the bottom line. If having considered everything, I find that the chances of success are great, I go in. Then I work very hard to make sure I succeed. There is no real formula for success. It is hard work and more hard work. And you have to monitor your investment. Remember, in most investments, you borrow money. The banks are interested in giving you the loan. But if you fail, they will have no mercy.'[2] But being a trailblazer has had its costs. The jealousy and the rumours that have accompanied Daim's business sucess are obvious examples.

---

1 Daim, quoted in S. Cheong, *Bumiputera Entrepreneurs in the KLSE*, CRS, 1996, p. 4.

2 M.S. Cheong and Adibah Amin, *Daim: The Man Behind the Enigma*, Pelanduk Publications, 1995, pp. 16-17.

Property has made Daim wealthy. But precisely how wealthy is difficult to ascertain. There are various estimates that float around, particularly on the Internet. But these are no doubt exaggerated for political reasons, and some, such as those described in Chapter 1, are simply ridiculous. I asked Daim during our discussions in Kuala Lumpur in 2000 how wealthy he was. His reply was elliptical to such a direct question. 'Put it this way, I'm not poor,' he laughed.

Getting Started

Daim made his entry to the business scene in the late 1960s. He did not do it alone. Initially, his two partners were Low Kiok Boo and Thamby Chik. Low was an important influence on Daim. 'He taught me business,' Daim told me. Daim watched him carefully and emulated him. Nonetheless, Daim did not stay in regular contact with Low after his early business associations with him, and less so on Daim's entry into politics. Partly this was due to Low spending a lot of time in Perth, Australia, and also because he suffered from a long-term, kidney-related illness. He passed away in April 2000, but not before approaching Daim to request that the Malaysian government donate more kidney dialysis machines to the hospital system. On the other hand, Daim still maintained regular contact with Thamby Chik until the latter's death. The two enjoyed each other's company and shared a common interest in badminton – they used to play together regularly.

Low, a client and subsequent friend, encouraged Daim to go into business in 1969. He told Daim that there was no way that a Malay lawyer could really prosper, as the Malay business sector was too small and Chinese business people would inevitably go to Chinese lawyers, or at least to Indian ones. Low was in the property business in the Malaysian state of Melaka with Thamby Chik, a local Malay businessman. Thamby was an ideal partner for a Chinese Malaysian. He had grown up in Singapore and Melaka and was fluent in Hokkien. Low encouraged Daim to join them. Daim agreed and the three decided to go into the salt business. First, they went to Thailand, Taiwan and Japan to study salt production. Subsequently, they decided on Kuala Selangor as the best place in Malaysia to start their own salt production operations. They cleared 600 acres on the coast, but it was not smooth sailing. They soon found that once the salt crystals started to form, it inevitably rained, dissolving the crystals. What little production they did garner was not competitive with imported salt. Then, in 1970, there was a great flood, which washed away their salt, and the venture almost went bankrupt.

Daim and his two co-investors decided to give the salt business away and opted for plastics production. The government awarded them a production licence, but shortly after several more licences were awarded. This meant that they faced more competition than they had expected. The venture was also hampered by an inadequate supply of good workers. Ultimately, the three investors closed one of the plants, but there were three others in Melaka. These, too, were not profitable, at least not at first, but they were not making significant losses either. With more nurturing they did become profitable and were listed on the local stock exchange.

Success in Real Estate

The proceeds from the plastics business were ploughed into yet another business. This time it was real estate. Daim established a property company, Syarikat Maluri Sdn Bhd. He took 60% of the new company's equity, and Thamby Chik and Low each had 20%. Daim bought a tract of state land in Cheras, on what was then the outskirts of Kuala Lumpur. Daim at first had difficulty obtaining a loan to purchase the land, but his close friend and fellow lawyer Alex Lee, with his ties to D&C Bank, helped to facilitate a M$5-6 million loan. (Lee had been in Cambridge about the time that Daim had studied there and had later accompanied Daim to the United States to lobby the Americans on tin at Mahathir's behest. He was later to become a deputy minister with the Gerakan party until retiring from politics in 1995. He died in a scuba diving accident off the coast of Papua New Guinea in October 1999.) Initial approval to purchase the land came from Harun Idris, who was then the chief minister of Selangor state. (Daim had known Harun from when he practiced law and Harun was the Legal Advisor for Selangor.) But approval from all the various other authorities took a number of years.

Excessive bureaucracy was not the only problem. Kuala Lumpur was declared the Federal Territory, and the Cheras land was designated Federal Territory land. So a whole new round of approvals had to be sought. The then mayor, Tan Sri Yaacob Latif, caused further difficulties, according to Daim, as did other politicians and federal and state authorities. Some officials demanded bribes for approvals, and so on. All approvals for the project were finally settled so that construction could begin in 1974 – three years after Daim and his co-investors first set about acquiring the land. (The experience must have been formative given Daim's later insistence as a minister that approvals be fast tracked and delays be reduced to a minimum.) The site was divided into single- and double-storey link housing, semi-detached houses and four-storey shoplets. By 1976, there was a housing boom, and Daim and his partners made a great deal of money, particularly from the sale of the shop-houses. Taman Maluri had been on the outskirts of Kuala Lumpur, but as the city grew, it became well within the city, which significantly added to its value. Beyond Maluri, for example, there are now more housing estates such as Taman Pandan Jaya, and these too are relatively central today.

Daim's creation of Taman Maluri was not easy. He did have some connections in government, but these were necessary rather than sufficient. He has said of this time, 'I faced it all – from sleepless nights, long hours in the office, begging banks, running so often to government departments and sometimes having to deal with petty-minded officers with big egos … I was given the run-arounds to test the patience of a saint. I swallowed my pride and learned to be patient.'[3] This is important. Connections helped to get things going as they often do across Asia, but Daim wasn't after a quick profit. He wanted to develop a real and sustainable business.

---

3 Cheong, op. cit., p. 2.

Later, Daim revealed in a speech to Malay business students a similar version of these struggles. 'We identified the land, drew up the plans, then went on the merry-go-round to get approvals. That was not easy at all,' he told the students. 'We had to deal with so many government departments and financial institutions. It was a very frustrating process. By then I knew business was not easy. Business is very complex where sometimes one is confronted with problems where there are no easy answers. But we must not be dismayed if we take a long time to find answers to the questions. We persevered and months later got all the necessary approvals and permits.'[4]

Said Daim, 'How did I succeed? I worked damn hard, and when I was not working, I was thinking. I went into areas that were new to Bumiputeras (Malays). Some may say I was lucky, that I went into property with the help of Harun when the State Government sold me land. But after me, many others were given even bigger pieces of land. Some are successful but others wanted quick money and just sold off their valuable pieces of land. They were not interested in taking risks. No risk, no gain. The Malays have to learn to work and sweat for their money. Easy come, easy go. Work hard and sweat for your money and you will value it.'[5] It is a lesson, one suspects, that Daim feels that too few even today have learned.

Research and attention to detail was the other key to success. Although he was the first big Malay property developer at that time, Daim did not encounter too many problems from Chinese contractors. One reason was that he did all the planning and calculations himself. He made sure that he understood each project in its smallest detail. He spent day and night on each site, and he cut out any unnecessary expenditure. Contractors were paid on time, or at least their payments were not unnecessarily held up. He developed the reputation for paying promptly once the services were delivered.

Daim then used what was left of the Maluri development as collateral for further borrowings for more investment, and then later in exchange for stakes in other companies. His success with the project also encouraged him to undertake further property developments. With the 300 acres at Maluri, plus 300 acres at Kepong, called Taman Bukit Maluri, and elsewhere, and then 2,000 acres in Jitra, Kedah, where the Universiti Utara (Northern University) was temporarily sited, Daim's aim of being a millionaire was fulfilled. Along the way, Daim made a M$100,000 donation to the UMNO political fund for the 1974 election. He gave it through Musa Hitam, who was then assistant minister for trade. Daim remembers that, at the time, the contribution caught the attention of Tun Razak, Malaysia's second prime minister, who reportedly was very pleased with the sum.[6] It was a significant amount of cash at the time.

---

4   Daim, Z., 'Managing business: My personal experience', speech to business students at Universiti Utara Malaysia (UUM), published in March 1995.

5   Cheong and Adibah Amin, op. cit., pp. 18-19.

6   Ibid., p. 15.

Daim and the Stock Market

Another source of Daim's wealth has been the stock market. At times he has been one of Malaysia's most active stock market players. Daim noticed in the 1970s that several Chinese Malaysian, including the later-to-be-disgraced Tan Koon Swan, were turning quick profits from investing in the stock market. Unlike today, no Malay investor had any great prominence in the stock market, so Daim decided to fill the gap. The first stock that he bought into was United Estates Projects Bhd (UEP). He acquired a 30% stake in the company for M$74.2 million from Bandar Raya Developments, the property arm of the Malaysian Chinese Association's investment company, Multi-Purpose Holdings Bhd (MPHB).

A company called Baktimu was given six months to pay for the UEP stake. While Daim sought financing for the deal, news spread that he was behind Baktimu. By then, Daim was known to have good links to the government, and UEP's share price began to rise. In six months, Daim and his partners made a large paper profit on their UEP holdings.[7]

Daim later sold the UEP interest to the government-controlled Sime Darby, a highly diversified publicly listed conglomerate, for a significant profit. Part of the transaction gave Daim a 7% stake in Sime Darby. The fact that the sale was to a government-controlled entity attracted a lot of criticism, of which Daim is well aware. He said to me that the price paid by Sime Darby was not excessive – people simply did not realise what a good buy the UEP stake was for Sime Darby and, ultimately, it made a lot of money on the acquisition. Controversial though it was, Daim's UEP play whetted his appetite for more stock market investing and he acquired stakes in other counters. By the time he was appointed to the cabinet in 1984, he was a substantial shareholder in many companies listed on the stock market. But then, in September 1986, the cabinet decided that all ministers should sell their interests in public companies. Daim subsequently sold his interests in the various listed companies that he had, including the interest in Sime Darby.

In the years before he was Minister of Finance and in the years after, Daim came to be viewed as the most powerful figure in the Malaysian corporate scene, and stocks surged on the basis of unconfirmed rumours that he was somehow linked to them. Indeed, guessing which stock is a 'Daim stock' became a popular pastime in Malaysia. Investors poured millions of dollars into this or that stock on the basis of rumours that Daim had bought into it or that he was somehow linked to it. Investors believed that such a linkage would become the basis for a takeover bid or that the company would win lucrative contracts from the government. I asked Daim how he felt when his name was linked so regularly to this or that stock, causing its price to rise. He replied that he regarded it as 'a nuisance'. No-one was wanting to work; everyone was wanting to play the stock market instead. To Daim the stock market had become a casino. Once when he was quoted as saying that stocks were over-valued, the market fell, and Lee Kuan Yew telephoned him to

---

7   P. Searle, *The Riddle of Malaysian Capitalism*, Allen & Unwin, Sydney, 1999, p. 138.

ask why he had said such a thing causing stocks even in Singapore to fall. Daim complained to me that once, even during a dental checkup, while he was laying flat out in the dentist's chair with dental instruments pushed into his mouth, his dentist wanted to know what stocks he should buy. He had a similar experience at the immigration counter whilst arriving in Singapore.

In January 1994, Daim even felt obliged to issue a press release to deny that he was linked to a range of companies that had rocketed in price on the strength of rumours of such an association. Specifically, he denied any involvement with Lien Hoe, AP Land, Seal Incorporated, Sin Heng Chan, Sri Hartamas, North Borneo Timbers, Binaan Setegap, Econstates, Anson Perdana and Glenealy. He said that shares in one of the companies had rocketed from M$1.70 to M$17.00 on the strength of the rumours, and that this was 'crazy'. It was just so easy to make money on the stock market but too many had forgotten that it was just as easy to lose it. Daim conceded that he did hold shares, but that he had largely cashed out of everything but blue chips. In a characteristic understatement, he said: 'I still play for pocket money. I need to make some money for the weekend spending but people say that I am a big player.' [8]

Daim's Later Business Involvements

Daim's corporate holdings today largely fall into three categories: property in Kuala Lumpur, shares on the KLSE, and banks outside Malaysia. Daim and his family are still developing Taman Maluri, a large residential area in Kuala Lumpur, the land for which he first acquired in the early 1970s. The property business is now in the hands of his daughter. The Daim family was to have participated in another large development, also in Kuala Lumpur, but plans were shelved during the 1997-98 economic crisis. The Economic Planning Unit awarded the privatisation and development of 189 acres of state-owned land in Kuala Lumpur in 1997 to a consortium in which Daim's family had a minority stake. Former Deputy Prime Minister Ghafar Baba also had a stake. The development was to cost M$8.1 billion.[9] But when I asked Daim about the project he seemed only vaguely aware of its details. His daughter, it seems, had carriage of the project and he was happy to leave it to her. But ultimately, the government cancelled the project and took back the land.

Daim continued to hold shares in companies listed on the KLSE after his second appointment as finance minister in 1998. That would suggest potential conflicts of interests. However, Daim claimed that his share portfolio was professionally managed and that he barely knew in what stocks his managers had invested. He argued that if he knew exactly what his holdings were, he would be too tempted to follow the fortunes of his stocks and it would become an excessive distraction. In any event, under cabinet rules, Daim said that ministers were

---

8   As reprinted in *Daim Speaks his Mind*, Pelanduk Publications, 1995.

9   'Big fish, big pond', *Far Eastern Economic Review*, 27 March 1997.

required to sign a statutory declaration, which was given to the prime minister, detailing their shareholdings in KLSE-listed stocks where that shareholding amounts to 2% or more of a company's total equity. To be fair, Daim's second stint as finance minister was barely out of choice. He was drafted into the role whilst Malaysia was in the midst of an economic and political crisis. Barely was there time to rearrange his extensive private business affairs and presumably requiring a wholesale sell-off of his shares would have seen him realize huge losses given the region-wide financial crisis. In any event, as of mid-2000, Daim was emphatic that he did not own more than 2% of any company listed on the KLSE.

The third pillar of the Daim family business empire encompassed private banking outside Malaysia. Being overseas, this had the advantage of being immune from conflicts-of-interest allegations back in Malaysia. Daim freely admits to having owned banks in the Czech Republic, Hungary, Bosnia-Herzegovina, Albania, Ghana, the Republic of Guinea, Mozambique, Tanzania, Gambia, Senegal, Bangladesh, Laos, Malta, Mauritius, Bosnia, and Indonesia. Not all are particularly profitable, though Daim describes some as 'very profitable'. He owned almost all of them outright, or with only some nominal equity participation from others. Collectively, they form the International Commercial Bank Group. The first bank was set up in the Czech Republic in April 1994 and within six years the Group had banks in eight countries. Each bank sought to provide the full range of conventional banking services, principally to local customers.

Daim was offered many more licences, for example in Morocco, Mauritania, Sudan, Namibia, Kenya, Qatar, Syria, Cambodia, Burma, Vietnam and Nigeria. He did not pursue these because for some, the terms was not acceptable, or the entry costs were too high. One gets the feeling too that unofficial demands might have been made and Daim says that he has always played by the rules, feeling that giving in to such demands leads one down a slippery slope.

How did Daim come to own so many foreign banks? He explains that his reputation as an economic manager among developing countries and their leaders is such that he was often offered a banking licence simply on the basis of his personal business and his public policy records. He maintains close connections with several African political leaders, and these are among the political connections that have yielded such commercial opportunities. Importantly, none of the banks in the International Commercial Bank Group was established until several years after Daim ceased being finance minister in 1991.

In the case of Turkey, Daim explained to me that he visited Turkey on (then) Prime Minister Erdoğan's invitation. Erdoğan also invited Daim to attend his party's conference where he was seated next to the prime minister. Erdoğan wanted Daim to invest in Turkey and offered him a bank. Daim's managers negotiated with the owners of the bank but for various reasons the deal fell through. In Pakistan, the then prime minister asked Daim to invest, although he says he didn't follow up, and in the Philippines, he had dinner at Malacanang Palace with then President Gloria Macapagal Arroyo who similarly invited Daim to invest in the Philippines, but again, he didn't pursue it. He was already rather stretched.

Daim claims that the rationale for his desire to control one bank in Malaysia was so that his expatriate Malaysian managers who look after his banks in Africa and Eastern Europe could return to Malaysia and work for his Malaysian bank rather than having to leave Daim's employment if they wished to return to Malaysia and remain in banking. To this end, Daim briefly controlled International Bank Malaysia. It was known as Hock Hua Bank (Sabah) Bhd until being acquired by Daim in 1997 and being renamed. (Daim says the choice of the name 'International Bank Malaysia' reflected his ambitions and focus for the bank.) On being appointed finance minister the second time, Daim was required to sell his interest in the bank. This he did, and he claims he did so at a loss. Nonetheless, rumours at the time suggested that the bank had been sold to a distant relative of Daim's and that it was being 'warehoused' for him so that he could take back control of it after leaving the ministry. Daim denied both accusations when I asked him about them. The bank did maintain a technical and management services agreement with Daim's International Commercial Bank Group. In any event, it was to be merged with Multi-Purpose Bank and several other financial institutions, a policy Daim devised while he was finance minister. So, whether it was being warehoused or not, Daim was unlikely to have another chance at controlling it, thanks to his own policy initiatives.

Some Tips on Staying out of Trouble

Daim is well known as a businessman, but what about his family? He has two daughters from his first marriage, a son from his second marriage, and two sons from his third marriage. At the time of writing, one daughter lives in Switzerland where she runs a head-hunting business. The other lives in Kuala Lumpur and is involved in managing the family's Maluri investments. The oldest son, who studied history in England at Cambridge University, operates his own business interests in and outside Malaysia. The two youngest sons currently are studying.

But despite Daim's many business involvements, few of his children and other relatives have high-profile business interests. This is unusual in Asia where conglomerates often are built around well-connected families. Rarely do his children or other relatives appear in the media with their business involvements. An exception is a nephew, Annuar Senawi, who came to notice in 2000 when he announced his intention to take over ailing listed company Idris Hydraulic. Annuar also controlled the listed hotel and resort company Landmarks Bhd. In any event, Annuar was a professional – a qualified actuary – and so could have been expected to find himself in business anyway. But apart from Annuar, Daim's other relatives are not as prominent in business as, say, the children of former Prime Minister Mahathir. Their lack of obvious business involvement seems almost anomalous, particularly given the innuendo that Daim tends to attract. Daim has not used his position as a senior member of the government to enrich his family, and particularly not his children.

In reviewing government contracts sometime in 2000, Daim was surprised to see that one of the successful tenderers had a name that was similar to 'Maluri'. A quick check was sought and it was found that the company concerned had no relationship to the company managed by his daughter and hence there was no reason for approval not to be given.

The key to avoiding accusations of nepotism and patronage, says Daim, is for officials to insist that their children stick to one core sector if they decide to go into business. If their interests become too widely diversified, then it appears that they have been opportunistic. They then become proper targets for criticism, or at least suspicion.

As for Daim himself, he says he fully complied with all restrictions and disclosure requirements made of him in his capacity as a minister. Ministers were required to make declarations of their assets and to provide those declarations to the prime minister every two years. The declarations were not made public and were provided only to the prime minister and not to, say, the Parliament, as happens in some other countries. I asked Daim at the time when he was still serving as finance minister whether he felt that such disclosure was sufficient. He replied that, 'Yes,' he thought that it was, but he felt that it would have been better if the ministers, and top civil servants, declared their assets to Parliament, and the Anti-Corruption Agency, respectively.

V

THE POLITICIAN

The partnership between Daim and Mahathir is the most successful political partnership Malaysia has seen. It is a relationship that stretched over fifty years. It endured a great deal, including speculation that it had either ended or was about to. The strength of the relationship and its importance to both politics and policy within the government virtually ensured that it would be the subject of constant speculation. Other senior politicians have come and gone. But Daim endured. When he did leave the government in 1991, it was of his own volition. And when Malaysia faced its darkest hour during the 1997-98 economic crisis, Mahathir drafted Daim back into the cabinet. The relationship between the two survived for as long as it did because Daim's loyalty to Mahathir was without question. Never was he a threat to Mahathir.

Daim and Mahathir are ideally suited. Both are straight shooters and given to telling unpalatable truths. Mahathir's controversial book *The Malay Dilemma*, which was first published in 1970, contained a great deal that was uncomplimentary about Malay society and culture. Daim similarly has no false illusions about Malay life and what needs to change. The two men have other important similarities. Both are impatient, dislike bureaucratic red tape, and are workaholics with enormous capacities for work. They are also nationalistic and pragmatists. If something doesn't work, then better to try something else. Results count for more than processes. Both are also Malay leaders who flout certain traditional Malay customs, such as the preference for obliqueness in conversation. Instead, both prefer to be direct or blunt, even at the risk of being offensive. In this aspect at least both are very un-Malay, but they remain proudly Malay nonetheless. At the personal level, though, they are courteous and sensitive to the other person's needs.

Cheong Mei Sui and Adibah Amin observed in 1995 in *Daim: The Man Behind the Enigma* that where Daim is sceptical, Mahathir is trusting; Daim has an almost gloomy view of human nature, whereas Mahathir's is more sanguine. According to Daim, Mahathir has a good heart of which people sometimes take advantage. Mahathir is an excellent public speaker and debater. Daim, on the other hand, prefers to work behind the scenes. Daim tends to be less compromising and less willing to suffer fools than is Mahathir. Loyalty is placed high on Mahathir's hierarchy of values, whereas Daim is largely indifferent. Mahathir is the master of rebuttal, whereas Daim prefers to ignore criticism rather than to defend himself. Perhaps Daim simply cannot be bothered; it also means avoiding conflict and disharmony, a preference that is traditional among Malays. The differences meant that Daim was an excellent source of alternative advice for Mahathir. That also meant that they did not always agree.

Though Daim and Mahathir are both from Alor Setar, in northern Malaysia, little can be read into that. It does not account for Daim's relationship with Mahathir and is perhaps more a coincidence than anything else. There is no evidence of some sort of Alor Setar 'putsch'. When I suggested to Daim that there might be an element of this at work he scoffed at the suggestion. He did say, though, that the fact he and Mahathir came from the same town at least meant that each knew who the other was and that they knew of each other's views. But that was as far as it went.

They were not childhood friends as is commonly supposed, especially as Mahathir is 12 years Daim's senior. Mahathir's house was on Jalan Pegawai. Daim's was not too far away on Lorong Kampung Padang. Daim's recollection of first meeting Mahathir was when Daim was still a schoolboy and aged 15 in 1953. Mahathir's brother-in-law Ghani was a close friend of Daim's elder brother Senawi. Mahathir was going back to university in Singapore and Senawi accompanied Ghani to the railway station to see him off. Daim accompanied Senawi. Daim's immediate impression of Mahathir was that he was very confident. It proved to be an accurate observation.

Political Beginnings

Daim's first involvement in the political process came while he was still a practicing lawyer and before his foray into business. In 1966, while a lawyer at Allen & Gledhill, the firm was appointed by the federal government to act for the governor of Sarawak state in a case against Sarawak's then chief minister, Stephen Kalong Ningkan. Daim's role is little realised in Malaysia today, but several senior Sarawakians have said to me that Daim's intervention at the time was critical.

Daim often had to travel to the state capital, Kuching, and on embarking on one such visit he met Musa Hitam, then UMNO executive secretary (and, later, deputy prime minister), at the Kuala Lumpur airport. Musa was going to Kuching too, on behalf of Tun Razak Hussein, who was then deputy prime minister. It was another link; another association that would help to draw Daim into politics.

Daim spent about a month in Sarawak meeting the leaders of the various parties and factions that were involved in moves to replace Stephen Ningkan's Sarawak National Party (SNAP) government. Earlier, a group of state Legislative Assembly members, mostly from the opposition Parti Pesaka and Parti Bumiputera, but also some SNAP members and independent Legislative Assembly members, had met with Prime Minister Tunku Abdul Rahman to inform him that Ningkan and his SNAP government no longer enjoyed the confidence of the Assembly. The prime minister had then sent the home affairs minister, Tun Dr Ismail, and the housing minister, Khaw Kai Boh, to ask Ningkan to resign. Ningkan refused. The governor, Tun Abang Haji Openg, then sacked Ningkan, and Tawi Sli took over as chief minister.

Ningkan sued Tawi Sli and sought a court declaration that his sacking was void and that he should remain as chief minister. Ningkan won the case. He was declared the rightful chief minister, and his sacking was declared null and void. That did not solve the basic problem that Ningkan no longer enjoyed the support of a majority in the state Legislative Assembly and effectively was leading a minority government that would be unable to have any or most of its bills passed. To get around this, Ningkan refused to call a meeting of the Assembly, as was his right, for a period of up to six months. Unrest began to break out in Sarawak and demonstrations were held against Ningkan.

Back in Kuala Lumpur, Daim was asked to attend a cabinet meeting chaired by Razak. Daim briefed the cabinet on the political situation in Sarawak and advised the cabinet that it should declare a state of emergency there in view of the rising tension and demonstrations. The cabinet was convinced and followed Daim's advice. A state of emergency was declared and Razak thanked Daim for all his help.

On the advice of Kuala Lumpur, the Sarawak governor suspended the Standing Orders of the Assembly and called a meeting of the Assembly using emergency powers. Daim helped the governor to draft the statement that the Assembly was to restrict its debate to the no confidence motion in Ningkan only. The Assembly met and the Ningkan administration was duly voted out. It then voted in Tawi Sli as the next chief minister.

Daim's spell at Allen & Gledhill also allowed his and Mahathir's paths to cross. They had not seen each other for 13 years, since their time in Alor Setar. Mahathir by this time was a Member of Parliament and an adviser to the UMNO Labour Bureau. He asked Daim to act for a group within the Sri Jaya Transport Workers' Union. Daim did so, but the action was lost.

The pair did not meet again for another few years. Mahathir had just completed the manuscript for *The Malay Dilemma* and was looking for a publisher. Daim and Mahathir's nephew, Ahmad Mustapha, owned a small publishing business called Karyawan. Mahathir showed Ahmad Mustapha a draft of the book. However, Mahathir lost his seat in the 1969 elections, he was then expelled from UMNO for his criticism of UMNO's leadership. On top of that, the 13 May 1969 riots broke out. With these distractions, and an economy that was deteriorating, the publisher decided to delay publication of the book. Furthermore, Daim and Ahmad wanted to concentrate on building up their publishing business rather than steering it into trouble. As Daim explained to me, 'We were still young and [*The Malay Dilemma*] was too controversial.' Mahathir decided to give it to another publisher. It was published and banned shortly after. The ban was not lifted until 1981 when Mahathir became prime minister. (It was, however, published and distributed by Times Publishing in Singapore throughout the 1970s and 1980s.) Was Daim surprised by the contents of *The Malay Dilemma* and did he agree with all that it said? He said to me that he was not surprised, because he had been reading Mahathir's regular columns in newspapers. He did not agree with all that is in it but does agree that 'it was and is still largely valid'.

Daim stayed away from politics for the next decade or so. He declined the offer by Razak of a seat in Sungei Petani in Kedah in the 1974 general election, preferring instead to concentrate on business. This did not mean that Daim had decided that he was not interested in a political career, but rather that he wanted to be successful in business first. Over the next several years, though, he did have reason to meet with Mahathir, who was by then the deputy prime minister. He pleaded the case, for example, to Mahathir for the release of Harun Idris, the former chief minister of Selangor, who had helped Daim by granting him the right to purchase the land for what became Daim's Taman Maluri project. Idris was serving a prison term for criminal breach of trust. Harun was an old friend and Daim felt that there was a political element to Harun's investigation and prosecution.[1] Mahathir tried to plead Harun's case with Hussein Onn who was then prime minister, but his approaches were firmly rejected. In turn, Daim wanted to directly plead Harun's case, but could not even get a meeting with Onn. Harun might well have been guilty, but many felt that Hussein Onn's insistence on prosecution was born of his desire to thwart the political ascendency of Harun, who was a political rival.

Daim also pleaded for Abdullah Ahmad, who had been detained on the charge of being involved in a communist conspiracy when he was deputy minister in the Prime Minister's Department. Daim viewed the allegations as untenable. When Mahathir became prime minister in 1981, he had Abdullah released from detention and secured a full pardon for Harun. Notwithstanding that, Harun later joined the opposition party Semangat '46, which sought to topple Mahathir. By mid-2000, Harun was very ill after having suffered a stroke. He approached Daim to ask if he might be readmitted to UMNO, and Daim approached Mahathir on Harun's behalf with the request.

Into the Centre

By 1980, Daim was regularly acting as an informal consultant on business matters to Mahathir, who was then deputy prime minister. Daim was candid with his criticism of government policies, and Mahathir seemed to accept that Daim's advice and opinions were genuine and not tainted by vested interests associated with any particular faction of UMNO. It was during this period that their relationship flourished. With Mahathir's backing, Daim rose rapidly to key positions in government and in UMNO. In 1980, Prime Minister Hussein Onn agreed to make Daim a senator on the recommendation of the then finance minister, Tunku Razaleigh Hamzah. When Mahathir became prime minister in 1981, he sent Daim on a number of missions. The first major task was to visit the United States to deal with the structure of the world tin market. The General Services Administration (GSA) had a huge stockpile of tin and it was releasing it on to the world market, causing the price of tin to be depressed. This was obviously harmful to Malaysia, one of the world's largest tin producers. Mahathir wanted Daim to negotiate

---

1   M.S. Cheong and Adibah Amin, *Daim: The Man Behind the Enigma*, Pelanduk Publications, 1995, p. 135.

with the GSA to see if the rate at which it released tin on to the world market could be slowed.

Daim went to Washington accompanied by Alex Lee, by then a senator, and Khalil Akasah, a former UMNO secretary, together with representatives of the government-controlled company Malaysian Mining Corporation, plus several representatives from the private sector. Meetings were arranged with several key American government officials and chairmen of various Senate committees. The trio made little progress in the first few meetings. Daim and Khalil met to discuss what strategies they might employ to make the Americans more sympathetic. They had noticed that the one thing they really seemed to care about was the threat of communism, so that became the basis of the trio's renewed strategy. They emphasised internal security, the big strides the Malaysian government had made in quelling the communist threat within Malaysia, and they explained the background to the Malaysian tin mining industry, where the mines were located, and the historical inroads that the communists had made among the tin miners many of whom were working class Hakka Chinese, a community that had a history of communist sympathies. The ground was laid for a more receptive treatment, and on another visit to the United States, Daim, together with government officials, was able to sign an agreement with the GSA to limit its sales to 3,000 tonnes annually for three years. It was a significant success for Daim.

Daim also assisted the Malaysian government in restoring its relations with Britain in the early 1980s. In October 1981, the Malaysian government announced a 'Buy British last' policy, after a series of problems between the two countries. One of the issues was the raising of university fees in Britain. Many Malaysians were studying in Britain, and as a result of the higher fees Malaysian students went to study in the United States, Canada and Australia instead. Mahathir even went so far as to make an official visit to France, where he invited French companies to come to Malaysia to do business. It was a calculated snub to the British.

At the time, Daim became close to the British High Commissioner to Kuala Lumpur, who increasingly was otherwise losing his access to the Malaysian government. Daim became something of an informal go-between between the British High Commission and the government. Daim was invited by the High Commission to go to London, and Mahathir approved of his going. There Daim met with the permanent secretary of the Foreign Office. He put across several proposals that would help to settle the dispute, something the British were keen to do, as British companies were losing millions of pounds worth of contracts in Malaysia. All the proposals were agreed to, including the return of the Carcosa residence in the hills near Kuala Lumpur. The historic home, which was built in 1898 and had been given to the British by Malaysia's first prime minister, Tunku Abdul Rahman, on Malaysia being granted independence, was being used by the British as the residence for their high commissioner. (It now serves as a boutique hotel and function centre.)

With Daim having paved the way, Mahathir then made an informal visit to London and met with the then prime minister, Margaret Thatcher. All went well, and Mahathir subsequently announced the cessation of the 'Buy British last' policy. Relations between the two countries were at last normalised.

Daim increasingly demonstrated his ability, and in 1982, during the lead-up to the general elections of that year, Mahathir offered the post of chief minister of Kedah, held at the time by Syed Nahar, to Daim. Daim declined the position. It had been many years since he had lived in the state and he had not yet achieved all that he felt he could achieve in Kuala Lumpur. The day before nominations closed for the 1982 elections, Mahathir called Daim and said that he wanted him to stand as the UMNO candidate for the federal Kuala Muda electorate in Kedah state. Daim agreed, despite not having stood for election before and not having campaign experience. With the help of his brothers, he campaigned and ultimately won the election.

In 1981, when Mahathir became prime minister, Mahathir asked Daim to take over either Bank Bumiputera or Ko-op Bersatu Bhd. Neither interested Daim. Daim enjoyed a challenge, but he had the good sense to choose those that were manageable. He did agree, though, when Mahathir, in his capacity as UMNO president, asked him to take over the management of Fleet Holdings, UMNO's main investment arm. At that stage, Fleet's main assets were several of the country's key newspapers. A business role suited Daim. But he also had heard that Deputy Prime Minister Musa was unhappy with Mahathir, and he could sense a possible challenge brewing. By holding the reins at Fleet, he could be sure that Musa's supporters would not hold key posts in the media. But Daim did more than just control Fleet so that others could not. He set about turning it into a conglomerate. UMNO was the largest political party in the country but its income base did not reflect that. Daim wanted to change that. But he could see that with UMNO owning more corporate assets, then the position of the Malays in the economy would be strengthened. Daim also understood how controlling Fleet and thus the newspaper assets it controlled could benefit the Malays and UMNO politically.

UMNO Inc

Initially, UMNO was financed by its members. But after its alliance with the Malaysian Chinese Association (MCA), and later with the Malaysian Indian Congress (MIC), UMNO's mode of financing changed. During the early days, the MCA assisted UMNO with financing for campaigning. But being Malay and largely rural, UMNO's support base almost by definition was unable to keep up with the party's growing financing needs. Gradually it was decided that the party should go into business. The MCA, being the main Chinese party, had an obvious base of wealthy constituents who were more than able to amply bankroll it. Not unreasonably, UMNO wanted its own source of funds to reduce its financial dependence on non-Malay supporters. Throughout the 1970s and then the

1980s, UMNO built up its own conglomerate in the form of the Fleet Group.[2] This entity had its origins in the Singapore-based Straits Times media group, which until 1973 controlled its Malaysian operations from Singapore. In that year, UMNO acquired the group's Malaysian operations. These were renamed the New Straits Times Press (Malaysia) Bhd (NSTP) and held by a new company called Fleet Holdings.

Supervision of Fleet was entrusted to successive UMNO treasurers. Between 1977 and 1982 this role was filled by Tunku Razaleigh. His management of Fleet was relatively low-key, mostly allowing it to expand on the basis of reinvested profits. He did, however, have Fleet acquire major investments in the Bank of Commerce and American Malaysian Insurance, in addition to NSTP. His relatively conservative style was in marked contrast to Daim, who was appointed a director of Fleet in 1982 and then UMNO treasurer (and Minister of Finance) in 1984. Daim's appointment was partly born out of Mahathir's dissatisfaction with the slow growth of UMNO's corporate investments. It was a watershed for UMNO's involvement in business. One of Daim's first moves was to place his protégés Wan Azmi Wan Hamzah and Tajudin Ramli into senior management positions within the Fleet Group. This allowed Daim to step away from the day-today management of UNMO's business interests when he was appointed to the Finance Ministry. Daim's appointment of professional managers, also meant that UMNO's businesses were used by Daim in the way that Peremba had been used – as an incubator to train and test Malay entrepreneurs whom he thought were promising.

Daim's appointment as UMNO Treasurer saw a rapid expansion of Fleet, under the professional managers appointed by Daim. They turned it into a highly diversified conglomerate of which interests in the media and finance sectors were only two of many. It no longer exists as a group but vestiges of it still remain and form some of the most prominent corporate assets in private hands today. The rapid expansion was aided by the patronage of the government, which awarded the group with lucrative contracts and concessions, and beneficial treatment in the allocation of Bumiputera loans and rights issues. Under Daim, Fleet grew to encompass the hotel and property group Faber Merlin Malaysia Bhd, the private television network Sistem Televisyen Malaysia Bhd (STMB) and the food retailer Cold Storage (Malaysia) Bhd. All three were listed on the stock exchange. A controlling stake was also acquired in the merchant bank Commerce International Merchant Bankers Bhd (CIMB). Fleet's acquisition binge was facilitated by a dizzying array of share market manoeuvrings such as rights issues and share swaps. Some of the transactions were so complex that at least one Malaysian academic built his academic career simply on untangling them. Their effect was to revolutionise how business is done in Malaysia.

---

2   UMNO's entry to business is analogous to the Kuomintang's investments in Taiwan, which are separate from those of the state and are designed to make the party financial independent of the state and its membership.

Inevitably, such a rapid transformation of UMNO's business interests drew criticism. Daim, particularly, attracted censure, especially during the 1987 UMNO party elections. Claims and counter claims were made as to what was the actual performance of Fleet's assets. Fleet had expanded rapidly, but when the 1985-86 recession struck, the group was in a precarious position, particularly with the collapse in property prices. The whole purpose of expanding Fleet was to give UMNO a strong source of funds, but with the recession the opposite proved true. Instead of helping to fund UMNO, UMNO was still having to fund it.

So, rather than having a corporate machine that generated vast profits to fund the party machine, senior UMNO officials ended up with a cash-hungry and unwieldy conglomerate that generated a lot of controversy and diverted the attention of the party's senior management away from politics. By the time of the 1985-86 recession, Daim had not only to contend with managing the recessed Malaysian economy but also with the growing mess of UMNO's finances. Banks were pressing UMNO for payment, and the position of the various Fleet Group companies continued to deteriorate. The interest bill alone on all the borrowings was running at around M$5 million a month. Assets needed to be sold to pay debts, but selling assets in the midst of a recession would have meant selling them at the worst possible time. It was not long before UMNO's corporate investments as a whole were technically insolvent.

Relief came on 4 February 1988 when UMNO was declared an illegal organisation and all its companies, assets and liabilities were seized by the Official Assignee. UMNO's investments were no longer Daim's problem. There was concern that the assets might be mismanaged – handling Fleet was difficult enough for Daim and Fleet's management, let alone for civil servants. Fortunately, the Official Assignee elected to sell them off, by which time asset prices had recovered. The proceeds from the sale were then turned over to UMNO. With the sale, UMNO and its successor, UMNO Bahru, could claim that it was no longer in business.

By 1990, UMNO had shares in a business empire that comprised some of the most important listed companies in Malaysia, including UEM, Hume Industries, Time Engineering, CIMA, Kinta Kellas, NSTP, Bank of Commerce and STMB. Halim Saad acquired control of the lot and folded them into Renong, which until then had been a small company listed on the KLSE.

Rumours soon circulated that Halim, through Renong, was holding stakes in all these companies on behalf of UMNO. There were suggestions too that Daim was also involved and that somehow, Daim was also secretly holding stakes either for UMNO, or for himself, or both. The rumours should have been nipped in the bud. Instead, they were allowed to go largely unchecked. If Daim can be accused fairly of anything, it is a failure to have better explained who owned what and to have done so in a timely, transparent and credible manner. He did not, and it became conventional wisdom that Renong was acting as UMNO's nominee in its control of these companies.

The rumours were such that by 1993, Halim felt compelled to meet with

Mahathir to confirm to the prime minister that he was indeed the owner of Renong and that he was not holding the stake on behalf of UMNO. Daim confirms that after the 1990 sale, no longer was there any commercial link, nominee or otherwise, between UMNO and Renong/UEM. He says that persistent rumours otherwise were a constant millstone around Halim's neck.

Another rumour which took hold, not just in the broader community but among even some government members, was that UMNO had accumulated net assets worth some M$20 billion. When it became clear that UMNO did not have access to such wealth, there were those who then wondered where the money had gone, not realising that such wealth had not existed in the first place. 'It seemed that the leadership had wondered which were my assets and which were the UMNO assets', Daim says. 'This was an unkind cut.' No doubt Daim feels it was particularly unkind because when he took over as party treasurer in 1984, UMNO's finances were a scandalous mess and he then spent the next six years rationalising and reorganising them. He had also found a way for UMNO to withdraw from the direct ownership of corporate assets.

Daim points out that Halim borrowed to buy UMNO's stake in various companies from the Official Assignee, and the price he paid gave UMNO a M$178.75 million profit. UMNO also ultimately made a M$50 million profit from the Fleet rescue deal. He says that as UMNO treasurer, the single biggest contribution he received on behalf of UMNO around that time was M$48 million, and that Halim himself made a donation before the 1990 election of M$20 million. But thereafter, donations from top Malay businessmen were not as great as might be imagined, largely because most of them had borrowed so heavily that they simply didn't have the spare cash. On top of that, UMNO had large outgoings, particularly at election time, when the cost of preparing for and fighting an election alone during the 1990s was believed to be around M$100 million.

UMNO's Later Investments

UMNO's need for money is the same as any political party elsewhere. Funds are principally required for election campaigns. Electoral laws restrict campaign spending to no more than a set amount per candidate, but the restriction applies only during the period of the official campaign (that is, from the time that the prime minister calls the election until the day of the election). Daim readily concedes that in reality much more than that is spent, generally in the lead-up to the calling of the election.

Today, UMNO is out of business in all senses and has been since the early 1990s. No longer are there stakes held in individual companies either directly or indirectly. But that is not to say that the party does not have investments. Daim says that the bulk of the party's assets at the national level are invested on the Kuala Lumpur Stock Exchange, not directly and not in any nominee arrangements but simply in mutual funds operated by both local and foreign firms. Consequently, UMNO does not show up on any company shareholder registry and nor should it. By 2000, Daim, as UMNO treasurer, claimed he had no knowledge of the companies in which the mutual funds invest UMNO's funds. He said it was all done on a purely professional and commercial basis and he was only interested in the bottom line.

Daim is unequivocal that political parties should not be involved in business. The potential for conflicts of interest are but one problem. 'There is bound to be some conflict,' he has said, 'But as long as things are done in the open and are declared, there is nothing wrong. My concern is that there are not enough capable and competent people to run the companies. Nobody wants to run business for political parties. What if the party loses the election?… Anyway the role of the Government is to run the country. Create the right environment so that business can thrive. Politicians should concentrate on politics. Draw the line clearly. Let businessmen be free to do business. When they do well, they can donate to the party.'[3] Daim, it seems, had experimented with broadening UMNO's role in business and ultimately learned that continuing with the experiment was a mistake. Daim's pragmatism is demonstrated again – if something doesn't work then try something else.

But does that mean that political parties should make a public declaration of their sources of finances? Perhaps they should be required to declare who their donors are and how much is donated, as is the rule in some other countries. 'Some of our coalition partners would not be very keen on that!' Daim laughed when I asked him. Still, Daim feels that the day is coming when such disclosures will be required in Malaysia. Renong, Daim disclosed in 2000, was a donor to UMNO but only around election time. But Daim claimed that Renong did not donate 'anything' for the 1999 elections because 'it didn't have any money'. That was true enough. In the wake of the 1997-98 economic crisis it was still fighting off insolvency.

But how does Daim justify the fact that UMNO was in business in the first place, and that he was instrumental in pushing it further down that route? UMNO had to be self-funding, he argues. Now that it is, it no longer needs to be, and nor should it be, in business. He believes that this should be so of all political parties. Of course, the argument is somewhat circular. Parties should not be in business, but they need to be self-funding. To become self-funding, then perhaps they might need to go into business. Whatever the case, UMNO can justifiably claim now to be out of active business, and has been so for many years. It retains some assets but these are mostly real estate investments such as the Putra World Trade Centre, the Pan Pacific Hotel and Menara Duta Onn, all in Kuala Lumpur, and these all earn an income. It also holds cash in fixed deposits. With these, it is self-sufficient, or at least it should be if these assets are managed well.

Into the Ministry

It is as finance minister that Daim has really made his mark on Malaysia. Mahathir made Daim finance minister in 1984. By then Daim had been the parliamentary

---

3   M.S. Cheong and Adibah Amin, op. cit., p. 126.

member for Kuala Muda for two years and, prior to that, had been a senator for two years. Although an UMNO member, he had not been an active participant in its internal machinations. Nonetheless, he concedes he was a keen observer. He was not aligned to either of the two major groupings in UMNO at that time – the supporters of Musa and the supporters of Razaleigh. For Mahathir, that was a considerable attraction. What he needed was a finance minister who would provide independent advice – a finance minister who would work for him and not be beholden to others.

The 1984 UMNO elections had deepened the rift between the two factions. Razaleigh had challenged Musa for the deputy president's post (which conventionally leads to the deputy prime ministership). Mahathir had made it clear to Razaleigh that he did not want him to challenge Musa, but Razaleigh proceeded anyway. Back in 1981, the two had vied for the same position and on that occasion Musa won. This time he won again. Subsequently, Mahathir demoted Razaleigh from the Finance Ministry to the Ministry of Trade and Industry. Daim explained to me that Mahathir had called him and explained that in the wake of Razaleigh's unsuccessful challenge, he felt that Razaleigh should be moved from the Finance Ministry, and that he wanted Daim to have the job. Musa wanted Abdullah Ahmad Badawi to be named finance minister, but it was to Daim that Mahathir offered the spot.

Daim did not accept immediately. He wanted time to reflect on the appointment and to consult with his family. Mahathir offered one week. Daim took a month. One of the reasons for his initial reluctance seems to be that he already had the prime minister's ear and was thus already influential. The position of finance minister would mean additional work and responsibility, but not necessarily significantly greater influence. It also would take Daim away from concentrating on his business interests. Daim's family left the decision to him, so he consulted with Anwar Ibrahim and Sanusi Junid, who was then national and rural development minister (and later chief minister of Kedah and, from March 2000, the president of the International Islamic University of Malaysia). Both said that he should accept.

Daim told Mahathir that he would accept, but asked him how long he intended to stay as prime minister, for Daim felt that he could leave when Mahathir did. Mahathir indicated that he would most likely retire in 1988. He was tiring and wanted to spend more time with his family and on his hobbies.[4] This satisfied Daim. It meant that he would then need to spend only four years in the cabinet. Daim says he later told Mahathir that he needed time to reorganise his business affairs to minimise questions as to conflicts of interest, although at the time, there was no ruling about ministers having investments.

Daim knew a lot about business when he was appointed as finance minister, but what did he know about economics? 'Not much,' was his candid response when I put the question to him. He did not rely on anyone in particular in the

---

4   Ibid., p. 37.

Finance Ministry to act as a tutor to him. Instead, he read as many economics textbooks as time would allow. He did, however, nominate Mustapa Mohamad to be a close adviser and confidante. Mustapa had been working as a lecturer when Daim first appointed him as his special assistant. (This lasted from 1984 to 1987, and from 1987 to 1991 he served as Daim's political secretary. He later became second finance minister but lost his parliamentary seat in the 1999 general elections.) Daim felt that it was important to at least be able to carry himself off as knowledgeable on the subject in meetings with his ministry officials.

One of Daim's earliest realisations was that the economy could not be run just like another business, albeit a big one. Said Daim, 'Managing an economy is not like managing a business organisation. In managing the national economy, the demands of the society impose the delicate need to balance a variety of expectations and hopes, which sometimes, can be at odds with one another.'[5] The bottom line is the main determinant for running a business, but there are many social and economic indicators that must be watched and taken into account when running an economy.

Not surprisingly, Daim's appointments as both finance minister and UMNO treasurer was met with criticism from within UMNO and from the opposition. Daim dismissed questions of possible conflicts of interest. He claimed that when cabinet decisions involved UMNO's corporate interests, he left the decision making to others. Furthermore, he had appointed professional managers to run UMNO's investments and largely absented himself from the day-to-day running of those investments.

Deputy Prime Minister Musa was also relatively hostile. Daim has said that each time Mahathir was overseas (which meant that Musa was left in charge), Musa would call Daim to his office and lecture him on this or that.[6] One of Musa's complaints seemed to be Daim's directness. If Daim did not like a policy, he would come straight out and say so. Musa, it seemed, preferred a more oblique approach, which certainly would have been more in keeping with traditional Malay ways. But this has never been Daim's style.

The rift between Daim and Musa worsened. Musa opposed many of Mahathir's policy positions, and soon it was clear that there was a rift between Mahathir and Musa. Nonetheless, within the cabinet, Mahathir had a solid core of supporters that included Daim, Anwar, Sanusi and Rafidah Aziz, who was then public enterprises minister. (Daim, Anwar and Sanusi were nicknamed 'AIDS', after their initials, by their UMNO opponents. The name, of course, was meant as an insult but Daim remembers it with amusement.) Musa ultimately resigned as deputy prime minister in 1986. Mahathir asked Anwar if he wanted to replace Musa, but Anwar declined, saying that he was not ready.

---

5 Speech by Daim to the National and International Chamber of Commerce and Industry (NICCI) Luncheon, Kuala Lumpur, 8 July 1999.

6 Cheong and Adibah Amin, op. cit., p. 38.

Malaysia's run of luck appeared to have reasserted itself with Daim's appointment. The country's long period of sustained economic growth meant that it had been able to afford successive governments in which ministers' over-riding concerns were with playing politics. In Daim, Malaysia was given, just at the right time as it was about to enter recession, a finance minister who cared little for politicking, but a great deal about the policy challenges at hand. He made a point of doing what he felt needed to be done and barely tempered his policy directions with political considerations – that was left to others.

Importantly, Daim was relatively immune from internal UMNO political pressure. 'From the time I joined the Government, I decided that I would not seek any elected office in UMNO. I was not prepared to be blackmailed with votes.'[7] Daim could afford to be indifferent to the sectional and parochial interests of his ministerial colleagues, and to a large degree he was. It suited his contrarian nature. What Daim was not immune from was controversy and shortly after his appointment, he met with the first significant patch of it.

The UMBC Controversy

Being both a senior government figure and a wealthy businessman is bound to lead to allegations of conflicts of interest. Daim faced many such allegations. Some are better founded than others, although Daim always seems to have a well-reasoned explanation as to why there was no conflict of interest or, if there was, how it was handled. He argues passionately that he always conducted his affairs with appropriate diligence and propriety. Others might prefer a more strict separation between business and policy, but Daim's conscience is clear. Besides, there is no suggestion that he ever broke any laws in his dealings while he served as a minister.

Nonetheless, the most controversial deal in which Daim was involved was the acquisition and sale of the United Malayan Banking Corporation (UMBC). UMBC was formed in 1960 by a group of Chinese businessmen headed by Chang Ming Thien. In 1976, the government-controlled Bumiputera unit trust Pernas acquired a 30% stake in the bank after it had come under scrutiny from Bank Negara. Its owners were suspected of misappropriating funds, which led to Bank Negara restructuring the bank's management and ownership. In November 1980, Chang sold his 56% stake to Multi-Purpose Holdings Bhd (MPHB), the MCA's business arm. MPBH was managed at the time by Tan Koon Swan and was listed on the KLSE.

The sale to the MCA was opposed by UMNO's Youth Wing. Its leadership objected to Malaysia's third-largest bank being controlled by the Chinese, particularly the Chinese party, and especially when the bank was already 30% owned by Bumiputera interests via Pernas. They wanted Pernas to have first right of refusal for Chang's controlling interest. The issue became politically sensitive and one that the government needed to defuse. Mahathir, who was acting prime minister at the time, asked Daim to see how the problem might be resolved. Daim

---

7   Ibid., p. 84.

had a meeting with Chang, who said that he was happy to sell to anyone if the price was right.

Finally, it was agreed that Pernas would raise its stake from 30% to 40.68%, that MPHB would buy 40.68%, and that the rest would go to a party or parties approved by the government. Ultimately, a company was formed to buy 11% of the remaining equity so that it, with Pernas, would control the bank.

The arrangement met with the approval of UMNO Youth, although it still preferred that Pernas should buy the MPHB stake in the bank. For UMNO Youth, the 'Malayisation' of the bank would be a symbolic victory over ethnic Chinese interests. The opportunity for the Malayisation would soon arise.

In 1982, the French government nationalised all of its banks. The consequence of this was that the hitherto private Banque Indosuez was now government-owned, including its branch operations in Malaysia. However, Malaysian laws prevent the operation of banks in Malaysia that are owned by foreign governments. Daim decided to purchase Banque Indosuez's Malaysian operations. Accordingly, the Malaysian French Bank was incorporated as a local bank, with Daim having a 51% controlling equity, through one of his family companies, Aslira Sdn Bhd. Other shareholders included Kuok Brothers Sdn Bhd (19%) and Banque Indosuez (30%).

In 1984 and prior to Daim being made finance minister, Tan Koon Swan approached Daim to see whether he would be interested in swapping his 51% stake in the Malaysian French Bank for MPHB's 40.68% stake in UMBC. MPHB did not have majority control of any bank and was keen to do so, even if it was a smaller bank. Politically, the move would satisfy both the MCA and UMNO Youth, in that the MCA would gain control of a bank and UMBC would become clearly Bumiputera-controlled. Mahathir approved the sale and Daim borrowed M$240 million to complete the transaction. The stake was bought by Daim through two family companies. (MPHB later increased its stake in Malaysian French Bank to 70% when it acquired the Kuok Brothers stake.)

Shortly after, in July 1984, Daim was made a cabinet minister when he accepted the finance portfolio. The final approval for Daim's acquisition of the UMBC stake was given in December 1984 – after Daim's appointment. As finance minister, Daim had certain responsibilities under the Banking Act which included granting approval for any arrangement involving the sale of shares in a bank that resulted in a change of management or control. So, on becoming minister, Daim was in the position of having to approve transactions in relation to the control of a bank by two of his own companies. It was an unfortunate situation brought about by the time that such transactions take given the highly regulated nature of the banking sector. The transaction had been in the pipeline for many months prior to his appointment. In fact, at the time of the negotiations, Daim says he had no inkling that Mahathir was thinking of offering him the finance portfolio. Even so, it did not look good, and later Daim and Mahathir's opponents, both within and outside UMNO, were able to make political capital from it.

During Daim's first week as minister, the file dealing with his acquisition of the UMBC stake reached his office. He sent it back to the secretary-general of the Treasury, stating that he could not deal with it as it related to his family's private companies. The then Acting Minister of Finance (Daim was away at a World Bank meeting) referred the matter to the cabinet, which agreed that the sale could proceed. Daim claims that he still did not deal with the file, but that it was signed off on when he was overseas, and that the approval was granted by the acting finance minister. This allowed Daim to claim that he was not a party to the approval. Such awkwardness often is the case when governments need ministers with hands-on business experience.

It was not the end of the controversial transactions, however. UMBC announced a rights issue, but Pernas declined to subscribe. This was reasonable, as UMBC was already in majority Bumiputera hands and Pernas had other investment priorities at the time. Pernas's unused rights were then passed to the Daim family companies that held stakes in UMBC, which exercised these rights as well as those it already had. As a consequence, Daim was able to lift his equity in UMBC from 40.68% to 50.38%, giving him outright control of the bank. Daim's companies required approval from the finance minister for this latest round of transactions. And again, the conflict-of-interest situation was side-stepped by cabinet (through the Acting Minister of Finance) giving the move approval, rather than Daim in his role as finance minister. Daim is unequivocal that he did nothing wrong. Nonetheless, the matter attracted much controversy. The *Asian Wall Street Journal*'s coverage of the UMBC deal so incensed the Malaysian government that it had the work permits of the paper's two Kuala Lumpur-based journalists revoked in September 1986.

Criticism that Daim took into account his own family businesses when he made policy decisions as finance minister were somewhat blunted, though, when, shortly after he acquired majority equity in UMBC, he introduced legislation that prevented individuals in future from owning more than 10% of a bank or financial institution's stock, or corporations from owning more than 20%. The measures meant that later, when Daim was required to sell his stake in UMBC, Pernas was one of the few organisations legally entitled to buy it as a block. Thus, the considerable premium that might have been attached to the UMBC stake, as it conferred control of a bank on the owner, was lost.

Still, the controversy surrounding Daim and his interests in UMBC did not stop there. The cabinet issued a directive in 1986 that ministers should sell their stakes in listed companies. The aim was to lessen the potential for conflicts of interest and, with Daim being both finance minister and the controller of a major local bank, there appeared to be plenty of such potential there. So, Daim was required to sell his stake in UMBC. The buyer of Daim's entire stake in UMBC was the government-controlled Pernas. It purchased the shares at Daim's cost price plus a mark-up to cover the holding costs. Daim still smarts at the memory of the forced sale: despite claims that he had profited, in fact the sale represented a loss for him, as he had to pay tax on the sale – ironically a tax introduced by Daim's own legislation.

Offers had come from non-Bumiputera interests, but to be fair to Daim, selling out to such interests would have invoked much fury, particularly from UMNO Youth. Given such sensitivities, Mahathir wanted the bank sold to a Bumiputera institution. Pernas was the obvious choice, notwithstanding that it had only recently rejected more shares in the rights issue. Pernas decided to buy the stake, and immediately asked the Treasury to give it the funds to do so. But Daim refused Pernas' request. It would have been outrageous for the finance minister to authorise the Treasury to give funds to Pernas so that it could buy his family's stake in a bank. Instead, Pernas was encouraged to seek the funds from the market. As Daim says, it was a good, commercial deal and he told Pernas so. They should be able to raise funds from the private sector on that basis, and if they could not then they should 'forget about it.'

Pernas managed to get a loan from commercial banks to buy the UMBC stake, but as Daim says, 'the attack on me never stopped. It just went on and on.' He complains that Pernas then gave the impression that it was forced to buy the stake and says that when he heard this he arranged for other buyers to buy the stake from Pernas but Pernas suddenly was not willing to sell, claiming it was a long-term investment. He says Pernas was bluffing when it suggested that it was forced to buy the stake. The Pernas management 'preferred the status quo so that if anything went wrong, the blame could be shifted to me.'

The UMBC controversy gained new life during the 1987 UMNO fight when Mahathir was challenged for leadership of the party by Tengku Razaleigh Hamzah. The Razaleigh faction raised it suggesting that there had been impropriety. Daim was aghast. Daim told me that 'I was angry with UMNO because during the fight between Team A (Mahathir's camp) and Team B (Razaleigh's camp), this was used as an issue against Team A, yet it was UMNO Youth that had objected to the Bank being sold to a non-Malay entity (the MCA) and I had to borrow to solve UMNO's objections. It cost me M$240 million! Instead of thanking me, they chose to forget the truth and use it as a political too. That's UMNO for you!'

The UMBC sale had been discussed in Cabinet and had subsequently been approved. As Daim says, 'Everybody seemed to be supportive until the 1987 UMNO fight when those who opposed Dr Mahathir suddenly made this an issue. I could not understand how those who supported it in the Cabinet could go out and oppose it now for political reasons. Where was their integrity?'

To comply with the cabinet directive, Daim and his family sold interests in 16 other companies in addition to the UMBC stake. Says Daim, 'recession was the worst of times to dispose of any assets especially shares. But I had made my choice. I agreed to serve the government and the government had made the decision that I had to dispose my shares. And I sold them.'

Included was a large interest in the Malaysian conglomerate Sime Darby. Daim told me that he had wanted to take the conglomerate over, but Mahathir had asked him not to do so. When Daim was forced to sell the shares in Sime Darby to comply with the cabinet directive, their price had fallen significantly from recent highs and Daim claims that he made no profit on the holding. 'After we sold and the market recovered, the shares went up double the price. The family could have made enough for a lifetime. But we sold and hardly made a profit,' Daim says. The UMBC saga attracted a lot of innuendo but as Daim says, 'Nobody said anything when we had to sell our Sime shares.'

Furthermore, the sale of the UMBC stake meant that Daim was hit with a M$10 million transfer tax, which he paid, although reluctantly. He was incensed at having to pay the tax when the sale was not of his own volition but was forced on him to comply with the cabinet directive. He launched court proceedings against the government to challenge the tax, but senior members of the government suggested that it might be best if he dropped them and 'forgot' about the tax. To this day, he is still annoyed that he had to pay the tax. 'M$10 million is a lot of money to be told just to forget about it,' he complained to me during our discussions.

Mahathir as Prime Minister – A Perspective from Daim

Looking beyond the day-to-day business of politics, what does Daim have to say about Mahathir? As we will see later, Daim was unequivocal in his support for Mahathir. Daim's role was very much that of the loyal lieutenant. But what did Daim feel that he could offer Mahathir? He was full of admiration for Mahathir's capacity for hard work. Mahathir is always very well briefed, Daim told me in 2000. For his part, Daim liked to advise Mahathir on the workings of business and the behaviour of business people. 'He is not fully smart on business. He doesn't always know how to tell who are the crooks and it is on this that I can advise,' Daim told me. He has also said, 'Mahathir's weakness was and still is trusting people; sometimes the wrong people. He would give people every chance to prove that they were indeed not against him. He never listened to warnings by friends. He always wanted concrete evidence first. Those close to him advised him to be wary of certain characters. He would call upon those characters, and after a short chat, he would be convinced of their support for him. He would then tell us not to worry about them. But we heard other stories and saw what they were doing.'[8] Daim prefered to be cynical where Mahathir was trusting and saw it as his role to advise accordingly.

In cabinet, Mahathir was not the aggressive dominator that many might assume. Rather than walk into the room, announce his position and then expect everyone to fall into line, Daim says that Mahathir tended to stay quiet, listen to the various positions, weigh them up, assess which points of view hold the numbers and who holds them, and then he announced his view. 'Mahathir is too smart to announce his view and expect others to follow,' says Daim.

Certainly, the view that Mahathir dominated the cabinet, the cabinet dominated the government, and the government dominated the Parliament and that, as a result, Malaysia under Mahathir was a *de facto* dictatorship, is a lot of nonsense.

8   Ibid., p. 136.

A long-lived dictatorship of the sort that Mahathir sometimes was accused of running could barely exist in Malaysia. Regional, multi-ethnic and multi-party politics are simply too complex and the compromise between all these conflicting interests too finely balanced for Mahathir or anyone else to consistently dominate and over-rule. But Mahathir did stamp his mark on government in Malaysia if for no other reason than by his force of personality. The stamp was applied carefully, though, and usually after a careful weighing up of the consequences. He was, as prime minister, a strong leader but also a coalitionist, both within and outside UMNO. Undoubtedly, the Asian tendency to support the leader gave Mahathir greater latitude than enjoyed by his prime ministerial colleagues in the West, but Mahathir's authority was tempered by political reality nonetheless. Such is the environment in which Daim the politician also had to learn to operate.

VI

THE ART OF POLITICS

Daim has often been described as a reluctant politician. It is nonsense. Daim loves politics. He has been UMNO treasurer, a member of Parliament and a cabinet minister – the latter not once, but twice. That is not the career pattern of someone who doesn't like politics. 'I am a politician through and through … I was just reluctant to hold office,' he has been quoted as saying.[1] He described himself to me as a 'student' of politics rather than a 'practitioner'. As his first stint as finance minister was drawing to a close, *The Economist* of 16 February 1991 said of Daim, 'He was that rare breed – a politician without political ambition.' But a politician nonetheless. As defence minister Najib Tun Razak said to me in late 2000, 'Tun would see politics as the pinnacle of himself as a person. He is proud of his record and he has every reason to be.'

Thong Yaw Hong, who served as secretary-general of the Ministry of Finance between 1979 and 1986, said of Daim: 'When Tun Daim assumed the post of finance minister, I had the impression that he was a reluctant minister. He was doing very well in his business and was drafted into the position. He had no political ambition to go further up the ladder. The fact helped him to make independent and unbiased decisions in the national interest.'[2] Thong was right. Daim was a reluctant minister, but he was not a reluctant politician. The power and the ability to achieve things attracted Daim to the position of cabinet minister, but the posturing and the protocol did not. He dislikes the formalities that come with being a politician. He is results-driven, and attending international forums is not something that he had either the patience or the time for. As Lee Kuan Yew said, 'He is an unusual politician. He is not a politician in the ordinary sense of the word because he is not interested in holding high public office. He is only interested in getting things done.'[3] During a conversation at his home in mid-2000, he said to me, with a wry look that was somewhere between triumphant and mischievous, that 'this time' as a minister he had yet to attend any international ministerial meetings at all. He had someone else to go on his behalf. He is a doer and not a poser but always pragmatic.

And what was Daim like as finance minister from the perspective of his government colleagues? As a minister, 'he [Daim] is very approachable and very

---

1 M.S. Cheong and Adibah Amin, *Daim: The Man Behind the Enigma*, Pelanduk Publications, 1995, p. 35.

2 Ibid., p. 170.

3 Ibid., p. 163.

quick to reply to letters', said defence minister Najib. Rarely in Najib's experience had Daim knocked back a request for extra funding for this or that ministerial program. 'Often you might not get all that you ask for, but Daim generally tries to accommodate you as much as he can', said Najib. In cabinet, Daim prefered to listen rather than to talk. 'He only talks when he has to,' Najib told me. Daim it seems prefers to talk to Mahathir and others in private ahead of or after a cabinet discussion, to voice his views or concerns. There is a practical aspect to this too. Cabinet presents a forum for the heads of the other parties in the coalition government to have their say and to be heard by the prime minister. Daim on the other hand had access to the prime minister and other senior UMNO figures that other party leaders might not have had.

The view from the back bench was also supportive. 'Tun is a hands on person and is very committed. He works long, long hours... He really looks into all the micro details, meets everyone and comes up with blueprints. He's not like other ministers who might want to be told what to say just an hour or two before they're due to make an announcement', said Dato' Jamaludin Jarjis, the now late and then chairman of the Back Benchers' Club and later Minister of Science, Technology and Innovation (among other portfolios) and Malaysia's ambassador to the United States. Daim had the reputation of being approachable and quick to respond to letters and queries. Daim, unlike some ministers, personally briefed government back benchers on upcoming bills of interest to them.

Tending the Grassroots

The pleasure that Daim took in being a politician was clear when he made return visits to his Merbok parliamentary constituency. It was a time for getting around and meeting people and catching up on local gossip. Merbok, which Daim held from 1986 to 2004 (between 1982 and 1986 he was the member for Kuala Muda), is centred on Alor Setar in northern Malaysia. It covers three state constituencies – Gurun, Bukit Selambau and Tanjung Dawai. Daim was an important player on the national stage but he was also an active local member. A local UMNO brochure produced for the 1999 national elections, which depicted the constituency in a series of panels, first showed Merbok prior to Daim being its representative. Local industry is summarised by pictures of a farmer tilling his padi field with a buffalo-drawn plough, women planting the padi, and a rubber tapper scoring the trunk of a rubber tree. The next panel shows Merbok with Daim as its representative. There are pictures of new mosques, new schools, a new Universiti Teknologi Mara building, new roads, heavy industry, and farmers using automated tillers and other such equipment. The final panel shows Merbok in the future, having had the benefit of further years of Daim as its member in Parliament. This time there are pictures of electronic circuitry, a satellite, a jet, a radio telescope and other such paraphernalia of the high-tech age. The message is clear: Daim stands for development.

Daim made it a practice to visit Merbok at least once a month in the wake of the November 1999 national elections in which UMNO lost significant ground, particularly to the opposition PAS. Grassroots campaigning became the catch-cry within UMNO after the elections, and Daim made a point of having as much contact with ordinary people as possible on the visits. He would fly to the constituency from Kuala Lumpur in the morning, spend the day travelling around the constituency, meeting, greeting and giving speeches, and then return to Kuala Lumpur in the evening. His UMNO division vice chairman, Suhaimi Abdul Razak, often accompanied Daim on these trips. Suhaimi, like Daim, was based in Kuala Lumpur but maintained close personal and family ties to Merbok.

I accompanied Daim and Suhaimi on one of these visits in April 2000. On the appointed day, Suhaimi and I waited on the tarmac at the private jet hangar at Subang, near Kuala Lumpur. We had been told to arrive early because Daim waits for no one; once he had arrived, the jet would take off. It was not too long before a blue Mercedes Benz drove on to the tarmac, with number plates that ended in '11' – Daim's preferred numbers that are on many of the cars in his private collection. The doors opened and out he stepped. He wore blue jeans, a loose cotton shirt and a pair of very scuffed Nike sandshoes with velcro straps instead of laces. Daim had lived up to his famous disregard for sartorial elegance. Everywhere we went, he was, quite simply, the worst-dressed person. Partly it is a matter of personal style and partly sensible politics. It is not good to be seen wandering around the *kampungs* dressed in a suit and tie as if one has just arrived from Kuala Lumpur. Not that Daim wears suits and ties in Kuala Lumpur. When it comes to clothing, he simply doesn't care. Once again, 'doing' takes precedence over 'posing'.

Daim spent the first half of the flight to Alor Setar flicking through the *Sun*, the *Star* and the *Berita Harian* newspapers. Newspapers are an essential tool of politicians everywhere. They inform on public opinion, current events and, perhaps most importantly, on what one's political colleagues have been doing. The other very important part of any newspaper, at least as far as Daim is concerned, is the sports section. These pages received as much attention as the news sections.

On landing at Alor Setar airport we were met by a group of local UMNO officials. After warm greetings all round, and particularly for Daim, the party made its way through the airport and into three Mercedes-Benzes and a Pajero, which, with a police motorcycle, formed the core of the convoy for the day's visit. We drove out of the airport compound and with little fanfare made our way down a highway.

The convoy stopped on a tollroad to pay the toll. Each car stopped, including the head car that carried Daim. That was something of a surprise. An official of Renong Group which operates many of Malaysia's tollroads, later said to me that even the prime minister's car must stop and pay the tolls on tollroads, even when travelling on official business.

The first stop for Daim and the rest of the convoy was a small village called Kampung Segantang Garam. A large meeting for local UMNO members and other interested people had assembled at an open-air meeting place by the side of a road surrounded by fields and with a picturesque backdrop of limestone mountains. Altogether around 120 people had gathered to hear from Daim. The various local UMNO officials took turns at making short speeches, which were followed by a speech from Daim himself. He wore a red baseball cap emblazoned with gold writing that spelled out 'UMNO Merbok'. Far from being the reluctant politician, he appeared to take considerable delight in the activities. He gave a chatty speech and looked carefully and gently into the audience. Behind him sat two rows of the local UMNO hierarchy. His was a consummate Malay performance. It was relaxed, assured, self-effacing and laced with gentle humour.

Although it was a rural audience, Daim talked to them about foreign reserves, the currency and the national economy. He talked *with* them, rather than down to them. It was symbolic of the Mahathir government's approach to the wider Malay constituency – not to avoid talking about weighty issues on the presumption that they will not be understood, but rather to talk about them in direct terms and in ways that *can* be understood.

At the end of the speech, Daim presented packets of money (from his own pocket, the local UMNO vice chairman said later) to four poor families. Next, he presented 15 new bicycles to local children from poor families, paid for by an UMNO charitable foundation. First he inspected the bicycles for the benefit of a local television camera crew, and then he shook the hand of each child in turn and handed each one a bicycle, which they excitedly rode off on. In turn, Daim was presented with a large basket of local fruits wrapped in orange cellophane.

After the ceremony was over, lunch was served for the visiting dignitaries and local UMNO hierarchy. Local dishes such as prawns, fish, stewed jackfruit, mango salad and sambal were served. The food was not grand but it was plentiful, and all who ate did so in the traditional Malay style – Daim included – without cutlery and by using their right hands, which were later washed with the aid of water kettles.

Daim then strode over to a group of waiting journalists and gave a sit-down media conference. Among the questions he was asked was his response to a statement by a senator in the Dewan Rakyat who had pointed out some anomalies with the administration of the Employees Provident Fund. Daim indicated that he agreed with the senator's concerns and said that the government was studying amendments to the fund.

After the media conference, the convoy moved on. The next stop was a mosque, where Daim and the others went for prayers. The afternoon rains had set in and Daim and the various members of the party filed out of the cars and into the mosque holding blue and white Barisan Nasional umbrellas aloft as they went. By this time the police motorcyclist was replaced by a police squad car with flashing lights which led the convoy. The convoy departed the mosque for the next venue. On the way, it stopped at the house of a prominent local UMNO official – an old friend of Daim's – to kill some time before the next event. Hot tea and cakes were served, photographs were taken and gossip was exchanged before it was time to leave for the next venue.

At Kampung Bujang there were more speeches, and an appearance by the newly-appointed Menteri Besar of Kedah, followed by a speech by Daim. Among the seven men on the stage, Daim was the most obvious, particularly with his scruffy Nike sports shoes. The other six wore black leather business shoes. Again, Daim's speech was very relaxed. For someone who is supposed to be ill at ease in public, Daim clearly enjoyed himself. Daim ended his speech by presenting a number of awards to people from the audience, with each one being called up in turn. That over, there was another table of food to be considered by Daim and his party and then a quick exit and on to the next venue.

The drive there almost came to grief, when several cars in the convoy almost collided with two buffaloes that had wandered on to the road. They looked more surprised than we. Eventually, the convoy arrived at a rubber estate staffed mostly by Tamil Indian workers. (There are many rubber plantations in Merbok.) A meeting venue had been set up on the lawns, and Daim, the Kedah Menteri Besar and other local UMNO officials sat down and listened to more speeches. Daim sat next to the estate manager who was English and very much a relic from the colonial days. He had been living in Malaysia for the past 50 years. He immediately tackled Daim about the distribution of welfare monies and about unanswered correspondence. The haranguing did not let up and lasted for the entire visit. Daim undertook to look into the problems and the unanswered letters. There was no amplification at this event. Daim had to give his third speech for the afternoon and it was difficult to hear all the proceedings. The speech was followed by another meal, including plenty of hot tea and traditional Malay coconut desserts. It was then back to the cars and the convoy moved on to yet another rubber estate.

On arrival, the party made its way into a large hall that had no electricity and, again, there was no amplification. At many of the meetings, Daim or the local senior party officials were handed envelopes that contained letters from voters voicing their concerns about various matters. At this meeting, one elderly Malay woman attempted to hand two envelopes to an UMNO official. 'No,' he said. 'Give it directly to Daim yourself.' 'We're trying to promote grassroots contact,' he later explained to me. The crowd of perhaps a hundred settled in the darkened hall, Daim was introduced, he spoke, he was presented with another basket of local fruits and other goods, before the party made its way to another table laden with local foods. After a brief snack, we were off again – to yet another appointment. If Daim felt tired, he showed no signs of it. This time the convoy had expanded to nine cars plus police vehicles.

We made our way to Sungei Petani, Kedah's second-largest town. There Daim opened a Goodyear tyre and auto services shop that had been established by a local Bumiputera cooperative. There were more speeches, another assembled audience and more food. One of the cooperative's managers spoke about their plans to expand aggressively into other areas. The new shop looked very bright with its shiny paint and trimmings, the crowd was impressively large, and management clearly had big plans. Who should upset proceedings? None other than the VIP guest – Daim himself, who duly announced in the middle of his speech that the cooperative's plans for such aggressive expansion went beyond the permitted scope and as such would be illegal. The audience was delighted by this very public show of Daim's well-known bluntness. The managers undoubtedly were somewhat embarrassed. Daim was unapologetic when I later mentioned the incident to him and seemed slightly amused at his having thrown a spanner in the works. The rules were clear, he said, but the managers had made it equally clear that they intended to breach them, unknowingly or not. So, he felt that he had little choice but to warn them.

Next, there was a visit to Daim's sister's house. A number of his close relatives still live in Alor Setar and Daim likes to call on them whenever he is in the area. (His elder brother, Hassan, passed away in July 2000 in Alor Setar – Daim and other family members were at his bedside at the time.) After that, the convoy sped out to the airport where Daim bade the local UMNO officials farewell and boarded his jet. Each of the gifts of fruits and local produce that were presented to Daim during the day were loaded aboard the jet and we took off for the return flight to Kuala Lumpur. A friend and party official – the one whose house we had called in on during the day – joined us on board. The mood was informal. Daim was especially relaxed, sinking back into his seat, his hands behind his head and his shoes off, engaging in light-hearted banter and local UMNO party gossip.

The only break in the gentle joviality was when Daim disappeared during the first part of the trip. Where had he gone? He had gone to the back of the jet to pray. He returned, wearing his socks but no shoes, and with his face still slightly wet from the ritual washing prior to Muslim prayers. It had been a long day, but it was not over. It was a Thursday, which meant that Daim would be hosting a prayer meeting at his house back in Kuala Lumpur. On landing at Subang, each of us climbed out of the jet and made our separate ways home to refresh, before it was on to Daim's house for the prayer meeting. The 'reluctant' politician seemed anything but.

The Parliamentarian

One of the requirements of being a politician is, of course, to attend Parliament. But attending Parliament, speaking in it and generally observing its rituals is one of the formalities that Daim, as a minister, seemed to prefer least. In Malaysia, Parliament is not the prime decision-making body, and while it has many of the trappings of a Westminster or a Congress, it doesn't function like either place. During Daim's time as minister, the government's sizeable majority, a poorly disciplined, organised and resourced opposition, and standing orders that favour the government of the day, meant that Parliament mostly rubber stamped the government's legislative program. That did not mean that there was no debate in Malaysia. There was, but the real debate occurred within the government, and particularly within its member parties, rather than in the Parliament. To Daim, Parliament was one of those formalities which being a minister meant he had to endure. Time had to be devoted to it, but for little obvious gain. Much more could be achieved in other forums, such as the cabinet. For Daim, Parliament was a necessary irritation, but an irritation nonetheless.

Many people assume that politicians are natural orators – including, unfortunately, many politicians. Whereas people in the private sector might seek professional training for public speaking, it is surprising how few politicians around the world do. Often it shows. Many are poor when it comes to speaking in public. Practising a speech is essential, something that Daim realised early on. His first budget speech, delivered in 1984, was critical to him. He had replaced Razaleigh, who was popular among business people and within UMNO, and many were sceptical of Daim's abilities and credentials. Daim has said, 'I was very nervous as the days got nearer for the Budget to be delivered.'[4] Daim had civil servants draft the speech. He then practised it over and over until he had memorised it, rewriting and polishing it as he went. He timed himself and had his personal assistant listen to his delivery and point out areas for improvement. The speech was a success and Daim received many congratulatory remarks. On taking office, one condition that he insisted on was that his budget speeches would not be televised. After the success of the delivery of the first budget, he changed his mind.

I attended one session of Parliament in early 2000 and was surprised to see just how relaxed it was. Daim was required to present the 2000 Budget to Parliament a second time on 25 February because national elections were called for late 1999 before the 2000 Budget could be passed. Analysts did not expect many changes, but nonetheless, there was keen interest to see what, if anything, would be changed, and whether the economic growth forecasts contained in the budget would be revised.

Daim was due to begin the budget speech in the Dewan Rakyat at 4pm on the Friday. It was an overcast afternoon with occasional bursts of rain. I first visited the Ministry of Finance to collect a visitor's pass for the Parliament building. The ministry, like many other government offices, at the time was located on Jalan Duta on the outskirts of Kuala Lumpur near the up-market Damansara Heights residential area. The foyer of the main block was crowded with local journalists and press photographers eager to catch a glimpse of Daim and his Deputies as they arrived and then left the building on their way to the Parliament, which is about a ten-minute drive away.

The Parliament itself comprised a tall office block alongside which sits a low-rise building that housed the Dewan Rakyat and its various antechambers, all set in large grounds with gardens and water features. The Parliament was surprisingly informal and casual. Once visitors had gained entry with the appropriate accreditation to the building, security was seemingly minimal. There were no bag checks, metal detectors to pass through, or any of the other usual security checks that one finds in other parliaments around the world. Outside the Dewan Rakyat chamber milled journalists, government officials, visitors, ministers and backbenchers. Visitors were free to wander seemingly where they liked. A series

---

4   Ibid., p. 70.

of lounges lined the long antechamber adjacent to the Dewan Rakyat chamber, and towards one end was a large, open-air garden encased with glass and which has a large pond at the bottom filled with dozens of over-sized carp. It all served to add to the air of informality.

The Dewan Rakyat chamber itself was relatively modest but attractively laid out nonetheless. There was blue carpet and highly carved wooden stalls at which government and opposition members sat. The ceiling soared to an array of white stone gables somewhat reminiscent of an old European church. At the rear of the chamber was the public gallery, which rose steeply.

The informality of the antechamber continued inside. Visitors with passes entered the chamber through the same doors as the politicians. In fact, access to and from the visitors' gallery for those entering from the antechamber actually took one on to the floor of the chamber and behind the last row of backbenchers' stalls. Such proximity to the chamber and to the politicians came as a complete surprise and differed considerably from the Houses of Parliament in London or even the relatively more relaxed Houses of Parliament in Canberra, Australia.

Daim began his budget speech precisely at 4pm. His green *baju Melayu* shirt contrasted with the purple *baju Melayu* worn by Mahathir, who sat at the far end of the front bench with Deputy Prime Minister Abdullah Badawi, MCA President Ling, Malaysian Indian Congress (MIC) President Samy Vellu and Sarawak Dayak People's Party leader Leo Moggie between the two men. There was a burst of camera flashes from the media photographers on the other side of the chamber as Daim rose to speak. His delivery was strong and sharp, with plenty of intonation in his voice. In fact, his speaking style was pleasant to listen to and well modulated. There were no theatrics, however; no hand waving or other dramatic flourishes. The performance was straight to the point but not hard work on the listener. Government members thumping their desks in appreciation at what they heard punctuated Daim's speech at various points. The visitors' gallery was almost empty. The public, it seems, shares Daim's view about the centrality of Parliament. The few who were there looked like students, plus a couple of businessmen who, with their searching glances around the chamber, appeared more eager that the various ministers noted their presence than anything else.

As expected, there was not too much that was new in the speech and accordingly, Daim, famous for his strong dislike of time wasting, kept the speech to just 40 minutes compared with the more traditional one-and-a-half to two hours for a regular budget speech. The more interesting action was going on elsewhere in the chamber. Mahathir sat throughout the proceedings alternately gazing at the ceiling, off into the distance or occasionally at Daim. Rarely, if at all, did he establish eye contact with any of his colleagues. Anwar Ibrahim's wife and newly-elected opposition member, Wan Azizah Wan Ismail, sat stony-faced on the front opposition benches, with her head down while she read the budget documents for almost the entirety of Daim's address. She neither looked at Daim nor conversed with her colleagues. Former finance minister Tunku Razaleigh arrived at the chamber slightly late – several minutes into Daim's speech. In fact, he was one of the last members to make it to the chamber. Ebullient as usual, he strode in, smiling and attempting to catch the eyes of as many of his colleagues as possible. He spoke to the member on his right side and then to the one on the left as he took his seat. He flicked through one of the budget papers already on his desk and then looked all around the chamber to acknowledge this or that colleague. The UMNO General Assembly was just a few months away and Razaleigh was still considering whether to stand for the vice presidency. The contrast between Mahathir's distance and Razaleigh's ebullience was clear.

Once it was all over, everyone in the chamber – politicians, officials, visitors and those few individuals in the public gallery – rose in unison and made their way to the various exits. Visitors with passes were encouraged to leave through the main doors to the Dewan Rakyat chamber – the same doors that the ministers and backbenchers were using, which meant that visitors, officials and parliamentarians alike were all squeezed together as they attempted to leave. Again, the relative informality of the occasion was a surprise. If Daim must attend Parliament, he is fortunate that it is Malaysia's. There are protocols and formalities to be observed, but they don't seem to be nearly as onerous as they could be.

The Manager

A minister must be both a politican and a manager. Too few are good at both. But how is management typically undertaken in Asia?[5] There is an analogy from history that is apt. After the Roman Empire crumbled, the rule of law was lost and the peoples of Europe were subjected to marauding bands of barbarians. To counteract the uncertainties of poor security and to fill the hiatus left by the Romans, a new system of social ordering emerged: the feudal system. It lasted in Europe from about AD 500 to 1800 – a period of 1,300 years – and involved simple peasant folk being organised under an aristocrat or lord. They supplied their labour to work his lands in exchange for the security he provided and a small part of what they produced. The mutual obligations between the lord and his peasants created a system of 'vassalage' – the owing of loyalty – whereby the peasants remained loyal to the lord and the lord to the king. The lord was omniscient and all chains of command, leadership and direction radiated from him. Those peasants whose loyalty was held in question lived on the periphery of the village, where they could never be quite sure of the degree to which the lord's umbrella of protection would cover them. The lords would form and reform coalitions, alternating between fighting each other and forming alliances, as expediency demanded.

To the vast majority of peasants in Europe during this time, the village was their whole world. They could expect to live and die without ever having cause to move much beyond it. Outsiders were not trusted, and with good reason. There

---

5   This section draws on similar passages in M. Backman, *Asian Eclipse: Exposing the Dark Side of Business in Asia,* John Wiley & Sons, Singapore, 1999.

was no social agreement or contract across feudal localities. Trust extended little further than the village boundary.

Today, many Asian managers behave as if they are feudal lords. In Southeast Asia, particularly, the business environment can be as fraught with dangers and devoid of the rule of law as life was in feudal Europe. Trust is not broadly extended, and offices and corporate structures have emerged to reflect this. Many Asian companies, government departments and even ministerial offices are like feudal villages, the employees like the villagers, and the founding patriarch, senior civil servant or cabinet minister, like a lord.

With trust in short supply outside the company, ministry or ministerial office, absolute loyalty is demanded within it. Staff follow orders – management is rarely participatory. Promotions often are not linked so much to merit as to the personal relationships junior staff might have with their superiors. Scaling the corporate ladder is a sign of one's trustworthiness; not necessarily of one's productivity. Loyalty, and even subservience and sycophancy, are rewarded; initiative, which by definition demonstrates a lack of dependence on senior staff, is not. Initiative, after all, carries with it the risk of showing up more senior staff, which causes them to lose face; therefore, it is disloyal, and thus not encouraged. Senior managers are always right even if they are wrong, and junior employees should not express their opinions before their seniors do, because it means that their superiors have no room to move should their view be contrary. They cannot be seen to be contradicted by a more junior staff member, as this would imply a loss of authority. The best course of action for an employee is to say only what is expected and to keep one's real feelings private. Form tends to win over content.

Pleasing the boss is often a far greater priority than, say, meeting targets – after all, everyone knows that numbers can easily be manipulated. A situation will be judged a success if it is handled 'correctly', even if the results are not what was desired. Staff expect their employer to look after them as a parent would a child, and, to promote the mutual dependence, employers usually oblige. Of course this is an extreme caricature. But behind such caricatures are grains of truth. The culture of harmony, dependence and community, rather than individualism, competition and productivity, underscores the village nature of many Asian firms and offices. So, to what extent is Daim a feudal manager or a modern manager?

Very much the latter, it seems. Certainly this was the case when he was a minister. He wants individuals to perform. He is not interested in observing seniority, even though the practice tends to be observed in most civil service structures. Nor is he too concerned with loyalty. An ability to deliver is what counts. For Wan Azmi Wan Hamzah, one of a coterie of young, promising Malays that Daim nurtured, Daim is not a hands-on manager, particularly once he has appointed those whom he finds competent. He said of their time at Peremba, 'While [Daim] is very clear and strong on vision and direction, he does not seek to actually sit on top of you on implementation … This allowed elbow-room for creativity in the people around

---

6   M.S. Cheong and Adibah Amin, op. cit., p. 182.

him, and many blossomed in this space and fresh air.'[6] In this regard, Daim is different to a traditional Asian manager, for whom there is more concern for methodology than outcomes and a strong preference to micro-manage, which tends to kill off creativity in subordinates. 'Tun is open to advice and alternative ideas. He will listen to you – he might not agree with you but when he makes a decision he expects you to follow', according to Professor Mahani, when I spoke with her in 2000.

Plenty of politicians are good at speech making, thinking up new policy and appealing to voters, but many fall down when it comes to administration. Daim's successor as finance minister, Anwar, for example, had the charisma and oratory skills to attract people, but when it came to day-to-day administration and dealing with the more mundane but nonetheless important aspects of being a minister, some say that, organisationally, he was very poor. Correspondence would go unanswered, decisions would be held over, and his office and desk tended to be a mess according to those who worked with Anwar while he was at the finance ministry.

Daim's style on those important but more mundane matters of administration could not be more different. The first thing that one noticed on entering Daim's office at the finance ministry was how relatively spartan it seemed. It was comfortable and functional but was not crowded with unnecessary mementoes or souvenirs. Towards one end of the room was his desk, and sitting at it, Daim looked somewhat dwarfed. During his first tenure as finance minister he issued a ruling that no file was to stay on any Treasury official's desk for more than three days. He practised what he preached. His desk was absolutely clear of papers bar one neat pile in front of him which he stacked in order of priority and which he worked his way through during the day.

Robert Louis Stevenson once said that 'Politics is perhaps the only profession for which no preparation is thought necessary'. One can learn to be a dentist, a lawyer or an architect, but it is difficult to learn to be a politician. Most politicians enter politics with little more than the hope that the experience gained from their past occupations might be useful for the next. It is a common mistake of many successful business people to enter Parliaments and ministries around the world and to assume that the job will be little different to running a private company. Daim quickly realised that there was a difference. 'If it's your own company, you are the boss and you can do what you like with the company and make very fast decisions. In the Government, you cannot make the decisions even if you want to do it. However powerful you may be, you are answerable to the Cabinet and to Parliament.'[7] On being appointed minister both times, Daim says he felt it necessary to make organisational changes at the Finance Ministry to improve its efficiency. He said to me that 'managing in the private sector is much easier' than managing in the public sector. In government there are many conflicting agendas

---

7   Ibid., p. 63.

and interests to manage. In the private sector there is only one agenda – that of the owner. Fortunately, the Finance Ministry was staffed with talented people who were able to help him find his way around. 'Some of the best civil servants are in the Ministry and many of them are experts in their field.'

The orderliness and functionality of Daim's office is carried through to his work method. Fellow cabinet minister and MIC president Samy Vellu said of Daim's working style, 'He talked very little but he was excellent in planning and meticulous in his work. He wrote the shortest letters as Finance Minister and I marvelled at that. There was only one occasion when he wrote me a long letter. It was in response to my query relating to Indians in senior positions in the United Asian Bank. He wrote two and a half pages explaining that there were enough Indians there and they would be given an opportunity to stay there even if a change took place in the bank. When I was Minister of Works, on many urgent matters concerning the Government and the people, he was always on hand to help. He made fast decisions. He never delayed things. He was a good listener. Although meetings with him were short, the salient points were covered.'[8]

This same lack of imperiousness, this wish to be helpful, was reflected in an anecdote told to me by KLSE chairman Azlan Hashim in 2000. In early 1999, foreign institutional investors started to complain that Malaysia's system for settling stock market trades was inadequate. The Delivery Versus Payment (DVP) mechanism that was in place complied with international standards and Malaysia and wasn't required to make changes. However, some institutional investors preferred the system that operated in the United States and wanted Malaysia to follow suit. According to Azlan Hashim, Daim was sympathetic. He realised that Malaysia was not obligated to change or enhance its existing system but wanted to be accommodating nonetheless. 'Tun is very customer focused – I can't but think that this has something to do with his business background,' Azlan said to me. So in July 1999, the KLSE launched the Institutional Settlement Service (ISS) which extended membership to the KLSE's clearing house beyond local stock brokerages to resident custodian banks and to institutional investors. The foreign fund managers were happy. Daim's desire to be accessible and helpful is epitomised by Azlan's observation, 'It's easy to get a meeting with Tun if there's something urgent.' It was a view shared by most of the people that I interviewed.

Surprisingly, Daim did not use a computer in his office at the finance ministry. All his computing and word processing was done for him. Nor did he use the Internet, at least not up until mid-2000. Mahathir is very technology savvy and has spearheaded Malaysia's thrusts into the Internet age. Daim, on the other hand, is not and claims that Mahathir is 'angry' with him for being so laggard when it comes to computers and information technology. His desk at home sports a computer. But that is more for his family to use, he says. This is not to say that he is unaware of the commercial opportunities that have arisen from the computer

---

8 Ibid., pp. 163-4.

age. When IT stocks were in favour in late 1999, Daim urged the immediate listing of Khazanah's wafer fab plant. He repeatedly said that the window to do so would close fast and that the government should seize the opportunity. His urgings fell on deaf ears and the optimum time passed by.

In work as in private, Daim has a strong dislike of formality and is softly spoken. He prefers to listen rather than to speak, particularly if in a group. He does not suffer inefficient staff. Said Daim, 'I am by nature impatient. I can't tolerate fools around me. I am interested in people who can work and deliver. It is better to have three intelligent, hardworking people and pay them well than to have twenty who get on your nerves. You will lose your temper because of them and in the end no work is done and you may have a heart attack in the process! It is better to get rid of the twenty and keep the three.'[9] He has no compunction in getting rid of under-performers. Daim said of his first tenure as minister, 'I know I antagonise a lot of people. When I joined the government I had a few removed from their jobs. They were unhappy and it is a well-known fact that I was very unpopular. I could not tolerate the undisciplined, the lazy, the disorganised and the corrupt. Under me they will have to work hard … If I didn't get rid of the deadwood, they would be cancerous. It wouldn't be fair to the rest. When you get rid of the useless, only the good remain. They will have an excellent environment to operate in and the organisation can only get better. They will be working amongst and competing against their peer group. They will sharpen their minds and hone their skills.'[10] Such a preparedness to dispense with under-performers is at odds with the historical Malay view of government and the civil service as being there to provide jobs and security, even if that means excessive featherbedding. It is not difficult to see how Daim's views and desire for modernity clashed with those of some sections of UMNO.

Daim saw it as his role to be more informed than his subordinates, or at least never to be less informed. He understands that knowledge is power. He does not mind his subordinates making mistakes, but he expects them to learn from those mistakes. Those who show a propensity not to learn are quickly shown the door. Daim readily concedes that he himself has made plenty of mistakes in life. The important thing, he believes, is to learn from them, but also to act quickly to fix them. For him, procrastination simply means more time wasting, and time wasted is money and opportunities lost, be it in business or in government.

As a minister, Daim was known to read all the papers that came to his office and he read all letters and minutes that left his office. One way to cut down on the paper work is to ask for oral briefings. Eventually he preferred them to written briefings. Having ministry officials come to his office and take him through a briefing saved time and allowed Daim to talk issues through and to give a quick oral response and on-the-spot decisions. He demanded written briefings for issues

9 Ibid., p. 4.

10 Ibid., pp. 4-5.

that he considered particularly important. And what were those? Unhesitatingly, he answered that mostly they related to the allocation of projects. He cited a recent decision on who should be awarded the contracts to build 550 schools. The task was big and involved a lot of money. Who should get such projects required a lot of deliberation to see that the contenders had the capability, to make sure that projects were distributed evenly, and to see that contenders supported the government. Balancing everyone's expectations and spreading around the largesse was a big task.

Punctuality is another must, as we saw in an earlier chapter. Said Mustapa Mohamad, 'Tun was also strict about punctuality and declined to see even dignitaries who came late. He also believed in having short meetings and said that it was inefficient to meet for more than one hour to discuss even the most important of matters.'[11] Nonetheless, sometimes meetings could be too short even for his liking. In 1985, when the Plaza Accord was signed by the G-7 economies to push up the yen to alleviate the trade imbalance between the United States and Japan, the fallout from the rapid appreciation of the yen was a dramatic blowout in the cost of servicing Malaysia's yen-denominated loans. The cabinet decided that Daim should go to Japan to discuss the problem with Japan's then finance minister Kiichi Miyazawa. However, when Daim found that the time allotted for the scheduled meeting with Miyazawa was just 15 minutes, he cancelled the visit. The Japanese lobbied Mahathir to change Daim's mind, as meetings had been organised for Daim with other dignitaries as well, but Daim was resolute. Daim believed the message to Malaysia was clear in the 15 minutes allotted, so he thought it proper to 'return the compliment'.[12]

Daim likes the same clarity in his speeches as he demands of those when they are briefing him. His speeches tended to be brief, to the point, with little padding, and contain a great deal of clarity. Speeches full of nebulous platitudes designed not to offend anyone, or written to avoid committing himself to anything, were not for him. Instead, usually they contained one major point that he wished to get across, and the rest of the speech was built around that point, to lend it support and to provide context. Often the major point was a direct exhortation to the audience, particularly if the audience was drawn from a specific sector, that they should do this or that, or try harder.

Daim spent a great proportion of his time as finance minister deciding on the allocation of projects. Decisions on projects still are vitally important to the government in its distribution of patronage and rounding up political support. But it is not as simple as rewarding friends and supporters. Government in multi-ethnic and multi-regional Malaysia requires a careful balancing of often conflicting interests. The impression gained is not so much that Daim enjoyed the power of allocating who was to undertake what project, but rather that

---

11 Ibid., p. 168.
12 Ibid., p. 137.

much time was spent simply trying to allocate projects so as to minimise adverse political fallout by carefully ensuring that everyone felt that they had their fair share. 'We are not going to give projects to people who oppose the government,' said Daim with disarming frankness during one of our 2000 meetings. Daim insisted, though, that bids be competitive and that projects were not awarded to those who could not undertake them. Political considerations were important, but they were not the only ones.

VII

REMODELLING SOCIETY

History has handed Malaysia a dilemma. The country's ethnic make-up is far from homogenous. The indigenous people, the Bumiputeras who are largely Malay, comprise more than 60% of Malaysia's 29 million strong population. Malaysia's Chinese account for around 24%, and Indians for 7%. Not only that, but the commercial power of the large Chinese Malaysian minority has been and remains significantly greater than is suggested by their numbers. It is a dilemma that could either have wrecked the country or be used to its advantage. Malaysia could have gone down either of two routes. It could have descended into ethnic turmoil and mayhem. It might have been another Bosnia, Cyprus, Northern Ireland or Rwanda. On the other hand, it might have utilised the ethnic mix to its advantage; used it as a strength, rather than seeing it only in terms of weakness. Fortunately, it chose the latter option. As Daim said when retabling the 2000 Budget in Parliament in February 2000, 'We have succeeded in nurturing our multi-racial society into an asset and mobilising this strength to forge a harmonious, developed and tolerant society. Unity and tolerance are the foundation for our success.' This does not mean that everyone has been happy with the direction Malaysia has taken and with every government policy. But the grumblings must be seen in context and against what might have been. The Malaysian government's management of the country's ethnic mix might not always have been perfect. Perhaps it could have done better. But what is important is that it could have done a lot worse – much, much worse. The proof of the appropriateness of the broad direction of government policy is where Malaysia finds itself today.

And today, Malaysia is surprisingly modern and sophisticated. Few outsiders who have not visited Malaysia understand just how developed the country is. Basically, Malaysia works. Modern Malaysia is very much Mahathir's creation and that of his government. His crowning glory is the fact that in 1997-98, in the face of the most serious economic collapse that Malaysia has ever endured, the country was not wracked by anti-Chinese riots as was Indonesia. Indeed, there was not a single racially motivated attack on any Chinese Malaysian business during the economic crisis. Although history has handed Malaysia a potentially explosive mix of ethnicities, the country has handled its domestic ethnic relations better than have many European nations. There are no equivalents in Malaysia of France's Jean-Marie Le Pen or Germany's Neo-Nazis.

The key to Mahathir's success has been the New Economic Policy (NEP). All too easily, the NEP was dismissed superficially in the West as 'racist' and therefore to be rejected. Race-based it certainly was, but given the choice between some targeted economic curtailment, and having their businesses looted and burned, it is not difficult to see which option most Chinese Malaysians preferred. Today, almost certainly most Malaysians of any ethnicity support the NEP and its successor, the National Development Policy (NDP), and judge them as successes. The NEP/NDP were augmented by a policy, largely overseen by Daim, of selecting particular Malay entrepreneurs for nurturing. Via privatisations and the awarding of infrastructure and other contracts, a whole class of Malay entrepreneurs was developed. As *Finance Asia* magazine said, 'As the economic tsar to Mahathir's political demagogue, Daim became the true architect of one of the most fundamental shifts of economic wealth to have occurred in the 20th century.'[1]

Daim on Being Malay

For all Daim's desire to modernise and his apparent political ruthlessness, he is enormously sympathetic to Malay culture. He respects it and is quietly proud of it. Many Chinese Malaysians might deride what they see as a Malay 'ineptitude' in business, the Malay tendency to spend windfalls on luxury goods rather than saving them for when they might be more needed, and so on, but they will often add, appreciatively, that Malays are very gentle people. Traditional Malay culture dictates that Malays should be very welcoming, sensitive to the needs of others and eager to be as hospitable as possible. But such traits have allowed Malays to be exploited by more aggressive cultures. From the intrinsic decency of traditional Malay culture comes self-worth and self-confidence. This Malay sense of decency is something that Daim is both proud of and which he feels sets the Malays apart. The trick is how to advance the Malays materially without them losing their moral sense and ethics.

Rarely does Daim miss an opportunity to push Malay interests in the business sphere. The vehemence with which he does so leads to speculation that he is anti-Chinese. But this does not necessarily follow. Such a label is simplistic. If he were genuinely anti-Chinese, he would not have had the Chinese business partners that he has had, nor the Chinese friends that he has. Furthermore, there are plenty of Chinese Malaysians who have been given breaks in business by Daim. Daim is admiring of the prowess in business of many Chinese, but recognises that differing cultural constraints between the Malays and the Chinese can put the Chinese as a group at a competitive advantage in business. When I asked Daim to name those Chinese Malaysian business groups that he feels have done the most in advancing the cause of Malays, perhaps by recruiting Malays as managers and so on, he was unable to name even a single group that he felt had performed adequately on this score. Partly, he suggested, it was because most Chinese businesses are family-owned and they find it difficult to employ outsiders, especially in senior roles. Even when Malay and Chinese partners do get together, Daim is sceptical of their success. 'I don't think Bumiputera-Chinese joint ventures have been that

---

1 'Financiers of the century: Daim Zainuddin', *Finance Asia*, December 1999/January 2000.

successful. I have been criticised for saying this but it's true. Most of the Chinese businesses are family owned. It's only human nature not to want to give away anything that one has worked so hard for so long. But I think if there is the right commitment towards partnership, it will work. If it fails, try again. Otherwise the Malays will have to get foreign partners for their joint ventures and the Chinese will be left out of a lot of opportunities in the long run.'[2] Thus, Daim believes that more must be done to promote genuine Malay-Chinese cooperation in business and that such cooperation is in the interests of the Chinese as well as the Malays.

Arguably, Mahathir has had a more inclusive view of the role of Malaysia's Chinese, but then so he should as prime minister. Historically, the traditional government response around the world towards middlemen minorities has been to try to eject or curtail them, be they Jews in Europe, Armenians in Asia Minor or Chinese in Southeast Asia. But back in 1970, in *The Malay Dilemma*, Mahathir acknowledged that it was almost impossible to imagine Malaysia without the Chinese in their roles as middlemen – shopkeepers and traders. 'They are an important and essential cog in the machinery of the Malaysian economy,' he wrote. Like Daim, Mahathir was unequivocally pro-Malay. But also like Daim, that did not mean he was anti-Chinese.

Daim experienced the commercial power of the Chinese as a child, although, importantly, he says that his first experience of racial prejudice was not in Malaysia but in South Africa on his visit there in 1957. In his hometown in Kedah state, the majority was Malay, but most of the shops and other businesses were owned and operated by local Chinese. According to Daim, 'The irony was that there's a place near my kampung called Pekan Melayu ["Malay Town" or "Malay Market"]. It [was] a business centre completely owned and run by the Chinese until Mahathir opened his clinic there.'[3] And that was hardly unusual up and down peninsular Malaysia's west coast. A formative experience for him, though, was a visit in 1956 to Kelantan, on Malaysia's east coast, where there are relatively few Chinese. Daim was struck by how, in these circumstances, the Malays turned out to be quite capable business people. In the markets, Malay women were robust and even aggressive in business. They could and were doing well. There were some Chinese shops, but these had nothing like the stranglehold over commerce that their counterparts had on the west coast. 'Kelantan, to some extent, showed Malay potential in business,' Daim said.[4] It was a formative visit for another reason: Daim has remained impressed ever since by the competence of Malay women as money managers and astute business people.

Mahathir's race-based policies were not born out of some notion of the inherent superiority of the Malays, but precisely the opposite. He argued, in *The Malay Dilemma*, that the Malays were relatively disadvantaged for a range of

---

2   S. Cheong, *Bumiputera Entrepreneurs in the KLSE*, CRS, 1996, p. 10.

3   M.S. Cheong and Adibah Amin, *Daim: The Man Behind the Enigma*, Pelanduk Publications, 1995, p. 116.

4   Ibid., p. 117.

reasons that included inherited characteristics, and cultural and environmental reasons. They had evolved in the fertile lowlands of Malaysia where life was relatively easy. On the other hand, the Chinese who came to Malaysia had evolved in the far rougher terrain of southern China and thus were more adept at survival. Relatively crude though Mahathir's analysis was, the fact remained that the Malays were losing ground and national stability consequently was at risk. The solution, Mahathir argued, was to implement special policies to allow the Malays to better compete. Not to do so would be to risk more bloodshed and anti-Chinese rampages along the lines of the 13 May 1969 riots in which hundreds of Chinese died. So, in effect, the NEP and Malaysia's other race-based policies have been as much for the benefit of Malaysia's Chinese as for the Malays. For his part, Daim said to me that although he would beg to differ on some of the detail, he was broadly sympathetic with the sentiments expressed in *The Malay Dilemma*.

A Rebalancing of Interests

Traditionally, the Malays largely tended the paddy fields. The Chinese then acquired the rice crop when it was harvested, including an amount of implied interest for having extended credit to the Malays. The Malays owned the land, but effectively they toiled for the Chinese. There was little wrong with this. The Malays had access to a system of easy credit in a way that no bank would provide, and the Chinese were able to trade in rice and make profits. The charging of interest is *haram*, or forbidden by Muslim law, so the system also provided a convenient way for Malays to avoid an overt association with the practice of usury. Of course, there was interest on the credit the Chinese provided, but for most Malays it didn't seem that way.

After independence, the implicit national contract between the Malays and the non-Malays was that the Malays would have the political power and the non-Malays (largely Chinese and Indians) would retain the commercial power. For some time this worked and there was stability. The Malay leadership felt that political power was what really counted. It was more honourable, whereas commerce and perhaps hard work were seen as coarse by some. The Chinese, on the other hand, saw commerce and hard work as principled. But ultimately, these perceptions changed and the national contract became less appropriate as new realities set in. The Malays, who had political control, could not see why they should not also have some commercial power; and the Chinese, who had a lot of commercial clout, could not see why that ought not to be reflected in politics as well.

Increasingly, the Chinese became involved in politics. The 1969 national elections delivered the Malay elite a rude shock. The ruling Alliance lost power in Penang, nearly lost in Perak and Selangor states, and in the National Parliament lost more seats to the opposition. No one should have been shocked, believes Daim. 'People go into politics to gain power.'[5] Increasingly, there was a mismatch

---

5   Ibid., p. 118.

of expectations on both sides. The Malays felt that their political power was being eroded without any corresponding advances in the economic field. The Chinese were prospering but felt that they had no say in the government of their country.

Tensions steadily rose and culminated in the 13 May 1969 riots in which a significant number of Chinese were killed. In the immediate aftermath of the riots, the National Operations Council was formed and took over the running of the government. Deputy Prime Minister Razak Hussein effectively became the leader. Shortly after, the prime minister, Tunku Abdul Rahman, stepped aside and Razak became prime minister. The national contract was clearly no longer appropriate and had to be redrawn. The result was the NEP, which came into force in 1972.

The Bumiputeras had only a 2% share in corporate equity at that time. The Chinese had a 20% share and foreigners 61%. The target was to increase the share of the Bumiputeras to 30%. According to Daim, no one is sure why the figure of 30% was chosen and not, say, 20% or 40%. The idea was not so much to redistribute wealth from one group and then give it to another, but rather to expand the economy and allow the Bumiputeras to have a greater share of the new wealth generated until their total share in corporate equity had reached 30%. That way, Chinese Malaysians would not have existing wealth taken from them and, while having a smaller share of new wealth, they would still retain a bigger share than the Malays.

But by 1992, the 30% target had not been met. Bumiputera equity participation had risen dramatically, but had reached only 20% of corporate holdings. Nonetheless, it can be argued that although the 30% target was specific, it was actually a tangible proxy for something less tangible and less measurable: ensuring harmony across Malaysia's various ethnic communities. In this regard, the NEP was a tremendous success.

Radically raising the profile of the Bumiputeras in the national economy was all very well, but unless there were Bumiputera managers to run the increased Bumiputera holdings, then all would be to little avail. So, unavoidably, huge investments in Bumiputera education and training were needed. Mahathir had cited education in *The Malay Dilemma* as an especially important means to promote greater equality between the Malays and the Chinese. In this, he was correct: education has been instrumental to largely banishing the class system in Western Europe too. The education system had to be changed, as well as there being increased funding. In the past, when Bumiputeras sought higher education, they tended to favour the arts and, upon graduation, join the civil service. What needed to be done now, was to substantially lift Bumiputera higher education participation rates, alter the types of courses favoured by Bumiputera students and then ensure that, on graduation, they sought careers in business and in the professions. With such ambitious goals, there was no alternative other than to introduce affirmative discrimination. The higher education Bumiputera intake was set at 55% and for non-Bumiputeras at 45%. These figures were tough on non-Bumiputeras, many of whom had to see their sons and daughters miss out on a place in Malaysia's higher education sector in favour of Bumiputera students, some of whom were less qualified, but the quotas were broadly in line with Malaysia's population mix.

Some years ago as part of my research for a study on Southeast Asian Chinese business success, I asked several of the office holders at one of Malaysia's leading Chinese chambers of commerce what they had most disliked about the NEP. 'The education policies,' came the quick reply. They hated the fact that quotas for Malay students meant that many of their children had to seek tertiary education overseas. But they said that by the mid-1990s their view had changed. Sending their children overseas had allowed them to forge new contacts and relationships that were good for business that they otherwise might not have had. Even more importantly, Mahathir's insistence on educating the Malays meant that there was now an educated class of Malay workers whom Chinese businessmen were happy to employ. No longer were the NEP's employment quotas for Malays seen as onerous. The 'shotgun' marriages of the past between Chinese employers and Malay employees had become affairs of mutual convenience.

The UDA and Peremba

Daim's most important contribution to the NEP was that he felt that it needed to be augmented. It was a view that Mahathir shared. Both men believed that raising the share of Malay equity in the economy was good, but that it wasn't good enough. Malays also had to be managers.

By 1977, Daim decided that he had made enough money to retire from business and it was time to go back to university. He enrolled at the University of California at Berkeley to do a course in urban planning. He remained in California for two years, studying and relaxing. During this time, his son Wira was born. Daim's earlier studies had been about passing exams rather than learning. He was then more interested in playing sport. The decision to enroll at Berkeley thus seemed to mark a change in attitude to his personal education. This time he enrolled out of a genuine desire to learn. Why the change? He told me that by 1977, he was almost 40 years old, and he felt that he had achieved all that he had wanted in business and that it was time to expand his horizons.

In 1978, Daim met Mahathir in Los Angeles and in San Francisco. Mahathir wanted Daim to return to Malaysia and stand in the general election that was to be held later that year. But Daim had just started the course at Berkeley and didn't want to return immediately. Daim next had an offer from Public Enterprises Minister Abdul Manan Othman, who was a personal friend and had studied in London with Daim, to become chairman of the Urban Development Authority (UDA). In the words of Daim, the UDA was a 'total mess'. Daim went to see Othman on his return to Malaysia in early 1979 and told him that he did not want to take on the chairmanship of the UDA. The Authority was too big, too bureaucratic and too diverse. It needed a full-time chairman, and Daim could only be available on a part-time basis. Instead, he suggested that the UDA should form a holding company into which all of its commercial property and other commercial assets should be folded. Daim agreed to manage this, as it was more an area that he felt matched his expertise. Hence, Peremba was established and Daim became its non-executive chairman.

Daim stayed at Peremba from 1979 to 1984. It wasn't long before he decided that Peremba could be used to develop a class of Malay entrepreneurs, rather than simply manage construction projects on behalf of the Malay population who otherwise had little in the way of a direct corporate role. He handpicked his officers. They were all young, and he felt that they were intelligent and would be able to withstand the demands he would make of them.

Some of those who would become Malaysia's most prominent Malay entrepreneurs had their starts with Daim and Peremba. Many were accountants; others were engineers. Wan Azmi Wan Hamzah, who later acquired Land and General Group and developed it into one of Malaysia's largest companies, describes his first meeting with Daim in 1979: 'I remember turning up at a site office in Taman Maluri, and was ushered into a back room, which was the office of Daim. I remember there was a collection of some very strange furniture – Malaccan Chinese antiques including what looked suspiciously like a bed. But there was this desk, very tidy, behind which sat a rather diminutive and tidy figure with a strong nose and neatly trimmed moustache. He introduced himself as "Daim" and before I could begin to work my sales pitch, he offered me the job of General Manager of Peremba Berhad.'[6]

Under Daim, Peremba embarked on many building projects across Malaysia. But why did the UDA and Peremba become involved in so many such projects that normally would not have been undertaken by the state but by the private sector? Daim's answer is straightforward. Prior to Peremba and the UDA, Chinese business people almost exclusively owned the buildings in the centres of Malaysia's cities and major towns. The role of Peremba was to shake up the structure of the ownership of Malaysia's central business districts to give them more a Malay, and not just a Chinese, hue. Sungei Wang Plaza in Kuala Lumpur's Bukit Bintang area is an excellent case in point. It was Malay-controlled but home to dozens of Chinese-run shops and was (and is) still largely patronised by Chinese shoppers. The fact that it was under Malay control prevented the whole complex from being an exclusively Chinese enclave.

Prominent Chinese Malaysian businessman Robert Kuok and his team worked with Daim's Peremba for the development of the UDA Bukit Nanas (UBN) project in Kuala Lumpur. It included the construction of Kuala Lumpur's Shangri-La hotel, part of what was to become Kuok's worldwide Shangri-La hotel chain. Kuok wanted his company to manage the construction project, which was not unreasonable. But Daim insisted that Peremba should do so, so that its staff could gain the experience of managing a large and costly project. Up until that point, Peremba's main claim to a successful project was the management of

---

6   Ibid., p. 173.

the completion of a M$10 million retail/office complex in Ipoh in Malaysia's north. The UBN/Shangri-La project was worth M$400 million. Daim saw the management of the project as the first major opportunity to put his vision of developing a class of young and capable Bumiputera professionals into practice – a team 'to develop the nation'. Peremba also constructed Sungei Wang Plaza and the Parkroyal Hotel in Kuala Lumpur, to name a few.

Daim was criticised during his period at Peremba for misusing the time of what were, after all, government employees. Key executives were used to do non-Peremba work such as that which involved UMNO's corporate interests. Wan Azmi Wan Hamzah has claimed that this misses the point. Daim had decided that Peremba was more than just a state-owned company charged with managing state-owned assets; rather, it was to be the incubator – the training ground – for a new class of Malay entrepreneurs. In this view, Peremba is better thought of as also being an institution that provided vocational training, or at least that is the defence. When I asked Daim about the efficacy of Peremba executives doing non-Peremba work he said that clearly they were, but outside office hours.

The government had gone into business to help achieve the NEP's 30% Bumiputera equity goal in 20 years. Many government business agencies were created, and civil servants were seconded to run them. The policy had not been a resounding success – something that was to greatly influence Daim in his decision to create a class of private-sector Malay entrepreneurs.

Many of the agencies became conglomerates in their own right. Accounts were not published, fraud and mismanagement were rife, and the agencies were largely unaccountable. Initially, the non-Malays were critical of the agencies' creation, but in time they became important beneficiaries of some of them. Daim pointed to the Urban Development Authority (UDA) as an example. The UDA was supposed to be profitable but never was. There were some achievements, but there could have been more. According to Daim, 'In terms of profit, UDA was a dismal failure, though it did help to bring Bumiputeras into the cities. In a way, this was its success. Had it been properly run and managed, it could have achieved tremendous success. It was typical of the new Malay predicament – a missed opportunity.'[7]

When the property crash came in 1972, rather than take over complete projects, the UDA took 30% stakes in many of them. This meant that the non-Malay developers were able to retain management and equity control, but at the same time gain a badly needed cash infusion courtesy of the UDA. 'Bumiputera' equity (so defined) might have risen in the property sector because of the UDA's actions, but Bumiputera control and management influence in the sector did not necessarily increase as well. Ultimately, the UDA succeeded in bailing out many Chinese developers, after which they were able to continue and ultimately thrive. Government money was spent, but the UDA's actions did not lead to any obvious greater Malay control in the property sector. It was a typical outcome of

---

7   Ibid., p. 122.

government programs around the world whereby the very group of people such programs are designed to help end up becoming its victims, whereas those it is supposed to curtail, at least in a relative sense, become the main beneficiaries. The phenomenon of 'middle-class' welfare subsidised by the taxes of the poor (rather than the other way round) in many developed countries is an example of this.

Bank Bumiputera was another agency designed to help the relative position of the Malays. It did some good, but a lot of mistakes were made as well. The bank was created before the 1969 riots, but after them new emphasis was placed on its role. The government poured huge sums of money into it, and its stated task was to provide credit to rural Malays who otherwise would have trouble obtaining funds from the formal financial system. Instead, it veered off into quite another direction, satisfying the aims of its ambitious managers rather than those of the government. As Daim has said, 'Bank Bumiputera expanded fast, went overseas and opened branches. It completely forgot its original role, ie to help Bumiputeras get finance to do business. Instead it went international through its subsidiaries overseas and lent more money to non-Bumiputeras than Bumiputeras. It became too ambitious. Management grew lax. After all, it was a government bank and was run like a government agency. It felt that if it faced problems, the Government would not allow it to go down. There was always the Treasury to bail it out.'[8]

Bank Bumiputera's managers had been given a bank to help rural Malays, but instead they wanted a bank that was a glitzy player on international capital markets. Ultimately, the management of Bank Bumiputera saw a series of enormous fiascos that brought international embarrassment to Malaysia and did much to mask any good that the NEP and Malaysia's other affirmative action policies achieved. The bank became a byword for all that was wrong with the government's affirmative action policies up until the creation of Peremba.

Enhancing the NEP

When Mahathir became prime minister in July 1981, he had an ambitious agenda for the economic transformation of the Malaysian economy and for the role that Malays would play in that transformation. The NEP had been successful to a point in giving Malays a greater share in national wealth and prosperity, but progress was slower than Mahathir would have liked. A greater share of corporate wealth now had Malay owners, but a class of Malay entrepreneurs was still to be created. The 'success' was more statistical than practical. What was needed was a mechanism by which Malays had a real chance at becoming entrepreneurs.

Mahathir had always been consistent in the need to develop a class of hand-picked Bumiputera entrepreneurs. He talked in *The Malay Dilemma* about the failure of the Rural and Industrial Development Authority (RIDA), a British colonial government body that was set up to develop a class of indigenous business people.

---

8   Ibid.

It gave capital only to the poorest Malays who had only the 'vaguest' notions of going into business. Those Malays with any hope of succeeding received no assistance. Mahathir arrived at the prime ministership with a desire to only pick winners, rather than to waste public funds on losers as the RIDA had done. The colonial initiative was simply welfarist.

Daim's work at Peremba dovetailed nicely with Mahathir's ambitions for the next phase of the NEP. Daim selected, nurtured and entrusted potential entrepreneurs. Some of those so treated went on to become big names in Malaysian business. As mentioned, there was Wan Azmi Wan Hamzah of Land and General Group, but also Halim Saad (who went on to head Renong Group), Mohamed Razali Rahman (who later acquired control of Peremba from the government), Hassan Abbas (who later had a share in Landmarks Group, among others) and Samsudin Abu Hassan (who later headed Landmarks Group). In Peremba, Daim's protégés were able to access some of the nation's biggest projects as their training grounds. Not all of Daim's protégés spent time in Peremba. Tajudin Ramli (who later acquired control of Malaysian Airlines), for example, was never in Peremba, but nonetheless was acquainted at the time with the group that was. Importantly, Peremba was not 100% Malay. Daim made sure that around 20% of senior officers were non-Malays. He felt that it was important for the Malays to have others to measure themselves against.

So that Daim could achieve all that he wanted as finance minister, and do it quickly, conventions were occasionally overturned. The independence of the central bank and other institutions was curtailed. Through his chairmanship of the securities supervisory agency, the Capital Issues Committee (CIC), central bank governor Tan Sri Aziz Taha had the power to block or alter the terms of proposed acquisitions, takeovers or new share issues of companies listed on the KLSE, and this put him in conflict with many prominent members of the new Bumiputera business elite. Aziz's power threatened Daim's desire for rapid change. Daim complained to Mahathir and, ultimately, Aziz's opposition to Daim's policies was over-ruled. In April 1985, Daim removed the central bank governor from the chairmanship of the CIC and the agency was relocated to the Treasury. It was thereby brought under Daim's direct authority, with its chairmanship passing to Thong Yaw Hong, the secretary-general of the Treasury and thus a senior bureaucrat in Daim's ministry. (The CIC was reconstituted within the Securities Commission in 1993.) The move significantly increased Daim's power over the business sector and signalled Aziz's departure as governor of the central bank. Aziz was too much like a traditional civil servant, too concerned with due process and insufficiently business-minded for the new order. There was a new 'can do' approach to government and its desire to energise the Malay business sector. The civil service, like Malaysia's other institutions, would now serve as an instrument to promote this new aim. The ends might still not have entirely justified the means, but they were now more important.

However, Daim didn't just want change at the top. He felt that there needed to be a cultural change among Malays generally about what was desirable employment and what wasn't. The civil service had been the saviour of the Malays – it had provided them with employment and status, but Daim saw that it had also become a trap. Rather than be the apparatus for the delivery of social services, it had become a shelter for the Malay community. The optimum career path among the Malays was one in the civil service that ultimately led to a secure government pension at the end. The civil service had become bloated. Duration of employment had become the means of advancement, rather than productivity. The civil service had grown to have a stultifying effect on Malay entrepreneurship and advancement. People don't become millionaires by joining the civil service unless they are corrupt, argued Daim. There is only one permanent head of each government ministry of which there is only a small, limited number, but in the private sector there is no limit to the number of successful business people. It was time for the educated Malays to venture beyond the safety and surety of government employment.

Daim made his views on the civil service very clear on becoming finance minister. He didn't just say that he felt that Malays should consider employment other than in the civil service. He froze recruitment. It was a daring move, considering that many Malay families saw a civil service career as a right, and, not unexpectedly, he was roundly criticised. Of course, there was an economic imperative as well. The deteriorating economy saw the government's finances quickly decline and Daim needed to control government spending. More than 60,000 graduates became unemployed after the move, and mostly they were Malay. They became a vocal and obvious pressure group that only abated with the improvement in the economy.

Daim's next target was the civil service pension scheme, which he decided to do away with. Instead, civil servants would be expected to rely on the Employees Provident Fund, just as private sector workers did. Again the ire was raised in traditional Malay quarters. Daim's response to claims that Malays would now feel insecure in their civil service jobs was unequivocal. 'Good!' he was quoted as saying. 'I don't want Malays to join the public sector. If no pension means fewer of them joining Government service, that will fit in well with plans for their progress.' And 'the challenge is outside. The Malays must go out. Face the world. Fight to survive. Anyway, the EPF was just as good as a pension. If the non-Malays were happy with the EPF, why not the Malays? What about those Malays already in the private sector?'[9]

Measures such as these ensured that the Malays would have to get out into the private sector. The next step was to ensure that, once there, they had somewhere to go. Chinese tended to employ other Chinese in their businesses and Indians other Indians. NEP employment quotas that forced private businesses to employ minimum numbers of Malay staff had helped provide jobs, but generally these were of a low level. What was needed was a Malay business sector that would employ Malay managers.

---

9   Ibid., p. 75.

Therein was the rationale for Daim's singling out a small group of Malay entrepreneurs for assistance and advancement. The cynical have suggested all manner of ulterior motives. For them, 'Daim's boys' were cronies rather than protégés. But was Daim doing anything different to what happens in large corporations where promising young new recruits are targeted for mentoring and advancement? There is another, albeit less sensational, explanation as well. It is only natural that managers and business owners prefer to employ people from their own social group or community. Accordingly, Chinese business people have tended to employ Chinese, Indians have tended to employ other Indians, and Malay business people, where they exist, prefer to employ other Malays. But with so few Malays in business, it meant that, outside the civil service, Malays had little access to the corporate world. Daim and Mahathir's development of a group of prominent Bumiputera entrepreneurs by allocating privatisation and infrastructure projects to them served to get around this problem. (Infrastructure projects tended to be awarded on a negotiated tender basis, whereas privatisations typically were awarded on a 'first come, first serve' basis, whereby budding entrepreneurs were encouraged to identify a government asset that might be suitable for privatisation and then put in a bid.) Each Malay entrepreneur would then employ other Malays, thus giving them a chance to experience management in the corporate sector – a chance they otherwise would not have. In time, they too would start their own businesses and repeat the process. So, behind each high-profile, government-assisted Malay entrepreneur might be dozens or even more Malay entrepreneurs, or at least Malay managers. As then KLSE chairman Azlan Hashim said to me in 2000, 'Daim's belief is that if you create ten Malay entrepreneurs and they in turn then create ten more then you will have a geometric progression. Of course you can't assume that each of the ten will be successful. It's not 10x10x10!' Nonetheless, if the government had relied only on the NEP's education and equity allocation policies, the whole process of creating a class of Malay entrepreneurs would have taken much longer, although the criticism would have been far less.

Daim's desire to quickly create a group of substantial Malay business people did not mean that those he was mentoring could do as they liked. 'Tun enforces rules without fear or favour. I have never had any problems with enforcing rules and taking action against any company,' KLSE chairman Azlan Hashim told me. In February 1998 the KLSE slapped a public reprimand and the maximum fine (then M$100,000) on UEM for breaching KLSE rules. The company had issued false information in regard to dates on which it had purchased shares in Renong.[10] At the time Daim had yet to be reappointed as a cabinet minister but he was serving as an economic adviser to the government and was still very powerful. UEM was controlled by one of Daim's handpicked, promising Malay entrepreneurs, Halim Saad, and historically was a company that was very close

---

10 KLSE press release, 'Public reprimand and fine on United Engineers (M) Berhad', issued on 18 February 1998.

to UMNO. Of all listed companies, UEM was probably the one that Daim might have been expected to have felt the most protective of. And yet as Azlan Hashim told me, when the public reprimand and fine were announced, there was not a murmur of discontent from Daim. Azlan continued, 'The fines were grossly inadequate and we lobbied the Securities Commission for increases in the maximum fine…We can now impose a maximum fine of M$1,000,000. Of course some might still laugh at this, but it is much better than what we had.'

Business Disciples

It is the business career of Halim Saad that is most closely associated with Daim. Halim was educated at the elite Malay College, Kuala Kangsar, an institution that also produced other prominent managers of UMNO's business interests, including Anuar Othman (later managing director of UEM), Khalid Hj Ahmad (later managing director of New Straits Times Press) and Amirullah Abdul Muhi Mayuddin (managing director of Projek Lebuhraya Utara Selatan, or Plus Bhd). Halim later studied in New Zealand where he qualified as a chartered accountant and gained a Bachelor of Commerce degree.

Halim's rise in business began when he joined Peremba in the early 1980s. There he quickly rose to the position of corporate services manager. He also assumed directorships in several UMNO-linked companies. But by the late 1980s, UMNO's heavy and obvious corporate involvement began to attract significant criticism, so, through a complex array of transactions, it transferred ownership of its assets to various Malay individuals. Many of the assets wound up being injected into Renong, then a little-known property company listed on the KLSE, and in 1990, Halim Saad acquired control of Renong. He was a key figure in the restructuring of UMNO's key corporate assets under the new vehicle.

One of the first and biggest privatised projects to be awarded to Halim (through his UEM) was the M$7 billion North-South Highway that runs the length of peninsular Malaysia. According to Daim, the highway originally was to be awarded to Halim (at the time his holdings were still linked to UMNO) without a tender, but, due to the controversy and complaints that erupted, the government decided to call for tenders. Six companies put in expressions of interest and of those, two put in final proposals. One was Halim's. His was not the cheapest, but it was judged to be the best because the other company's bid allowed for only a single carriageway along some sections of the route. According to Daim, this is how the other bid was able to be cheaper than Halim's. Halim was also accused of being unqualified for the job, lacking experience and expertise. But as Daim points out, none of the six bidders was qualified at the time. Regardless of the controversy over how the contract was decided, what cannot be denied is that construction of the highway was a huge achievement that has greatly benefited the Malaysian economy ever since. UEM successfully raised the required capital, set about hiring the right expertise to get the job done, and then completed the project fifteen months ahead of the original schedule. Despite there being substantial cost over-runs, overall it was a milestone achievement for Malay business. Halim's success with the highway allowed him more latitude later on. Halim's companies were later awarded the rights to build a light rail system in Kuala Lumpur, a national fibre-optic network, a second crossing to Singapore, stadiums and other highways.

Halim's early association with Daim was very important to his start in business, but thereafter Halim was very much his own man. The proof of this is that Halim has on occasions embarked on strategies or taken routes that either surprised Daim or that he says that he himself would not have chosen. An approach made by expatriate Malaysian investor Khoo Teck Puat in 1996 to acquire a stake in Renong is a case in point.

According to Daim, Khoo offered to swap all, or almost all, of his stake in Standard Chartered Bank with Halim for a large chunk of Renong. (Khoo's stake in the UK bank of almost 15% was valued at around US$1.6 billion in 1998.) The deal seemed an astonishingly good one to Daim. Halim would be getting a large tranche in a blue chip bank of world standing in return for giving up part of his stake in Renong, much of which was yet to prove profitable. The deal would not have handed control of Renong to Khoo but would have left him as one of its largest single shareholders. Daim says he even flew to Singapore to personally examine and approve the deal. But Halim later rejected it, much to Daim's surprise. 'I couldn't believe it,' Daim said to me. 'Sometimes, I don't know who he gets his advice from.' The episode highlighted the closeness but also the independence of the two men.

According to Daim, Khoo, who had been one of the founders of Maybank, had lost control of the bank after he had been found to have had the bank inappropriately lend to his other interests. In exchange for relinquishing his control of the bank, the Malaysian authorities allowed Khoo to keep various landed properties in Singapore that had been part of Maybank's property portfolio. It was a typically Malaysian outcome whereby the vanquished are allowed to preserve some 'face' and some assets. Khoo decided to make his home in Singapore from where he acquired control of Standard Chartered Bank. Daim says that Khoo was so keen on buying into Renong that he ended his self-imposed exile from Malaysia to call in on Daim at his office in Kuala Lumpur. Daim told me that he would have been happy to have acquired the Standard Chartered stake himself, but at the time he didn't have any assets to swap. Instead, Daim emphasised to Halim that it was a good deal, and if Halim had listened and acted on Daim's advice, then Halim would have been saved when the financial crisis swept through the region in 1998.

As mentioned, Wan Azmi Wan Hamzah is another prominent Malay entrepreneur who emerged from Peremba. He was born in Kelantan in 1950 and is the son of former Supreme Court judge Wan Hamzah Wan Mohamed Salleh. He qualified as a chartered accountant in the United Kingdom and worked briefly for the Guthrie Corporation in the 1970s. He joined the UMNO-controlled New Straits Times Press Group in 1977 where he rose to become financial controller.

Two years later he joined Peremba, which was then headed by Daim. The two became close friends and in 1983 he became managing director of United Estates Projects Bhd (UEP), a listed company that Daim controlled, and a director of the UMNO-controlled Fleet Group and some of its subsidiaries. After he became finance minister, Daim appointed Wan Azmi in 1985 as chief executive officer of the government-owned Malayan Banking Bhd. Wan Azmi was 36 at the time – an age that is young for such a senior post by the standards of Western, mature economies, but less so for many fast-growing developing countries where the market for skilled labour and professionals can be very tight. Wan Azmi stayed with the bank for less than two years. His time there was difficult. It coincided with the recession and he had to call in the loans of many of his Bumiputera business friends. The Maminco tin scandal broke at about the same time and it emerged that Malayan Banking, along with Bank Bumiputera, had extended loans to a company set up by the Malaysian government in an ill-fated attempt to corner the world tin market.

Daim facilitated the sale to Wan Azmi of an 8% stake in an ailing timber company called General Lumber, owned by Raleigh Bhd, on Wan Azmi's departure from Malayan Banking. (Raleigh had been part of Daim's private business interests prior to relinquishing it after becoming finance minister in 1984. Daim had sold his interest in Raleigh to several business associates.) Wan Azmi had little trouble raising the finance needed for the stake, particularly given his good connections in the banking sector, having just resigned as head of one of the country's major commercial banks. His strong political connections were also a considerable help. He subsequently raised his direct interest in General Lumber to almost 15% and became chairman of the company. Its public listing meant that it could readily raise cash to expand and to diversify. Wan Azmi and his brother-in-law, Nik Mahmood Haji Nik Hassan, then set about creating one of the few fully integrated timber operations in Southeast Asia. Diversification into stockbroking, chemicals and property development saw the lumber aspect of the company decrease in relative importance. Accordingly, the company's name was changed to Land and General Bhd in December 1991. Wan Azmi had succeeded in transforming the company from a small and unprofitable concern to one that was large and highly profitable. Wan Azmi stayed close to Daim. As is further discussed in Chapter 14, in 1998, when the NEAC was established in response to the economic crisis, he was appointed by Daim to his small but powerful NEAC Working Group.

Tajudin Ramli was another young Malay selected by Daim for mentoring. He was born in impoverished circumstances in Kedah but became one of Malaysia's most prominent entrepreneurs. He had served as a general manager of the UDA Merchant Bank. Later, he and Daim acquired control of the formerly British-owned Raleigh, which in turn was sold to Vincent Tan. Tajudin's Alpine Resources was later awarded Malaysia's first mobile telephone licence in partnership with the government-controlled telephone company Telekom. In 1989, another of Tajudin's companies, Technology Resources Industries (TRI), bought out Telekom's share in what had become Cellular Communications Network (Malaysia), or Celcom. This gave Tajudin complete control over the country's only national mobile network. Other mobile phone operators were licensed in later years, but Celcom remained Malaysia's largest mobile operator.

In 1994, Tajudin acquired from the government a 32% controlling stake in Malaysia's national airline, Malaysian Airline System (MAS). It was Malaysia's biggest-ever corporate deal. MAS was already deeply troubled. Tajudin set about cutting costs at MAS and this quickly showed results. In 1996, MAS reported a 67% increase in profits over the previous year to almost US$100 million and revenues were up 17.6% to US$2.3 billion. But with the arrival of the 1997-98 economic crisis his debt levels increased significantly and the revenues fell for most of his companies. MAS began to lose money and Tajudin seemed unable to turn the situation around. By early 2001, Tajudin had sold his stake in the airline back to the government.

Manufacturing Millionaires

The sale of MAS back to the government was a significant backwards step for Daim's system of tutelage. The 1997-98 region-wide economic crisis did much damage to the business interests of the handpicked entrepreneurs. Many had grown too fast and had over-borrowed. But still Daim and Mahathir had no doubts as to the efficacy of building a class of Bumiputera business moguls. To have simply relied on the NEP, with its emphasis of holding equity in trust for the Malays, did very little for Malay entrepreneurialism. Mahathir was quoted in 1979 as saying, 'The best way to keep the shares between the Bumiputera hands is to hand them over to the Bumiputera most capable of retaining them, which means the well-to-do.' Daim urged party members, when addressing the 1985 UMNO General Assembly, to 'strive to attain the nature of the two Ms – not Mahathir-Musa, but Malay Millionaires.'[11] Without Daim's intervention with his strategy of deliberately selecting Malay entrepreneurs for propulsion into the upper echelons of business, the NEP's main success would have been merely the increase in corporate equity under Malay ownership.

The strategy proved highly controversial. A later chapter looks at some of the debate that enveloped the policy particularly in the wake of the 1997-98 economic crisis. But while Mahathir and Daim were intent on sharpening the NEP, around the corner lay a broader distraction: the economy.

---

11 As quoted in E.T. Gomez, *Political Business: Corporate Involvement of Malaysian Political Parties*, James Cook University, 1994, p. 7.

VIII

THE END OF MALAYSIA?

The world economy had been kind to Malaysia for much of the twentieth century. Generally, international commodity prices had remained high, and when individual commodities fell from fashion, another that Malaysia happened to be abundant in would take its place. Managing any economy under such benign circumstances was no great feat. The Malay elite could play at politics, content in the knowledge that the economy would hum along regardless. But all that changed in the mid-1980s. Commodity prices collapsed – not just one or two, but practically for all of Malaysia's major commodity exports such as tin, palm oil and crude petroleum – and they did so in unison. On top of that, the Plaza Accord, which was signed in 1985 by the G-7 economies to push up the yen to alleviate the trade imbalance between the United States and Japan, saw the yen rapidly appreciate, and the cost of servicing Malaysia's yen-denominated foreign debt followed.

Soon after the budget for the 1985 year was delivered, the first cracks had begun to appear. Commodity prices started to slide. The economy continued to deteriorate as the year wore on. The budget forecasts started to look shaky, and ultimately some were way out. One such forecast was that for the price of a barrel of crude oil, which was supposed to remain at US$29; instead, it plunged to US$9 during the year. In 1985, the country experienced for the first time a current account deficit, something that also had not been predicted in the budget. Gradually it became clear that many of the banks and finance companies were in significant difficulty. By mid-1985, the recession was in full swing. The situation was not helped by a string of scandals, particularly in the banking sector, that served to weaken the economy and confidence.

Government-controlled Bank Bumiputera had suffered throughout the 1970s and 1980s from bad management and imprudent borrowing. Bad loans accumulated, and by 1986 a government inquiry deduced that the bank had lost more than M$2 billion. Other crises occurred with other prominent financial institutions such as Perwira Habib Bank, Supreme Finance, First Malaysia Finance, KL Finance, Kewangan Usaha Bersatu Bhd (KUBB) and Pekembarjaya. On top of these came a crisis that involved many of the deposit-taking cooperatives that serviced the Chinese community, particularly Malaysian Chinese Association (MCA) members. Many ordinary savers faced the threat of losing billions in ringgit with the collapse of many of these institutions. Next came the Cooperative Central Bank scandal, which lost more than M$700 million, forcing the government to intervene and bail it out. Insurance companies were also facing problems. There was a contagion effect that spread from the financial system to the rest of the economy, particularly to many Bumiputera enterprises.

Daim was finance minister, so in the eyes of many he was to blame. And yet the previous finance minister, Razaleigh, had also been chairman of Bank Bumiputera, Petronas and Pernas, among others. His efforts earned him the moniker of 'Bapak Ekonomi' ('Father of the Economy'). While Razaleigh was the finance minister, commodities prices had generally held up, so that the Malaysian economy did not have to pedal very fast to do very well. This allowed a whole range of excesses to be masked, and gradually over time they accumulated, so that when the recession did hit Malaysia, rather than resting on a strong framework, the economy had a range of structural weaknesses that exacerbated the downturn and hindered recovery. Perhaps more fairly, many of the problems that occurred in the lead-up to the 1985 recession can be laid at Razaleigh's door. Arguably, Mahathir did him an enormous political favour by demoting him when he did. He escaped being tarred by a brush – the recession – to which he was a contributor.

The new realities came as a shock for a country that had known only positive economic growth since independence. Daim came to office without having any experience of managing a ministry. To have to do it as Malaysia's worst economic crisis to date engulfed the country must have been extremely daunting. 'I think I practically aged ten years overnight,' Daim is reported to have said.[1] Daim's difficulties were hampered by the fact that in the early stages very few people actually had much confidence in his abilities. To many, he had spent insufficient time working away within UMNO; he had not worked his way to the top. Instead, he owed his position to Mahathir. So, seemingly, he had come from nowhere, and rather than spend time building bridges to his colleagues he concentrated on administering Malaysia's economy.

Daim said to me in London in 2015 that dealing with this first economic crisis was the hardest thing that he ever had to do. It was far harder than dealing with the region-wide crisis that engulfed Malaysia in 1997 which led to his being called back as finance minister a second time. He had to learn the job at once and constantly make momentous decisions. 'I was one year into the job and everything was collapsing around me, but steel is forged in the hottest fire,' he said to me.

Bank Bumiputera

The first major problem that Daim faced was the Bumiputera Malaysia Finance affair. It erupted shortly before he took office and was the biggest loan scandal that Malaysia had faced (out of quite a number). Bumiputera Malaysia Finance (BMF) Ltd was a Hong Kong subsidiary of the government-owned Bank Bumiputera Malaysia Bhd (BBMB). It was revealed that between 1979 and 1982, BMF had extended huge loans to three property-based companies in Hong Kong. George Tan and his Carrian Group borrowed more than US$70 million

---

1   M.S. Cheong and Adibah Amin, *Daim: The Man Behind the Enigma*, Pelanduk Publications, 1995, p. 62.

from BMF between June 1979 and October 1982. Between November 1979 and September 1982, the Kevin Hsu group of companies borrowed around US$123 million, and Chung Ching Man and his Eda Investments borrowed around US$40 million between September and December 1981. Between late 1982 and late 1983, all three borrowers became insolvent and defaulted on their loans. Absurdly, Carrian and Kevin Hsu accounted for almost 80% of BMF's total loans portfolio. It was utterly imprudent that so much had been lent to so few, and completely scandalous that a bank that existed to lend to rural Malays should be lending at all to wealthy Hong Kong-based Chinese businessmen. By late 1993, when Carrian and Eda were liquidated, BMF had accumulated losses equivalent to M$2.5 billion, or more than twice Bank Bumiputera's shareholders' capital of M$1.22 billion. Ultimately, a whole range of improper and fraudulent practices was uncovered.

The scandal caused a public sensation in Malaysia (and elsewhere), which was compounded when the deputy head of Bank Bumiputera's Internal Audit Department, who had been seconded to work with BMF in Hong Kong as an assistant general manager, was found strangled in July 1983 in a banana grove in Hong Kong's New Territories. Mak Foon Than, a Malaysian, was subsequently arrested and tried for the murder. In October 1983, George Tan and Bentley Ho (Carrian's executive director) were arrested by Hong Kong police on charges of falsifying accounts with intent to defraud Carrian's other shareholders. Ultimately, it became evident that George Tan had bribed BMF employees to authorise the loans to his companies. The former BMF chairman, Lorrain Esme Osman, was imprisoned in Hong Kong for his part in the affair, as were a number of other BMF officials.

The problems at Bank Bumiputera had a long genesis and all that time, Tunku Razaleigh, Daim's predecessor, had been finance minister. Although he personally had no direct involvement in the fraud (he successfully sued three newspapers in Hong Kong and London that implied that he did), the administrative buck stopped (or should have stopped) with him. Nonetheless, he distanced himself from the affair and appeared to claim that he had no final authority over the bank, as did Mahathir.[2]

The government's handling of the affair vacillated between ineptitude and paralysis – it simply didn't know what to do. The opposition rightly hammered the government over the whole affair for months, and the international media was scathing. The government had no clear response to the crisis until after Daim was appointed finance minister. His appointment served as a circuit breaker to the confusion and apparent inaction. Being new to the portfolio, and untainted by the scandal, he was able immediately to set about making changes.

There were calls for a Royal Commission into the affair. These were ignored by Mahathir. But although the government had an overwhelming majority in Parliament, the public outcry was such that it had to do something. It opted for

---

2   B.T. Khoo, *Paradoxes of Mahathirism*, Oxford University Press, 1995, p. 128.

setting up a Bank Bumiputera 'in-house panel of inquiry', later known as the 'Committee of Inquiry' headed by Ahmad Noordin, a former auditor-general. Mahathir initially refused to make public the committee's final report, claiming that its contents might expose the government to libel suits. There was strong public pressure for the release of the report, however, and then Ahmad Noordin and Chooi Mun Sou, two of the three committee members, announced that they were willing to take responsibility for its publication. The government then acceded and allowed the report's publication, but only after it produced its own parallel report, the 'White Paper on the BMF', so as 'to be fair to everybody'.[3]

Daim appointed a new chairman of the bank, but the new appointee was unable to introduce the changes that were needed. Management and internal supervision at the bank had been allowed to go unchecked for so long that a poor management culture had set in. Daim replaced the new chairman with yet another one. To solve the problem of the bank's insolvency, the government decided to sell it to Petronas. It was hardly ideal to use the state-owned oil company to bail out a government bank beset with mismanagement. Nor was it ideal to have a state-owned oil company suddenly diversify into banking. Indeed, the Petronas Act actually prohibited Petronas from investing outside oil-related activities, and had to be amended retrospectively. But, according to Daim, Petronas was the only entity in Malaysia at the time with enough money. Closing the bank down would have been politically untenable given its identification with Malay interests. Daim felt there was no other option.

So, in September 1984, Daim called a press conference to announce that Petronas would buy Bank Bumiputera. Petronas would acquire 86.7% of BBMB held by Pernas for M$933 million and, at the same time, inject M$300 million into the bank. It would then also purchase non-performing loans for M$1.255 billion. This would leave Petronas with 90% of BBMB's enlarged equity. The commercial arm of the Ministry of Finance would hold the remaining 10%. The restructuring also involved BBMB selling its stake in Malayan Banking Bhd, then Malaysia's second-largest bank, to Pernas for a profit of M$589 million to further strengthen its capital base. The bulk of BMB's non-performing loans would then be written off, leaving the bank with a capital base of M$1.1 billion.

Having to deal with the BMF fiasco so soon after his appointment to the cabinet appears to have had an indelible impact on Daim's policy priorities throughout his ministerial career. Banking reform was an important policy interest of his both during his first and second stints as finance minister. Frequently, he invoked the memory of the inherent waste and the expense of cleaning up BMF and Bank Bumiputera as justification for his plans to reform Malaysian banking. Nonetheless, Daim remains sympathetic to what Bank Bumiputera was set up to achieve. I asked him if all the trouble the bank had caused the government over the years meant that it might have been better had it never been established. 'No,' he said, the bank had still been important as a source of credit for small Malay

---

3   Ibid., p. 231.

businessmen who would not otherwise have been able to borrow elsewhere. Given this, Daim still feels that Bank Bumiputera has had a net positive impact on Malaysia.

In 1991, Daim announced the government's intention to privatise Bank Bumiputera, but it was not until 1994 that Samsudin Abu Hassan, one of the group of young Malay business people to be mentored by Daim, commenced discussions with the bank on his possible acquisition. The deal did not go through. One sticking point was that the then finance minister, Anwar Ibrahim, was not pleased that Samsudin had first made an approach to the bank rather than to his ministry. Also, Samsudin was seen as very much associated with Daim and, by that stage, Daim and Anwar had already started to criticise each other in the media.[4]

Maminco

The next fiasco that Daim had to contend with was the government's involvement in what became known as the Maminco affair. On 8 July 1981, just eight days before Mahathir became prime minister, the then prime minister, Hussein Onn, chaired a cabinet meeting which approved a price support scheme for tin and the creation of Maminco Sdn Bhd, a government-owned company that would provide the means by which the government would manage the scheme. What started out as a price support scheme evolved to become a plan to corner the world market for tin. Initially, Maminco's plan involved purchasing tin futures on the London Metal Exchange (LME). Maminco did this secretly, without revealing that it was the purchaser. Its action pushed the price of tin from £6,880 per tonne in July 1981 to a high of £8,970 in February 1982. Briefly, it seemed that the plan was working. Sellers who had sold tin short soon had to enter the market to buy tin to meet the contracts they had entered. Tin became scarce, and the buyers had to bid against each other to buy what tin was available. The Malaysian government even earned an extra US$100 million in increased tin exports and duties.[5]

Unfortunately for the Malaysians, the scheme did what all such schemes do, which is to stimulate production of the commodity whose price is being supported. Those doing the cornering must then try even harder to keep the price at the new, higher level. Tin flowed on to the world market, and that flow threatened to become a flood when the United States General Services Administration decided to unload some of its tin stockpile in response to the favourable market conditions, further exerting a downward pressure on the tin price. About that time, Maminco switched its strategy from one of price support to outright market cornering. It made large spot purchases of tin so that those with futures contracts to supply tin had to scramble to buy tin to meet their commitments. By February 1982, tin prices had reached their peak and many LME traders were in financial

4 'Who gets what', *Far Eastern Economic Review*, 5 May 1994.

5 Khoo, op. cit., p. 231.

trouble. To ease their plight, the LME intervened and changed its rules. Traders could pay a fine in lieu of meeting their contracts in the event of a default. It also sharply reduced the penalties for the late meeting of contracts. Not surprisingly, Mahathir cried foul. The LME's sudden changing of the rules of the game was questionable, but then so was the attempt to corner the market. Tin prices correspondingly collapsed, and with it Maminco's plans. It was left with a huge stockpile of tin and massive debts. The Malaysian government then attempted to hide the losses with some creative accounting.

For five years, the government denied that it had been the mystery buyer, until Mahathir, at the urging of Daim, felt that there was little choice but to come clean. (Daim said to me that he had never supported the Maminco price support plan.) Daim wrote off the M$660 million in losses and closed the account to which they had been booked. For Daim, the situation could not be saved and it was better to come out in the open and admit that it was all a mistake. Denials beget denials and the situation had become untenable.

Daim's experience of the aftermath of the Maminco scheme helped to confirm in his mind the dangers of price support schemes. He is a supporter of the international Islamic movement, but he is no fan of the oil price-setting cartel OPEC, which mostly comprises Middle Eastern oil-producing countries. He believes that market forces should determine the price for oil. But what about the price for rubber, which is a major employer in his Merbok constituency? Malaysia and Thailand agreed in early 2000 to set up a US$80 million fund to help 'stabilise' rubber prices. The two countries planned to buy as much as 140,000 tonnes of rubber from the International Natural Rubber Organisation (INRO). Malaysia pulled out of the organisation in 1999 and Thailand withdrew in March 2000, claiming that INRO had failed to increase rubber prices. I asked Daim whether he felt that such a scheme echoed the Maminco scheme. 'No,' he claimed, the creation of the rubber fund was more for psychological influence than anything else. The mere announcement of its creation drove up rubber prices, he claims; and in any event, both governments only drew on about half the money that had been set aside in the fund to buy up rubber. Once again, Daim's policy pragmatism is demonstrated; he is no ideologue.

Pan-El

Daim's next problem was a major stock market scandal – the Pan-Electric Industries (Pan-El) debacle that erupted at the end of 1985. It would have been just another company collapse brought on by a combination of recession, mismanagement and fraud, but for the fact that Member of Parliament and MCA president Tan Koon Swan was embroiled in it. Tan and his supporters had just won a bitter 20-month power struggle within the Malaysian Chinese Association (MCA). Tan was seen as pro-business and pro-UMNO. Accordingly, he had the support of most senior UMNO members. Daim had reservations at first about Tan – Tan and his supporters had at times been openly critical of the

NEP – but ultimately he, too, gave Tan his tacit support. The trouble for Tan was that while his political star was rising, his personal finances were collapsing in a heap along with Pan-El.

Pan-Electric Industries, which had operated in Singapore for 25 years, was ordered into receivership on 30 November 1985 after it had defaulted on loans that approached S$400 million. It was just six days after Tan and his group were victorious in the MCA elections. Pan-El shares were traded on both the KLSE and the Stock Exchange of Singapore (SES). On 19 November, trading in the stock had been suspended on the SES along with shares in two other companies that held a lot of Pan-El's equity – Sigma International and Growth Industrial Holdings. Singapore's Monetary Authority (MAS) decided that it would close the SES for three days from 2 December to head off panic selling that could lead to a market crash. The head of the MAS informed Daim of what the Singaporeans intended to do. Malaysia was left with little option but to close its exchange as well – the two exchanges were linked and it was not possible to close one without affecting the other. If the KLSE remained open, Pan-El shares would be dumped in Malaysia, possibly leading to a market collapse there. Pan-El's collapse was the culmination of what has been described as 'years of syndicate-led market manipulation in many quoted companies, involving among other things, complex forward share contracts, webs of inter-broker credit and speculative ramping of share prices'.[6]

In January 1986, Tan was arrested in Singapore by the Commercial Activities Investigation Department. He was later imprisoned for two years and fined S$500,000. On his release in December 1987 he was charged, convicted and imprisoned in Malaysia for similar offences relating to Pan-El. He was forced to give up his parliamentary seat and the MCA presidency.

The Pan-El debacle and the moves by the SES convinced Daim that the KLSE should be split from the SES. Although Malaysia was an independent nation, the link between the KLSE and the SES meant that Malaysia did not have full control over its own stock market. Daim set up a committee to study the matter and to make recommendations. He also took the opportunity to reform the structure of the stockbroking sector in Malaysia. (These moves are examined in Chapter 18.) For Daim, the Pan-El debacle could be turned into a policy opportunity. In the maze of vested and often conflicting interests that is Malaysian politics, genuine economic reform often is only really possible in the face of some debacle or crisis. Only then can the multitude of vested interests be cut through. The next crisis that Daim had to face was economy-wide – modern Malaysia's first recession. It provided Daim with ample cover and justification for reform on many fronts.

---

6   Ibid., p. 216.

IX

DAIM'S PRESCRIPTIONS

The scandals and the collapse in international commodity prices of 1985 had arrived with little warning. In fact, the economic sunshine had continued to fall on Malaysia throughout 1984. But the storm was closing in. Daim had to prepare his inaugural budget in the latter part of that year. As far as budgets go, it was plain sailing. No one suspected that recession was about to hit the country. Daim ultimately went along with all the recommendations and forecasts that were supplied by officials. There was little reason not to. But as the previous chapter described, the budget projections were ultimately way off.

The dramatically deteriorating situation called for quick action and some major decisions. If Daim was to be successful in managing the economy through the storm, it was inevitable that some toes would be trodden on. Daim insisted that borrowers repay their loans no matter what political allegiances and influence they felt they could claim. He stood firm on this issue and it made him some enemies. Representations were quietly made to the prime minister that Daim should be removed. But Daim retained Mahathir's confidence and he remained resolute. Daim was very much of the view that the government, too, should live within its means, whereas his predecessor at the Finance Ministry, Tunku Razaleigh, preferred to spend and inflate the economy, in the hope that later inflation would generate higher tax receipts to pay for previous high spending. This was fine when the economy was growing, but it was a high-risk strategy should growth suddenly cease. And that is what happened in the mid-1980s.

Daim's immediate and greatest priority was to rein in government spending. According to Daim, 'In the private sector when we borrow we have to pay and pay quickly. But in the case of Government, I noticed that year in and year out, we kept borrowing and the debt kept on increasing and no attempt was made to reduce it. The excuse given was that if people are prepared to lend to us, it shows they have confidence in us.'[1]

Collectively, the country was a net debtor as well, despite it having substantial foreign reserves. Reserves stood at M$9 billion, but borrowing was M$20 billion when Daim became finance minister. This made no sense to him. There seemed to be little point in accumulating foreign debt and growing reserves at the same time. The country was 'flush' with cash, so Daim thought Malaysia should take advantage of it. The solution, he believed, was to encourage borrowing from within the country. The central bank was instructed to cut back on approvals for

---

1   M.S. Cheong and Adibah Amin, *Daim: The Man Behind the Enigma*, Pelanduk Publications, 1995, p. 73.

foreign loans, forcing companies to borrow locally. It turned out to be an excellent decision. When the 1997-98 Asian economic crisis struck, those countries most affected tended to be those with the highest foreign borrowings. Malaysia's external debts were relatively low. So the major impact of the collapse of the ringgit during the crisis was to make Malaysia's exports even more competitive.

Cutting Spending

Daim immediately reduced the need for public sector borrowings. Greater efficiencies in tax collection were introduced, so that the Inland Revenue Department substantially increased taxation revenues. He slashed government spending, which upset those in the civil service as well as those in the private sector who had become reliant on government contracts. Daim halved the development allocation for the Fifth Malaysia Plan from M$74 billion to M$37 billion in 1985. Only when commodity prices started to recover did he restore some of this funding back to M$47 billion. Cuts such as these were particularly politically brave given that development fund money was typically used in rural areas – UMNO's heartland – both to boost the rural economy and to ensure support for UMNO at election time.

Daim also tightened spending controls over government departments, agencies and state sector companies. Ministers' allowances were cut and their privileges reviewed. Nothing is more likely to upset politicians in any country and have them running to the leader to complain than having their entitlements scrutinised and reduced. The move was a measure of Daim's relative indifference to the opinions of his colleagues in his determination to do what he felt was appropriate. One measure was to downgrade the vehicle entitlement of ministers from a Mercedes Benz 280SE to a 230E.[2] It might not sound like a particularly savage measure, but the internal political fall-out that Daim had to endure was out of all proportion to the money he hoped to save the government from the measure.

State-owned companies came under particular scrutiny from Daim. Many had been used to dispense politically motivated patronage. The managers in some had also awarded themselves excessive rates of pay and benefits. In the past, when they incurred losses, they were usually able to approach the Treasury for a top-up. As a consequence, they faced a 'soft budget constraint' whereby their managers never really had to face the consequences of their mismanagement. Not surprisingly, many made more losses than they should. Daim introduced greater monitoring of the companies' budgets and started to fire some of the more incompetent and profligate managers. It was a significant change in the way things had been done and an open challenge to the traditional Malay way of doing things, whereby loyalty tended to be valued more than performance. Daim quickly developed a reputation as the government's toughest minister.

To encourage economic growth, the Cabinet Committee suggested that 80,000 low-cost homes be built annually for three years. Housing was chosen

2   Ibid., p. 44.

both for its socially useful effects and for the spin-offs, such as stimulating demand in the cement, timber and steel industries. Daim wanted Malaysians to grow more fruit and vegetables as well. When he suggested this as a means of occupying unemployed university graduates – whose numbers swelled to around 60,000 at one stage – he was criticised. For Daim, many graduates had become too comfortable and thought only of staying in air-conditioned rooms and riding in new Mercedes-Benzes. He felt that if more chose to become taxi drivers and foodstall operators while waiting for graduate employment to turn up, it would be a benefit for them in later life.[3] Meetings were called with the various chief ministers to push the urgency of making land available for low-cost housing. This was met with a great deal of resentment. Some complained that they had no land; others did not want the involvement of the federal government in something that was ostensibly a state issue. In the end, only about 8,000 homes were built during each of the three years. Daim's suggestion that additional land be provided for fruit and vegetable cultivation was also largely ignored. Malaysia's plurality means that not every battle can be won – even when it is the finance minister giving the orders.

The 1987 and 1988 Budgets

Daim cut government spending in 1986, but it was not enough. His cabinet colleagues, who thought that his tight-fistedness was one-off, were sorely disappointed. He went back for more in the 1987 and 1988 budgets.

The 1987 Budget had three broad aims:
- To reduce the role of the public sector in the economy and to strengthen its financial position.
- To promote the growth of exports and to reduce imports in order to improve the balance of payments.
- To improve the environment for an expansion of private sector investment and to stimulate business confidence.

The budget contained some real cost-cutting measures but also plenty of symbolism. The symbolic measures might not have added up to huge cost savings for the government but were important for the message they sent. Among the measures Daim proposed were:
- The allowances and privileges of ministers, deputy ministers and other members of the administration would be reviewed with a view to either reducing or abolishing them altogether. The entertainment and housing allowances, as well as allowances for official travel, would be reduced by 10-20%. All allowances that were paid during vacation travel would be abolished. The government would only pay the cost of the passage of ministers, deputy ministers and their spouses. These measures had immediate effect.

---

3   Ibid., p. 97.

- There were politicians and civil servants who received, or might be eligible to receive, more than one government pension. The government would impose a tax of 100% on such second and subsequent pensions.
- The entertainment and housing allowances of superscale officers would be reduced by 10%.
- The mileage allowance for travel on government duty for government officers would be reduced. Tighter controls would be implemented to determine what was, and what was not, necessary travel. The government would also take steps to reduce expenditure on travel for conferences and seminars overseas.
- The size of public sector employment would be controlled by measures such as earlier retirements, redeployment of excess staff and abolition of posts.
- The number and size of diplomatic missions and other overseas offices would be reviewed to economise on expenditure. Missions of lesser priority would be closed.
- Privatisation would be made more speedy and effective. The government would identify services and projects that could be privatised, and publicly invite interested parties to participate in the process. The government was prepared to offer the Malayan Railway for sale by leasing it at a nominal M$1.00 to any operator willing to operate it on a commercial basis.
- The scholarship scheme was to be modified. The allocation for the scheme was to be restructured so that 80% of it would be for loans and only 20% would be for actual scholarships.
- New employees and those not yet contributing to the Employees Provident Fund would be required to do so. They would then not be eligible for a government pension. In the long run, they would save the government significant sums, as retirement incomes would then be privately provided.

Despite the expenditure cuts and planned privatisations, the government was still to run a budget deficit in 1987 of M$2,718 million. Partly, this was due to the recession and a consequent fall in taxation receipts of M$1,100 million. Daim proposed further measures to bring the budget back to surplus by 1989. These included:
- Interest rates on government housing and car loans would be increased from 4% to 6%. The increase would also apply to members of the administration and would cover both new and existing loans. Category D civil servants would be exempted from the increase.
- More stringent conditions on the eligibility for government housing loans would be implemented immediately and would apply for both civil servants and members of the administration.
- Greater cost recovery via user pays. Fees and payments for outpatient treatment, including medicine and hospitalisation, would be imposed or increased. Lower-income people would continue to receive medical treatment without charge.

- Agencies would be amalgamated to reduce duplication of functions and to achieve greater work efficiency and savings on operating costs.

Daim announced further pro-business measures in the 1987 Budget. The share transfer tax was reduced, the existing exemption was extended to group restructuring to alleviate the property market slowdown, real property gains tax was lowered, exemptions from stamp duty were widened, the tax exemption on compensation for loss of employment to help the companies concerned and their retrenched employees was increased, double deduction for approved training by the manufacturing sector to upgrade skills was introduced, and exemptions from the need to acquire a manufacturing licence were extended. Daim felt that the government had done a lot for business. He now expected business to do its share in pulling Malaysia out of recession. As will be described later, he was and continued to be disappointed with corporate Malaysia's efforts.

When Daim presented his 1988 Budget in October 1987, the economy was on the mend. Public expenditure was more under control, the current account of the balance of payments had returned to surplus, Malaysia's foreign reserves had strengthened and the ringgit had stabilised. Partly it was due to better macroeconomic management. It was also partly due to the cyclical upturn of commodity prices on world markets. Daim was not satisfied, however. He declared that many of the old problems remained and were still to be resolved. Economic growth, unemployment and the government's budgetary position were still all unsatisfactory. The private sector was still not playing an adequate enough role. To provide more encouragement for the private sector, but also to improve public sector finances, Daim proposed:

- The compulsory payment of company tax by instalment.
- The abolition of the 3% company excess profit tax.
- The reinvestment allowance for capital expenditure to rise from 25% to 40%.
- A luxury sales tax to be imposed on items such as shark's fin, teak and sailing vessels.

The most significant consequence of Daim's cost cutting and his other measures was the improvement of the finances of the Malaysian government. In the 1984 Budget, the budget deficit was a high of 8.9% of gross domestic product (GDP). By 1988 it was down to 3.6%, and when Daim stepped down in 1991 it was 2% of GDP.[4] The absolute level of Malaysia's foreign debt followed suit. It grew, stabilised and then contracted. It grew by 34.7% in 1983, 17.6% in 1984, 14.2% in 1985 and 18.9% in 1986, but then in 1987, it declined by 0.3%, followed by a 6.7% decline the year after that and a 10.3% decline the next year.[5]

---

4   Ibid., p. 162.

5   Ibid., p. 45.

The Banks and Monetary Policy

Malaysia's banks and other financial institutions were in a weakened state by the time the full force of the recession hit in mid-1985. The recession served to further weaken the sector. Many businesses were unable to repay their loans, and the banks in their already weakened state were in no position to be lenient with bad debtors. Cabinet colleagues also appealed to Daim to ask the banks to relax, but he refused. His view was simple: if you borrow, you should repay. He felt that Malaysian business people lacked financial discipline and it was time for a cultural change. In any event, the banks simply needed the money.

Daim did, however, encourage the banks to give those business people who were in difficulty because of the recession more time to get their affairs in order. But he told them to 'go for' those business people who had come into difficulty because of their own mismanagement or their own extravagance. Many had borrowed not so much to plough into potentially profitable investment, but rather to surround themselves with the trappings of success before necessarily achieving it. Too many business people had emerged with extravagant offices with expensive fit-outs and top-of-the-range Mercedes-Benzes without having created the wealth to justify it all. The self-serving rationale for much of this was that they felt they needed to look successful in order to become successful. 'As if confidence came by showing off!' Daim is quoted as saying.[6] Many of these business people were forced into bankruptcy, or were threatened with bankruptcy unless they agreed to forego their assets so that they could be turned over to those with better business acumen. Daim's tough stance did not win him too many friends. And, of course, when he was less than tough on some, perhaps because he felt they had done the right thing and deserved another chance, or maybe they still had a place in Daim's overall scheme of things, he appeared to be playing favourites and being selective. Such are the risks of any government that seeks to intervene in an economy to 'pick winners'. Many of those offended and put out were supporters of the government and, more particularly, of UMNO.

To help those Bumiputera businessmen whom the government deemed to be genuinely affected by the recession, rather than simply being victims of their own mismanagement, the government arranged a meeting between bankers and the Malay Chamber of Commerce, at which a fund was launched to help 'deserving' businesses. The fund, the Entrepreneurs' Rehabilitation Fund (or TPU – *Tabung Pemulihan Usahawan*), was to help entrepreneurs affected by the recession by giving them loans for viable projects. Those who no longer had any projects but were thought to have good management teams were awarded government contracts. Of course, it helped to be well-connected and to have been an UMNO supporter, but at the same time, Mahathir and Daim did not intend to allow the recession to derail the gains that had been made by the NEP.

Another measure that Daim pushed for was a softening of interest rates. The government was unable to simply demand lower interest rates, as the central

---

6   Ibid., p. 84.

bank, Bank Negara, had a degree of independence from the government which the then governor, Tan Sri Aziz Taha, was keen to demonstrate. Daim, who tends to be more concerned with outcomes than the niceties of things such as central bank autonomy, sought to bring the bank more under his control. The erosion of the bank's powers was highlighted in 1985 when, following pressure from Daim, Tan Sri Aziz Taha quit. Aziz had favoured running a tight monetary policy and resisted political pressure in his policy making. Daim, on the other hand, favoured a more expansionary monetary policy with cheaper and easier credit. It would allow businesses more easily to service their debts and enable the government to pursue its share-ownership policies whereby more Malaysians could acquire stakes in companies by using credit to buy shares. (Independence might have been subverted or lost, but the bank is still regarded as professional.) Daim said it was Bank Negara's poor and inadequate supervision that caused failures resulting in the banking crisis and the BMF scandal. He felt that when the country was in crisis then the government must have the power to implement its policies. In any event, Daim's judgment on loosening monetary policy was ultimately proven correct.

The general weakness in the Malaysian economy and the run on deposit-taking cooperatives led to large losses among some of Malaysia's banks and finance companies by 1986. Alarmed, central bank officials moved in 1987 to bring down real interest rates. They bargained that, despite Malaysia's then open capital account and the ease with which Malaysians could shift deposits to Singapore, the leakage would be manageable if real interest rates on deposits were no less than 2 percentage points below international rates. As it turned out, they were actually 3.4 percentage points below the London Interbank Offer Rate (LIBOR) during 1987-88. This allowed the spread between deposits and loan interest rates – essentially, the banks' profit margins – to widen and the banks to recapitalise. The plan worked. In 1986, the combined losses of Malaysia's banks were M$337 million. By 1988, the sector was profitable in net terms – to the tune of M$794 million.[7] It's the same approach that governments in Western Europe had to take in 2009 when their banks were engulfed in a banking crisis.

Floating the Ringgit

Another very important reform measure was the floating of the ringgit. The ringgit had been pegged to the Singapore dollar at the rate of 1.10. Practical and pragmatic as ever and dismissive of false notions of national pride, Daim commented: 'At 1.10, no investor would be interested in Malaysia as Singapore had better infrastructure, a government seen to be clean and efficient and a better work force.'[8] Daim said to me during our discussions that another significant reason to float the ringgit was that at its artificially overvalued level, Malaysians

---

7 World Bank, *The East Asian Miracle*, Oxford University Press, 1993, p. 240.

8 Cheong and Adibah Amin, op. cit., p. 46.

wanted to do much of their shopping in Singapore where the prices of goods and services were low in ringgit terms. This led to a massive leakage from the Malaysian economy in favour of Singapore – something that could be ill-afforded while Malaysia was in recession.

Daim subsequently removed the link between the Singapore dollar and the ringgit, and the ringgit was allowed to find its own value in the marketplace. Demand and supply determined its value, rather than how the Singapore dollar had traded on any particular day.

Immediately, it significantly depreciated, which was seen by his detractors as 'proof' of Daim's incompetence. Of course, what the depreciation did was to make Malaysia more internationally competitive for investments and for its exports, and was important in allowing Malaysia to trade its way out of its problems. Rising inflation, too, was blamed on Daim. To some degree, this was a fairer criticism. Much of it was due to the decision to float the ringgit, whereby it depreciated, making imports relatively more expensive in ringgit terms, but this was more the inevitable consequence of the float rather than a specific policy failing.

Encouraging Foreign Investment

There were other structural problems that had to be attended to. Malaysia is very fertile and has abundant natural resources. When tin boomed, Malaysia produced tin and became one of the world's largest producers. When rubber prices boomed, it produced rubber and was one of the biggest producers. When palm oil boomed, it produced that and became the world's number one producer. These have represented relatively easy earnings for Malaysia, but it has also made its economy susceptible to highly volatile international commodity prices. Daim has called this the 'curse of the commodities'. Malaysia was so rich in commodities that it was in danger of being too relaxed.

Daim and Mahathir decided to develop new strategies for the Malaysian economy. What was needed was an industrial base that focused on manufacturing and value adding. Generally, economies that have a proportion of their exports as simple and elaborately transformed manufactures tend to be less susceptible to external shocks. What Daim and Mahathir wanted to do was to put in place measures that would transform the mix that was the Malaysian economy in favour of manufacturing, so that the economy would be less vulnerable to another commodity price-induced recession.

In addition, the redistributive tenets of the NEP had been based on an expanding economy, which was now contracting. Without growth, redistribution meant taking from one group and giving to another, rather than expanding the pie and then allowing one group or another to have what had previously not been there. Substantial redistribution under such circumstances is politically untenable, particularly in a country with Malaysia's racial mix. Malaysia needed new investment, particularly from overseas. To attract that investment, Malaysia's foreign investment rules needed to be overhauled.

During September 1986, Mahathir announced changes to the proportions of equity that foreign investors could hold in projects in Malaysia. The new rules allowed foreigners to have 100% equity in manufacturing operations, in certain circumstances. Up until then, the maximum amount had been 49%.

Under the NEP, foreign participation had been set at 30% under the equity structure formula for Bumiputeras, 40% for non-Bumiputeras and 30% for foreigners. Under the new rules, a foreign company would be allowed to have 100% equity if it:

- Exported 50% or more of its products.
- Sold 50% or more of its products to companies in free trade zones or licensed manufacturing warehouses.
- Employed 350 or more full-time Malaysian workers.
- Adopted an employment policy at all levels that reflects the racial composition of Malaysia.

However, if the foreign equity was less than 100%, the balance taken up by Malaysians should conform to the NEP. The new rules were to come into force on 1 October 1986 and end in December 1990. Foreign companies would also find it easier to bring in expatriate staff. A company with foreign paid-up capital of US$2 million would automatically be allowed five expatriate workers at any level during the first ten years. Changes of expatriate personnel also would not require fresh working permits. These new arrangements made approvals for expatriates in Malaysia among the most liberal of the Southeast Asian economies.

The new conditions applied to new foreign investments in industries whose products would not compete for the Malaysian market and to foreign-owned, or partly foreign-owned, industries that would not compete with existing local industries. They had an immediate impact on direct foreign investment (DFI). DFI approvals averaged US$300 million a year in 1983-85, but jumped to US$2 billion by 1988. Not only that, but the investments became more dynamic. In 1988, a quarter of the investment came from Japan, followed by Taiwan, China and the United States, whereas during the previous ten years the greatest source of DFI had been Singapore. New investments were directed into electrical and electronic products, chemical products, rubber products, basic metal products and petroleum. More of the investments were dedicated to exports than ever before. Over time, the benefits to the Malaysian economy and to Malaysians have been substantial. Foreign investment has meant substantial human capital formation. In 1985, for example, the 13 American semiconductor manufacturers in Malaysia spent more than US$100 million on training Malaysians, mostly technicians and engineers. By the late 1980s, more than 85,000 Malaysians were employed in the electronics industries and many of these were formerly poor, rural Malay women.[9] Results such as these clearly demonstrated the virtues of foreign investment.

---

9   World Bank, op. cit., pp. 302-3.

Daim and Mahathir also decided to press ahead with the government's promotion of heavy industry. Major projects were fostered with government subsidies and, particularly, tariff protection. Car manufacturing in Malaysia was promoted with heavy tariffs so that by 2000, the flagship passenger car produced in Malaysia, the Proton, was protected with average tariffs of some 200%. Daim justified measures such as these by citing the high unemployment the Malaysian economy faced in the mid-1980s. But it has not been without cost. Tariffs, by protecting local industry from foreign competition, tend to lead to resource misallocation and inefficiency. Daim claims that one benefit of Proton has been the spin-off industries in Malaysia to support the car's manufacture. Nonetheless, he conceded in 2000 that Proton's parent company probably was only profitable because of the tariffs, and that Proton, like many other heavy industries in Malaysia, was in need of a strategic partner. Daim said that he even went to the US to meet a potential investor that was interested to bring Proton to the US but was shocked to find that the agreement with Mitsubishi did not allow exports. He went to Japan to renegotiate with Mitsubishi but at that meeting, Proton's executives sided with Mitsubishi. Daim thereafter felt that it was a waste of time dealing with the consequences of getting into the sector when no proper study had been done as to its feasibility in the first place.

Some of the other heavy industry projects that the government promoted were more obvious failures. The most spectacular example was steel maker Perwaja Terengganu, founded in 1982, which was an extraordinary debacle, and cost Malaysians many billions of ringgit in waste and probable malpractice. The government acknowledged in 1996 that Perwaja was insolvent. By the end of 1998, the company's net liabilities were an extraordinary M$9.1 billion, and by July 1999 the plant was running at 37% capacity and down to operating with night shifts only in order to keep costs down. Daim said to me soon after that one of the problems with the steel maker was that the technology installed at its main plant by Mitsubishi of Japan was defective. He claimed that due to his personal interventions with the Japanese government, Malaysia got 'every cent back' from the Japanese for the plant. Nonetheless, to Daim this served to underscore just what a poor performer Perwaja had been, because it still made huge losses even though the technology at its main plant was practically free. According to Daim, he and Mahathir had agreed by mid-2000 that Perwaja should find a strategic and equity partner. I asked him if he would be happy to allow foreign ownership in Perwaja to rise above the maximum threshold of 30%. 'Anything!' Daim joked. 'Even 70% to offload it.'

By the time Daim was appointed finance minister, the Malaysian government had already set up Heavy Industries Corporation of Malaysia (HICOM) and Perwaja. Neither was being run profitably. Daim put these businesses on a more commercial footing. It is not clear if Daim would have supported their founding had he been in cabinet at the time they were set up. He said to me that if the proposal to support and build up heavy industries such as HICOM and Perwaja were to be brought to the cabinet in say 2000, it would not have his support. It would not be appropriate to found and develop such industries in Malaysia 'in the present situation', he said.

Nevertheless, in terms of the broader policy objective of tilting the Malaysian economy in favour of manufacturing, the measures were a resounding success. Around 1985, manufacturing contributed just 20% to the national economy. By 2000, it accounted for 37% of Malaysia's GDP.

Moderating Wages Growth

Other obstacles and distractions presented themselves. Macroeconomic management was further complicated by the attitude of the Congress of Unionised Employees in the Public Services (CUEPACS). Malaysia was facing its most difficult economic circumstances for decades, but the union argued for pay increases in its meetings on salary revisions for civil servants that were held with the government. Government revenues were falling due to the recession, but a wages hike at that time for civil servants would have pushed the government budget further into deficit.

It was not the time to be raising recurrent expenditure by granting pay rises to civil servants if the government wanted to balance its books, but the union was insistent. Some sections of the movement threatened industrial action. With an election around the corner and the economy already weakened, the government could not afford for there to be strikes. The cabinet considered that in the event of a strike it might need to invoke emergency powers and even to call on the military to allow emergency services to continue. It decided to grant pay increases to civil servants in categories C and D, despite Daim's objections.

The government did well in the subsequent elections. Daim then called for a voluntary moratorium on wage rises in both the private and public sectors for three years. He added in his 1987 Budget speech that the moratorium would become mandatory should economic conditions worsen.

Exhorting Business

Daim's recession budgets provided various incentives for business and removed or lessened some of the taxation and other shackles. He always emphasised the centrality of the private sector. 'The Government strongly believes in being realistic and responsive to meet the demands of the private sector, both domestic and foreign.'[10] Daim's attitude was that the government was there to work with the corporate sector, rather than to issue edicts to it from on high. But it was not a one-way street. He expected the private sector to do its share as well and not always wait to be led by the government.

Daim variously urged, cajoled and threatened the private sector to take a greater role in the Malaysian economy. He was responsible for many of the

10 Cheong and Adibah Amin, op. cit., p. 82.

11 Ibid., p. 83.

incentives that have been offered to the sector to encourage it to lead rather than to follow, and he became exasperated when it did not rise to meet his high expectations. After he introduced a range of concessions, such as lower electricity tariffs and reduced taxes, in 1985, Daim felt that the private sector's response was insufficient. He mused publicly at a September 1985 conference in Penang whether 'the private sector in this country is really more efficient and aggressive than the public sector'.[11] It is difficult to think of a more pointed chastisement. 'The private sector must not only be more efficient and aggressive but also be trustworthy, have a sense of integrity and responsibility and be prepared to place national interest before self-interest,' Daim has also said.[12]

Daim was still not satisfied with the performance of the private sector by the time he delivered the 1987 Budget speech to the Parliament in October 1986. He criticised it for its lack of confidence. 'Confidence is an attitude of mind. So long as we continue to harbour doubts and suspicions and remain content to believe in wild and baseless rumours, we will always have a crisis of confidence.'

Again, in a speech to the Malaysian Institute of Directors' Roundtable Conference on 30 October 1986, Daim exhorted the private sector to do better. 'In the recent budget, further measures have been announced to encourage private sector activity. I hope that, as directors, you will translate the hopes and intentions of the government into reality. In the past there has been a gap, indeed a substantial gap, between the government's expectations and actual private sector performance ... One of the problems with the private sector is that, it is always looking towards the government for more incentives and tax reductions ... Yet each time we meet the private sector the request is still for more concessions.'[13] As will be mentioned later, Daim was as unimpressed with the private sector's efforts and responsiveness in the 1997-98 economic crisis as he was in the 1985-87 recession.

Appraisal

Daim's efforts in pulling Malaysia out of the 1985 recession attracted much criticism. As is the way of Malaysian politics, much of it was not direct and in the open, but muttered by way of innuendo and rumour. But the results of Daim's measures were plain for everyone to see.

From a negative growth rate of 1% in 1985, the economy grew by just over 2% in 1986 and by 5.2% in 1987. Between 1988 and 1990, the economy grew at an average annual rate of 9.1%. Unemployment fell from a peak of 8.3% in 1986 to 6% in 1990. Between 1985 and 1990, the value of manufactured exports rose almost fourfold, from M$12.47 billion to M$48.05 billion – an average growth rate for the period of 31%. The new rules on investment had also encouraged a massive inflow of investment, particularly from Taiwan, Japan and Singapore.

---

12 Ibid., p. 82.

13 As reprinted in *Daim Speaks his Mind*, Pelanduk Publications, 1995.

Manufacturing sector employment also rose 12% per annum in that time. The figures spoke for themselves. Certainly, commodity prices on world markets had recovered, but that does not account for the switch to manufactured exports. The figures were an unambiguous endorsement of Daim's austerity measures and general economic management.

By the time Daim became finance minister in 1984, there was no way to avert the cumulative consequences of years of fiscal laxity and inadequate prudential supervision. Only with a lot of persistence and in the face of occasionally vehement criticism was Daim able to bring in measures that he felt would help Malaysia to recover. His policy prescriptions might not always have been right, but judging by the controversy and disquiet they sometimes caused, clearly they were what he thought was right, rather than what he thought would prove popular.

Daim's management of the economy during the 1985 economic crisis included many brave decisions, particularly given the cultural and political context in which he operated. Perhaps he did not go far enough in many areas, but credit is certainly due to him for what he did achieve. Many of his political colleagues, let alone the rest of the population, were barely conversant in economics. The Malay cultural predisposition to patronage also made it difficult to cut out all the government-provided benefits that could or should have been eliminated. The implementation of severe cutbacks in public spending, the liberalisation of equity guidelines which had the effect of reducing opportunities for Malays, and the restriction of bank credit and the refusal to yield to the special pleadings of several prominent Bumiputera businessmen for a debt moratorium on the repayment of their loans, all served to alienate Daim from the one constituency that naturally should have been his – Malay business people.

Nonetheless, the fact that Daim attempted to take some of these steps at all took much resolve. It was not the best way to win friends amoing his political colleagues. Said Sanusi Junid, former agriculture minister: 'Tun's most significant contribution to the Malaysian economy was his ruthless and timely intervention in a professional way when the Malaysian economy was in recession. Being ruthlessly efficient, he was prepared to make tough and unpopular decisions to reverse recessionary trends, such as cutting expenses where necessary.'[14]

Mahathir was under tremendous pressure for much of the time to fire Daim – it was his unwavering trust in Daim, and perhaps the knowledge that Daim could be the foil for all the hard decisions that he knew had to be made, that allowed Daim the room to get on with the task at hand without having to be unduly concerned with the minutiae of UMNO politicking. Daim could have opted for the easy road and, like his predecessors, simply borrowed yet more money to reflate the economy, but Daim the businessman knew that borrowing without due regard for the day that the lender would call in the loans was no way to build anything, and certainly not an economy.

---

14 Cheong and Adibah Amin, op. cit., p. 166.

Innuendo has always followed Daim. Partly this is due to his resolute indifference to it and his absolute lack of interest in countering it. In this context, it is sometimes forgotten that his stewardship of the Malaysian economy during the mid-1980s recession won high praise internationally as well.

According to Australian academic Peter Searle, 'Finance Minister Daim Zainuddin's resolution in promoting far-reaching (and successful) structural adjustments in the mid-1980s showed a capacity to over-ride the interests of the politically important Malay middle class and the growing Malay business community.'[15]

The *Far Eastern Economic Review* said of Daim in September 1988 that he had made a 'huge contribution to one of the most rapid and successful structural adjustments among developing economies', and talked of his 'great contribution [to] ... the cutback in Government spending in response to Malaysia's worst ever recession'. Also, 'it now seems likely that his management of the economy will be seen as having played a crucial role in preventing Malaysia from sliding into chronic indebtedness and in putting the country back on course for newly industrialised country status'. And 'Malaysia's tapping of a good portion of the foreign investment that has been pouring into the region for the past two years is testimony to Daim's pragmatism and his ability to convince Mahathir that social restructuring should take second place to economic growth'.

The London-based *Economist* magazine was equally as supportive. It said, 'When Mr Daim, a businessman and friend of Dr Mahathir, took over the portfolio in 1984, things looked bleak. Malaysia had a heavily taxed, tightly regulated and badly indebted economy. Prices for its main exports – rubber, palm oil and tin – were tumbling. Mr Daim seemed to relish the criticism he attracted from populist politicians for his deregulation of the economy and his tight fistedness. The measures he forced through have yielded handsome dividends ...'[16] Only rarely have finance ministers around the world attracted such praise. Daim had shown himself to be a superb policy maker, not just by the standards of Malaysia, but of the world.

---

15 P. Searle, *The Riddle of Malaysian Capitalism*, Allen & Unwin, Sydney, 1999, p. 8.

16 *The Economist*, 16 February 1991.

X

THE 1987 POLITICAL CRISIS

Restoring Malaysia's economy back to health was no easy task. For not only did Daim have to restore it, he also had to restructure it. The task was made all the more difficult by constant, low-grade bickering within UMNO. But by 1987, the sniping erupted into open warfare. Musa had resigned as deputy prime minister and from the cabinet, but did not resign from the position of deputy president of UMNO. Groupings had formed around Musa and Tunku Razaleigh, who was trade minister.

For a time, the government was in danger of being paralysed by infighting. The cabinet split, and the focus for much of the internal discontent with the leadership was the one senior figure in the government without a protective power base within UMNO – namely Daim.

Early in 1986, Mahathir had floated the idea within the senior ranks of the government of calling an early election later that year, which would have been a full year before the current term was due to expire. Mahathir thought that the economy would continue to deteriorate and so, politically, it made sense to hold the election sooner rather than later. Deputy Prime Minister Ghafar was enthusiastic. Daim, though, was not. He felt that the economy was on the mend, but more importantly, that the election should be held after the upcoming 1987 internal UMNO elections. Daim believed that if the general elections were held before the UMNO ones, UMNO stalwarts who were not given positions in the new government after the general elections would then cause trouble at the UMNO elections. Mahathir would be able to call for loyalty and unity at the UMNO elections ahead of the general elections, something that he could not do if the timings were reversed. Again, Daim, the so-called disinterested politician, was showing his flair for politics, along with a Machiavellian streak.

Mahathir was not convinced that the economy would recover as quickly as Daim had forecast. There was also a view that if the government was returned at the national elections with a big majority, then the positions of Mahathir and the other senior UMNO officials would be strengthened ahead of the UMNO elections. Mahathir duly called national elections for 3 August 1986.

UMNO did very well at the elections. It won all but one of the seats that its candidates contested. (Its coalition partners did not do as well, but the government was safely returned.) Mahathir announced the new cabinet on 11 August. There were very few changes. Mahathir tends to prefer continuity and preserving the status quo. Nor did he take the opportunity to remove those whose support of him was open to question. This preference for continuity contrasted with Daim's, who had little hesitation in firing those whom he believed were under-performing or disloyal.

The next hurdle was the UMNO elections. Most UMNO elections feature rumours and rumblings of possible challenges to the senior officials. Often such challenges do not materialise, and if they do, they are usually not serious. Early on, the rumours started as usual, but this time they developed a serious tone almost immediately. Out of the swirl of rumour emerged a clear challenge to the position of Mahathir by the trade minister, Razaleigh.

Mahathir at first did not believe that Razaleigh would challenge him for the UMNO presidency. thinking he was simply testing his level of support. However, when Musa emerged as Razaleigh's running mate, the true nature of the threat emerged. The rivalry between the Razaleigh-Musa camp and the Mahathir group intensified. One of the more obvious targets for the malcontents in the party was Daim. Politically, Daim was the creation of Mahathir and he lacked grassroots support within UMNO. To his detractors, of whom there were many, he had 'parachuted from above'.[1] And as government member of parliament Jamaludin Jarjis said to me in late 2000, 'Being Mahathir's finance minister means that if you want to get at Mahathir you can attack Daim…A lot of the brickbats thrown at Daim are because of politics and not because of his doing.' This was as true in 1987 as it was in 2000 when Daim was again finance minister.

In early 1987, the economy had yet to show signs of recovery, so Daim's management of it was an obvious point for attack. Everyone blamed Mahathir for appointing Daim as the finance minister. Few understood how the economy functioned. All they knew was that it was a mess and Daim was the minister in charge. The recession had hit everyone hard, and especially UMNO businessmen who were delegates to the UMNO Assembly. Several of them had also been nominated as candidates in the 1986 general election. They had won their seats, but with Mahathir's minimal reshuffle they had been rewarded with nothing. They were fertile targets for the malcontents of the Razaleigh-Musa camp. But it was not simply all about personality and patronage. There were policy differences between the two camps, too. The Mahathir camp was aligned with the privatisation, 'can do', private sector push, whereas the Razaleigh-Musa camp had a vague preference for the more traditionalist, softly-softly approach where the state had an important, if paternalistic, role to play. Mahathir and Daim had become impatient with the results of the NEP and sought to speed up the creation of a class of Bumiputera entrepreneurs, but the latter camp held more to the NEP as it was originally conceived.

On top of all this, Razaleigh asserted that the Malaysian economy could be fixed in 'six months'. It was an outrageous claim from the man who had been responsible for so many of the structural problems in the economy that had built up during his time as finance minister. Nonetheless, it was an appealing message

---

1   M.S. Cheong and Adibah Amin, *Daim: The Man Behind the Enigma*, Pelanduk Publications, 1995, p. 103.

for many in the UMNO membership whose understanding of economics was unsophisticated, both because of its simplicity and its quick-fix nature.

There were other sources of dissatisfaction, too. Razaleigh was disappointed at repeatedly being denied the deputy prime ministership, Musa had lost Mahathir's trust, Abdullah Badawi (who had aligned himself with the Razaleigh-Musa group) resented Anwar Ibrahim's intrusion into Penang, and Rais Yatim was unhappy with what he saw as the 'personality cult' that had been built up around Mahathir.[2]

In the lead-up to the UMNO conference, Daim went overseas for meetings and then to Mecca to undertake the minor Hajj, or *Umrah*. But Mahathir called him back earlier than scheduled. He had grown increasingly worried as party infighting intensified. There were also rumours that the Sultan of Brunei was involved and was providing financial support to the Razaleigh-Musa camp. Daim was asked to approach the Sultan to see if the rumours were true. The Sultan denied any involvement whatsoever. He was nonetheless keenly interested in developments in Kuala Lumpur. There was another irritation. Hundreds, possibly thousands, of poison pen letters – an anonymous means of attack and politicking – which are an unfortunate aspect of elections and campaigning in Malaysia, seemingly more so than anywhere else, were circulated in the run-up to the Assembly.

Mahathir wanted a clean UMNO election. He disliked overt campaigning and did not approve of the use of money in fighting internal UMNO elections. Indeed, Daim claims that Mahathir never used his own money or anyone else's to bolster his own position within UMNO. However, for the 1987 elections, money was already part of the process. Mahathir was concerned and asked Daim to monitor this emerging phenomenon in UMNO. Daim told Mahathir that he would organize things to counter this. It is claimed that Daim set about organising the money that was required to gather in support from around the country. When I asked Daim about this, he responded that the claims that the Mahathir camp had raised money to curry internal UMNO influence were untrue. 'We were very confident; we thought that we would win easily, so there was no need,' he said.

Daim joined Mahathir and his other supporters for a trip around peninsular Malaysia on a 'meet the people' exercise aimed at gathering support and answering some of the allegations raised by those allied to the Razaleigh-Musa camp. Apart from his efforts in his own constituency, Daim had not gone out campaigning in a party election, and he quickly decided that for him, the exercise was not a good use of time. Generally, it was only supporters who turned out to see Mahathir at formally organised events. Of course the prime minister was obligated to be seen out and about, campaigning among the public but for other, lesser figures, there seemed to be little point in preaching to the converted. Daim believed that the

---

2 B.T. Khoo, *Paradoxes of Mahathirism*, Oxford University Press, 1995, p. 265.

challenge was to penetrate the opposition, and that wasn't going to be achieved by publicly campaigning around Malaysia.

The UMNO election day was 24 April 1987. The day itself, like the preceding ones, was filled with unbelievable tension. Malaysia came to a standstill as business, particularly, waited to see what would happen. The likely numbers were counted and re-counted, and money and promises of post-victory positions flowed. Ultimately, Mahathir won, but only just. The results were officially announced at 9pm that night and again at the convention the next day. Out of 1,479 votes cast by the delegates, 761 were for Mahathir and 718 for Razaleigh. Mahathir had won by just 43 votes, or a margin of just 1.45%. Had 22 of Mahathir's votes gone to Razaleigh, it would have been he and not Mahathir who was elected president of UMNO and thus, by convention, prime minister of Malaysia. The deputy prime minister, Ghafar Baba, also won only narrowly against his challenger Musa Hitam, by just 40 votes. Both sides were stunned and in a state of disbelief.

Razaleigh came up on stage to personally congratulate Mahathir, but the latter's response to the gesture was perfunctory at best. His victory was a shock to the challengers – they had expected to win. But it was also a shock to the Mahathir team because the victory was so narrow. They had calculated a win by as many as 200 votes. Partly, the confusion arose because many of the delegates simply did not vote in accordance with the wishes of their divisions – 66.2% of UMNO divisions had voted in favour of Mahathir, but just 51.45% of their delegates did so at the UMNO Assembly.

How had Razaleigh come within a handful of votes of seizing the prime ministership from Mahathir and gaining control of Malaysia's government? Much of the support that he received is attributable to his time as finance minister. He was a Tunku, or prince, from the royal family of Kelantan. True to Malay traditions, he had a paternalistic view of his role as a member of the social elite. He went around the country as finance minister and gave on-the-spot grants. Many rural folk viewed the grants as if they came from Razaleigh personally rather than from the government, and he was remembered for it. For eight years as finance minister he was able to dispense money courtesy of the government while he largely received the credit. It allowed him to build up a powerful network of supporters around the country. This, coupled with his highly personable nature, political skills and ability to remember names, made him a formidable grassroots politician. Mahathir, on the other hand, was a good orator, media performer and policy person, but was not at ease on a one-to-one level. For many, Musa's departure to the Razaleigh camp was important. Musa had received Mahathir's strong support in the face of his vacillations. He had also been Mahathir's deputy prime minister. Many seemed to feel that if Musa could no longer stand being in Mahathir's government, then things must have been truly wrong – allegations of Mahathir's dictatorial style must have had some credence.

Daim told me in 2000 that he saw quite a lot of Razaleigh – the two had been friends for a long time and remained so. Both had studied in London at the same time. Razaleigh completed an arts degree with a major in economics in Belfast, after which he moved to London to do law. He intended to study with Daim, but Daim had already qualified. Razaleigh returned to Kelantan when his father died, but did not return to London to complete his law degree. Instead, he took several banking jobs in Kuala Lumpur where he and Daim often caught up. Razaleigh soon decided to go into politics and he used Kelantan as a base. Was Razaleigh obstructionist or difficult in cabinet after Daim took over his finance portfolio? It might be expected that he could have been if he was eager to protect his old turf or even his policy legacy. 'No,' says Daim. 'He never disagreed with me in cabinet.' As for Musa Hitam, Daim said to me that he didn't see him. 'He sends me his speeches,' Daim remarked with a wry smile when I asked him if he sees Musa these days. The two were not close in government – Daim found Musa imperious and too eager to pull rank when he was deputy prime minister.

Mahathir decided to reshuffle his cabinet in the aftermath of the 1987 UMNO elections. Sanusi, Anwar and Rafidah agreed to meet at Daim's house. On hearing of the meeting, Mahathir wanted to attend as well. He was the first to arrive.[3] Daim, uncompromising as ever, suggested that Mahathir fire all those who had not supported him. Daim's view was very much a 'winner takes all' approach and it had the support of the others but was rejected by Mahathir. Mahathir wanted to opt for reconciliation. According to Daim, Mahathir kept repeating that 'winners do not take all and losers do not lose everything'.[4] For Daim, this only encouraged more division in the party. He felt that dissenters needed to be shown the consequences of their actions. Ultimately, the decision was made easy for Mahathir. His main protagonist, Razaleigh, offered his resignation from the cabinet, an offer that Mahathir accepted.

The next day, Mahathir announced the new cabinet. Three ministers and four deputy ministers were dropped. They were the defence minister, Datuk Abdullah Ahmad Badawi (even though he had just been elected an UMNO vice president at the UMNO elections); a minister in the Prime Minister's Department, Datuk Abdul Ajib Ahmad; the welfare services minister, Datuk Shahrir Abdul Samad; the deputy foreign affairs minister, Datuk Abdul Kadir Sheikh Fadzir; the deputy primary industries minister, Datuk Radzi Sheikh Ahmad; the deputy transport minister, Datin Paduka Rahmah Osman; and the deputy energy, telecommunications and post minister, Datuk Zainal Abidin Zin. Foreign minister Datuk Rais Yatim, like Razaleigh, resigned his post earlier. All had been supporters of the Razaleigh-Musa alliance. (Abdullah Ahmad Badawi returned to favour in the wake of Anwar Ibrahim's sacking as deputy prime minister and finance minister in 1998. He was first given the deputy prime ministership. He was then awarded the deputy presidency of UMNO and publicly named by Mahathir as his heir apparent. He served as prime minister between 2003 and

---

3 Cheong and Adibah Amin, op. cit., p. 109.

4 Ibid.

2009. Rais Yatim also later returned to the cabinet as a minister in the Prime Minister's Department.)

The whole affair had been a tumultuous upheaval for UMNO and for the government. But to the dismay of the latter, which was eager to concentrate on repairing the economy, it was not the end of the trouble. Twelve members (and later 11 after one dropped out) of UMNO who were dissatisfied with Mahathir's win at the UMNO elections, challenged the result in court. The plaintiffs complained that about 78 of the conference delegates were not entitled to attend, let alone vote. The court upheld the election results but delivered an astonishing broadside. It determined that UMNO was an illegal organisation. It was a result that no one had expected.

The court found that UMNO had 30 unapproved branches in four divisions. These had held their annual general meetings and elected delegates or sent observers to the divisional conferences which, in turn, elected delegates to the 24 April 1987 UMNO Assembly. Section 12(3) of the Societies Act deemed that a society (including a political party such as UMNO) is illegal if it has unapproved branches. The decision even questioned the position of Mahathir as prime minister. UMNO's corporate assets were then placed with the Official Assignee. Mahathir, Daim and their supporters were left with no party, no assets and uncertain positions. It was an astonishing outcome. They had to move quickly to ensure the legality of their positions. On 15 February 1988, they registered a new political party, UMNO Bahru (or New UMNO), with Mahathir as president, Ghafar Baba as deputy, Mohamad Rahmat as secretary-general and Daim as treasurer. Uncertainty about the legality of UMNO's control of its assets and uncertainty caused by the manoeuvring of Razaleigh lasted through 1988 and into 1989.

Razaleigh and his supporters formed their own political party. They attempted to register it under the name of UMNO Malaysia, but this was rejected. The name 'Semangat '46' was ultimately accepted. (One of those to join Semangat '46 was Harun Idris, who had been close to Daim in the past.) The new party had only limited success politically. It won just eight seats in the federal Parliament in the 1990 elections and only six in 1995, before it and Razaleigh rejoined UMNO in 1996.

Daim's Departure

In many Southeast Asian cultures, it is not appropriate to resign from a high post when someone even higher was responsible for giving it to you. Resignation in such circumstances might be interpreted as a loss of face to the more senior party. After all, one's position is not yours to resign away; it can only be taken from you. This traditional view is now changing. Nonetheless, Daim's resignation in March 1991 from the position of finance minister was unusual. It was unusual in Malay society, but also unusual anywhere. Politicians who are at the height of their powers and who have no obvious reason to leave, rarely resign of their own volition, in Malaysia or elsewhere. Perhaps the most analogous resignation to Daim's was that of the Australian treasurer, John Dawkins, in 1993. Dawkins had only recently been appointed treasurer – the equivalent of finance minister in Malaysia. But having attained that goal, and after a long career in politics, he decided it was time to do something else. With no warning, he simply walked into the House of Representatives of the Australian Parliament one afternoon while it was sitting and requested leave to make a special statement. With that he announced his immediate resignation and, with little else said, walked out. It was done with the minimum of fuss. Everyone was surprised when it happened but not surprised overall, given the character of Dawkins. And so it should have been with Daim. But with Malaysia being Malaysia, few could accept that Daim's departure had no ulterior motive or rationale.

For some time, there had been open speculation that Daim wanted to leave. He had already stayed longer than his original commitment to Mahathir when he had been appointed. Nonetheless, when the resignation came, it created a considerable stir. As is usual in Malaysian politics, little is taken at face value and all manner of opinions were proffered as to why Daim had decided to resign. The idea that he simply had had enough and wanted to do something else was too simple and too benign. All manner of rumours circulated in Kuala Lumpur as to what the 'real' reason could be.

According to Daim, 'When I accepted office, I did not intend to stay long. Little did I realise the problems ahead. Whoever thought the recession would hit so hard? Whoever dreamt of a split in UMNO? First, problem after economic problem delayed my departure from office. Had I left earlier, people would have criticised me and I would have gone down in history as a failure. It was a challenge I could not resist. In fact it was a challenge tailored for me. I accepted it and sat down to work to find solutions to the problems. Just when I thought I had found the answers and that the results were about to show, the fight within UMNO started and the main issue was the way we were running the economy. It was so easy to mislead the misinformed.'[5]

Daim actually fully intended to leave prior to the October 1990 general election. He did not even want to stand for re-election in his parliamentary seat, but Mahathir convinced him to stand again. He then asked Mahathir not to include him in the new cabinet. Mahathir agreed at first but then asked him to stay on for one more budget. Accordingly, after that budget – delivered on 14 December 1991 – Daim tendered his resignation. After returning from leave, he and Mahathir discussed the timing of his departure and his successor. There were three possible candidates, apart from Mahathir himself. There was Sanusi, who was agriculture minister; Rafidah, the trade and industry minister; and Anwar, the education minister. Sanusi was in poor health and was happy in his current post. Rafidah had already declared in the media that she did not want the finance post. Daim felt that Anwar would be interested. The next problem was who should take Anwar's position as education minister. That post was high-profile and highly politicised.

---

5   Ibid., p. 144.

It was seen as a senior position and a stepping stone to the prime ministership. Consequently, Mahathir thought it was time to depoliticise it. It would be offered to a member of the government from a party outside UMNO. It was also decided that Abdullah Badawi, who had been removed after being associated with the Razaleigh-Musa team in 1987, would be invited back into the cabinet to fill the vacancy caused by Daim's departure.[6]

Upon Daim's resignation, Mahathir recommended Daim for the Seri Setia Mahkota award – Malaysia's highest – which carries with it the title of 'Tun'. Although Daim claims he wanted to give up all his posts, he stayed on as UMNO treasurer and a member of the Political Bureau, UMNO's most powerful internal body.

Logically, it was an ideal time to resign. The economy was back on track after the 1985 recession, the government's own budgetary position had improved considerably, and the NEP had made enormous strides in improving the relative position of the Malays (not without a lot of waste and inefficiency along the way, but the successes were fairly clear). Daim had presented seven budgets as finance minister and one can imagine that there would have been little challenge in producing an eighth, especially for a man who had already demonstrated a capacity to achieve outside politics. Indeed, he told me in mid-2000 that he had 'stayed too long' during his first stint as finance minister and that he had become 'bored' with the work which had become 'routine'. Daim's resignation, when it came, might have been a surprise, but it wasn't out of character.

6   The description of choosing a successor to Daim closely follows that in Cheong and Adibah Amin, ibid.

XI

BUSINESS, THE MARKET & PRIVATISATION

Daim's contribution to Malaysia during the 1984-91 period as finance minister was much more than simply as an astute economic manager for tough times. What he did was to change the way the state operates, particularly in its relations with the private sector. It is a contribution far more fundamental than merely captaining the economic ship, for he was both captain and engineer. It was a change that was enduring as well. Many of his policies were continued after he left the finance ministry.

Some have argued that Daim brought to Malaysia the view that the state, party and business need not operate as distinct entities. That is to say that Daim's vision is a corporatist one in which each of the three institutions is pressed into service to help achieve national development goals. Certainly, Daim does not see that business and government should be in 'conflict', but rather that there should be a 'commonness' of interests.[1] His approach has had an enormous and controversial impact on government policy and the structure of Malaysia's business sector and its relationship with government. Mahathir gave the cooperative, rather than competitive, approach the label 'Malaysia Inc' in 1983, but it was Daim that set about giving Malaysia Inc its definition.

Daim is not short of pro-market rhetoric. He was at his most liberal in an address to a 1994 international symposium organised by the Writers' Academy of Malaysia when he said, 'As free men, we celebrate the demise of Communism, the end of totalitarianism and the disintegration of the command economy. As free marketers, we rejoice in the triumph of democracy and the principles of the market economy even as we recall the prophetic vision of Victor Hugo who said more than a century ago: "Markets, open to trade, and minds open to ideas, will become the sole battlefield." '[2] Daim claims to have been inspired by no particular political leader around the world, but he does admit to an admiration for Margaret Thatcher and, in particular, her handling of the trade unions in Britain.

Although disposed to the free market view, Daim is definitely not in the *laissez-faire* camp. He said at that same symposium, 'Experience has shown that it is highly improbable that a purely free market mechanism will fulfill the development objectives aspired by developing nations in Asia. Excessive reliance on market

---

1   P. Searle, *The Riddle of Malaysian Capitalism*, Allen & Unwin, Sydney, 1999, p. 104.

2   As reprinted in *Daim Speaks his Mind*, Pelanduk Publications, 1995.

forces can lead to a concentration of economic power as well as create wide disparities in income, which may result in creating instability in the social fabric of Asian societies.'[3] This is not an unreasonable view given Malaysia's experience whereby Chinese Malaysians as a group were doing disproportionately well in the national economy compared with the Malay community. It became the justification for massive government intervention in Malaysia's economy. And when that still did not yield the desired results, Daim's solution was even more direct intervention.

Privatisation was a key component of the Daim vision. It served several aims. One was to raise money for the government's coffers. This could then be used to pay off debts and support rural development. Another was to reduce the risk to the government of future losses of otherwise state-run businesses. A third aim was to promote the government's affirmative action and redistributive policies that favoured the Malays. By selling off state-run companies to Malay business people, the government was able quickly and significantly to increase the country's stock of Malay entrepreneurs.

Although Daim privatised, he wanted to influence private sector outcomes too. He claims to be pro-market, but is also a heavy interventionist. The two seem at odds. Perhaps the easiest way to reconcile these two, apparently contradictory, notions is to see Daim as more pro-private sector than pro-free market. His view seems to be that the state has little role in owning and running enterprises, but that does not mean that it cannot cajole and push the private sector. For Daim, the umpire should not own the sports field, but he can be a player. His later support for the capital and currency controls that were introduced in 1998 reflect this. He was happy to see the market for the ringgit suspended because he could also see that it would give Malaysian business some breathing space.

There were instances, however, when Daim was wary of privatisation. In cabinet, he argued against government land being sold directly to private entrepreneurs. Instead, he preferred that government land destined for privatization be held by a land bank trust under the auspices of the government's Khazanah sovereign wealth fund on behalf of all Malaysians. Daim felt that when Kuala Lumpur and its environs were made a Federal Territory, the land acquired by the Federal Government from the State of Selangor was a very precious commodity deserving of special status and treatment. It should not have been given to private companies and individuals, irrespective of race. But cabinet rejected Daim's position.

Apart from the need for redistributive policies, both Mahathir and Daim have justified the government's intervention in the economy by portraying the government as a quasi-shareholder in Malaysia's business sector. 'The Government after all is an indirect shareholder of all your companies,' Daim told the Malaysian Institute of Directors' Roundtable Conference in October 1986. 'If you make more money, government revenues will increase.'[4] It is a sentiment

---

3   Ibid.

4   Ibid.

repeated again, fourteen years later by Mahathir, when he wrote in his book *The Malaysian Currency Crisis* that 'The government wants to see business profitable because it has a 28% stake in the profits made through corporate tax'.[5] So, the government has an interest in what the private sector does and how it performs, and so on that basis can expect to intervene, according to Daim and Mahathir.

The view of government and business in 'partnership' is one that Mahathir and Daim stressed time and time again. But by mid-2000, Daim at least had changed his views somewhat on the cooperative or corporatist model. Always pro-business in his orientation, he nonetheless has consistently expressed disappointment with Malaysia's business sector. It had not led in the way that he felt that it should have; nor had it responded to the incentives and opportunities that he had offered as finance minister to the degree that it should have.

The very essence of 'Malaysia Inc' was this partnership, but by mid-2000 Daim felt that it was more a one-way street, particularly in the wake of the successful lobbying of the government by business to have his banking and stockbroking merger policies reversed. (This is discussed at length in Chapter 18.) 'When we had Malaysia Inc, we thought we could work together and plan together, but [in the wake of the economic crisis] Malaysia Inc served to benefit vested interests too much,' he told me. 'If there is a failure with Malaysia Inc, it's that the private sector uses its influence with the government too much.' Daim's disappointment with the business sector in Malaysia was a constant theme that ran through my many discussions with him. He was as critical of Malaysian business after the 1997-98 economic crisis as he was during the 1985-87 recession. 'The private sector thinks the government is there for its convenience,' he said to me.

Disappointed though he might be at the Malaysian business sector's seemingly perpetual inability to rise to the challenges he feels are laid down for it, Daim nonetheless remains a staunch advocate and defender of the sector's legitimacy. Certainly, business people are better at running businesses than civil servants. Relatively few civil servants have private sector experience and thus little direct knowledge of how business functions. Businesses should very definitely be run by business people and not government workers, is Daim's view.

Privatisation

Daim brought privatisation to Malaysia. Prior to his appointment as finance minister, selling off state-run assets was almost unthinkable. They were an essential part of the UMNO patronage machine – and an important employer of Malays; a convenient refuge where they could be employed with all the cosseted conditions expected of the state sector. It was conventional wisdom that the state should own and operate many businesses and that these should be a natural place of employment for Malays. Conventional wisdom, that is, until Daim came along.

---

5   Mahathir Mohamad, *The Malaysian Currency Crisis: How it Happened and Why*, Pelanduk Publications, 2000, p. 9.

Said Daim, 'It's my strong belief that the Government should not get involved in business. We [the Government] have more than one thousand companies and most are not doing well. They are a financial burden to the Government. I have always held the view that the Government's role is to create the right environment so that the private sector can do well, not to participate or compete with the private sector.'[6]

Nonetheless, the desire to privatise and the need to dispense patronage were not necessarily at odds with one another. Instead of rewarding supporters of the government with a job in a state-owned company, the government could now reward them with a small concession to operate this or that business. This has meant that privatisation in Malaysia has been both broad and deep. The national airline was sold off but then so too were the concessions to operate the snack shops on the Butterworth to Penang ferry services. Privatisation and the need to dispense patronage created a myriad of small Malay-owned businesses right across Malaysia that otherwise would not have existed.

Daim's belief in the importance of privatisation is difficult to over-emphasise. Hardly a major speech went by without him extolling its virtues. When it came to that one issue, if Margaret Thatcher was privatisation's greatest proponent in the developed world, then Daim was one of its greatest proponents in the developing one. For Daim, there is no need to convince people of the virtues of privatisation. The ideological battle had long been won and its virtues were self-evident.

Daim's push for privatisation had Mahathir's full support. (Administratively, proposals for privatization were handled not by the Ministry of Finance but by the Economic Planning Unit in the Prime Minister's Unit.) Mahathir was not greatly impressed with the NEP's fixation with quotas such as the 30% target for Bumiputera ownership of corporate equity. As mentioned, reaching the target might well be a Pyrrhic victory if Malays achieved ownership but not the management. For Mahathir, the 30% figure was more a proxy that would, or should, suggest Bumiputera management over the economy, and there was a danger that the proxy would prove to be a very poor one unless Bumiputeras were actually running major private companies and making decisions. For Mahathir, the NEP made no sense unless Bumiputeras could manage and not squander their new-found wealth.[7] It was a view that Daim shared. Privatising would allow existing businesses to be placed under Malay private sector management. The justification for privatisation was also couched in terms of 'efficiency', 'private enterprise' and 'productivity'. It was a significant shift from the principles and nomenclature of the statist protection approach that had evolved with the NEP.

Daim did not privatise gingerly. He did so with a vengeance. Indeed, Daim's enthusiasm for complex business transactions and share swaps — an enthusiasm that he largely introduced to the local business sector — often meant that he

---

6   M.S. Cheong and Adibah Amin, *Daim: The Man Behind the Enigma*, Pelanduk Publications, 1995, p. 154.

7   B.T. Khoo, *Paradoxes of Mahathirism*, Oxford University Press, 1995, p. 128.

could achieve his aims with the minimum of public attention. He was able to work behind the scenes while Mahathir grabbed the headlines. Major state-owned companies that were either partly or fully privatised (sometimes by simply part-listing them on the Kuala Lumpur Stock Exchange) during Daim's first stint as finance minister included Malaysian Airlines System (MAS), Tenaga Nasional, Airod, Sports Toto, North-South Highway, Jabatan Telekom, Malaysia International Shipping Corporation (MISC), Eon, Labuan Water Supply, Port Kelang Container Terminal and Cement Industries of Malaysia. A more complete list appears in Figure 1.

Figure 1
Major Privatisations during Daim's First Period as Finance Minister[8]

Privatised Project	Year of Privatisation	Form of Privatisation
Jalan Kuching/Jalan Kepong Interchange	1984	Build-Operate-Transfer
Malaysia Airlines System	1985	Sale of equity on the KLSE
Tenaga Nasional	1985	Corporatisation & part-privatisation via a KLSE listing
Airod	1985	Lease
Sports Toto (M) Bhd	1985	Sale of equity on the KLSE
Malaysia International Shipping Corporation (MISC)	1986	Sale of equity on the KLSE
Port Klang Container Terminal	1986	Lease & sale of assets
Kuala Lumpur Interchange	1987	Build-Operate-Transfer
Labuan Water Supply	1987	Build-Operate-Transfer
North-South Highway	1988	Build-Operate-Transfer
Tradewinds (M) Bhd	1988	Sale of equity on the KLSE
Syarikat Telekom (M) Bhd	1990	Sale of equity on the KLSE
Edaran Otomobil Nasional	1990	Sale of equity on the KLSE
Cement Industries of Malaysia	1990	Sale of equity on the KLSE
Food Industries of Malaysia	1990	Management buy-out
Peremba	1990	Management buy-out
Pernas International Hotel and Properties Bhd	1990	Sale of equity via a share placement
Perusahaan Otomobil Nasional Bhd (Proton)	1991	Part sale of equity

The speed with which many privatisations occurred, and the fact that many proceeded without tender or, when they did, the tender was not open and public, attracted much criticism. Alleges Edmund Terence Gomez in his book *Political Business: Corporate Involvement of Malaysian Political Parties*: 'Soon after the privatisation policy was put into effect, however, allegations of extensive political nepotism and patronage emerged. These allegations were probably not all unfounded in view of the absence of an independent and accountable monitoring body to ensure proper implementation of the policy. The possibilities, thus, for windfall gains were high. For example, the policy's commitment to the NEP objectives and its "first come, first serve" premise provided an ideal opportunity for political leaders and politically-connected businessmen to gain priority over other independent companies. Since privatisation in most cases did not even involve the formality of an open tender system, many beneficiaries were chosen solely on the basis of political and personal connections.'[9]

Gomez's criticisms might be too harsh. Connections were obviously important to securing privatisation deals, but to say that 'many' beneficiaries were chosen 'solely' for that reason is excessive. Daim does not deny that connections were important, but he rejects the notion that any projects were given to those whom he felt did not have the capacity for undertaking them. Thus, connections sometimes might have been a necessary condition, but they were not sufficient. Perceived ability was also important, even if in hindsight the supposition was not always proven true. Occasionally, Daim was defensive of the government's privatisation programs, but he was never apologetic. He told a seminar in July 1990, 'The Malaysian Government is not ashamed to proclaim that it is pro-business in its policies. Thus it will continue the policy of privatisation, with probably even greater vigour, to sell off public enterprises which can be better run by the private sector.'[10]

Perhaps some of the veiled accusations and suggestions of impropriety are warranted, but what seems more likely, in the absence of any credible research or claims, is that at the nub of their criticism is a dislike of Daim's pro-business stance. The real argument for many of them, particularly those in local academia, derives more from their clinging to outmoded tenets of socialism than from any over-riding concern for due process. Simply, many critics were uncomfortable with privatisation, no matter how it was carried out. As such, much of the criticism they levied, irrespective of its merits, seems to have been offered up to legitimise their real concerns, which were essentially ideological. Essentially they were socialists in a world being swept by pragmatism and a widespread preference for market solutions.

---

8 E.T. Gomez, *Political Business: Corporate Involvement of Malaysian Political Parties*, James Cook University, 1994, p. 16.

9 Ibid., p. 17.

10 As reprinted in *Daim Speaks his Mind*, op. cit.

What regrets, if any, did Daim have about how Malaysia's privatisation program was conducted? His response was typically blunt: 'My one regret was that I had not been able to speed the privatisation process even further.'[11] He has argued that putting many of the privatisation projects to tender wasn't feasible. Foreigners would not have been permitted to control most of the assets that were offered, and beyond that there simply were too few Malaysian entrepreneurs, especially in the early days, who were capable and willing to bid for many of the projects or assets on offer. An open bidding process could well be called, but what would be the point if there was only one or perhaps no suitable bidders? Precious time would be lost, particularly for a government that was in a hurry. At one stage, the government even offered Malayan Railways for M$1.00 but there were no takers.[12]

HICOM's privatisation provides a useful case study about how things were done in Malaysia, or, as Daim would argue, had to be done. HICOM was created in the early 1980s to be the vehicle for the government's heavy industrialisation push. It targeted a number of large-scale, capital-intensive projects for development, including iron and steel, nonferrous metals, machinery and equipment, pulp and paper products, and petrochemicals. By 1988, HICOM had set up nine companies that employed a total of 4,350 workers. The companies were involved in steel, cement, and motor vehicle and motorcycle assembling and manufacturing. The highest profile among these investments was the Proton car project, a joint venture with Mitsubishi of Japan that aimed to produce 100,000 units per year.

In 1995, businessman Yahaya Ahmad (who later died in a helicopter crash) told Daim during a flight to Myanmar, to where Daim was leading a business delegation, that he wanted to buy the state-owned car assembler Proton. It would be a bold move, but Daim came up with an even more audacious idea. Why not buy Proton's parent, HICOM, with all its subsidiaries, including the five that were listed on the KLSE, Proton being among them? Yahaya wrote to Mahathir with the suggestion, and Mahathir eventually gave the deal his approval. So, on 27 October 1995, Yahaya's privately held Mega Consolidated announced that it was to buy 32% of HICOM from Khazanah Holdings, the government's investment arm. (It had been set up in 1994 to invest in strategic industries that the government felt would strengthen the economy.) Yahaya paid M$1.7 billion for the stake – which represented almost a 10% premium on the company's share price that had prevailed when the deal was announced. Yahaya paid for the deal with a series of complex share manoeuvres on the KLSE that ultimately saw HICOM having to issue almost M$1 billion in bonds and warrants. Nonetheless, the government received a good price, and HICOM was privatised.[13] Who wants to bid for a company that is making losses, Daim wryly observed later.

Malaysia's privatisation program proceeded well into the 1990s, after Daim

---

11 Cheong and Adibah Amin, op. cit., p. 76.

12 Ibid.

13 'Shroff: Smooth operator', *Far Eastern Economic Review*, 23 November 1995.

had resigned as finance minister. More than 200 projects were privatised in the first half of the 1990s alone. To support the private sector in the privatisation effort, the government provided soft loans, tax incentives and other concessionary terms. These forms of support were given particularly for privatised projects with a high social component, such as sewerage, roads and highways, power, and light rail, to ensure that these services were provided at affordable prices to the end-users after privatisation. Daim claimed in 1999 that since its inception in 1983, the privatisation program had saved the government M$73 billion in capital expenditure. The government had received M$14 billion in revenue from the sale of assets and equity as well as tax revenue that otherwise would not have been collected. Over 97,000 employees, or 11.4% of the total public sector workforce, were transferred to the private sector.[14] And there were less tangible or measurable benefits as well, such as increased efficiency, productivity and responsiveness to customers' needs.

Daim is a passionate advocate of privatisation, but he does not support the open-slather kind. He believes that majority equity should be retained in Malaysian hands, and under his watch only 30% of the equity in most privatised businesses was permitted to be owned by foreigners. He said to me that he used to tell Eastern European leaders, where privatisation had gone much further, 'Now that you have independence, what have you got left given that everything has been privatised and sold to foreigners?' Daim is all for privatisation, but he is also an economic nationalist.

I asked Daim whether he could foresee a time when significant government-linked companies such as the telecommunications company Telekom and the power company Tenaga Nasional would be 100% in private hands. 'No!' was the emphatic answer. Such companies are 'strategic' and, as such, the government should retain a golden share of the equity. Not only that, but Daim claimed that private investors *wanted* the government to retain majority equity and remain in control of such companies, because it made them feel 'safer'. Government control was likely to mean that the existing privileges accorded to them would remain and that such companies could expect to be bailed out by the government in future should they run into trouble.

The Malaysian government's headlong rush into privatisation and contracting out was not without problems. Mistakes were made. Some assets were privatised that shouldn't have been. Some companies were established, too, that with the benefit of hindsight Malaysia might have done better without. The Perwaja steel project, discussed in Chapter 9, is one of the more obvious examples that even Daim is willing to concede was a failure.

In a speech in 1999, Daim formally conceded that the service provided by an entity might deteriorate after privatisation. 'Although the standard of efficiency has generally been higher with corporatisation and privatisation, this need not be

---

14 Speech by Daim to the Washington SyCip Policy Forum, Asian Institute of Management, Manila, 4 March 1999.

true in every case. Sometimes, it is best to keep the service under the public sector if the quality of service actually deteriorates after privatisation. The government has to be vigilant at all times. When a service has been privatised, the government has to ensure that the increase in quality and productivity is higher than the rise in the cost of providing it.'[15] Professor Mahani Zainal Abidin of Universiti Malaya agreed. 'The model of privatisation should not be applied to everything,' she told me in December 2000. Then defence minister Najib Tun Razak was equally circumspect. He said to me in relation to the privatisation program that 'the macro figures look very impressive' but observed that 'what has led to criticism has been the specific management of certain projects.'

The haste to privatise, particularly in the 1990s often meant that the necessary regulatory framework was hurriedly formulated. The result was weak regulatory authorities with vague mandates, which were not able to effectively supervise the privatised entities to ensure compliance of standards of service. Some projects perhaps should never have been privatised. Malaysia was swept up in the world-wide desire to privatise at all costs. Marginally viable entities were privatised in the hope of making them viable. Some could only survive in private hands with government-supported loans or concessions and some of these went beyond reason.

The project that most readily comes to Daim's mind as one that should not have been privatised is the national sewerage system. It was privatised in 1993 when Anwar was minister for finance, but by early 2000 it was clear that the private sector could not profitably run the scheme. It was to be operated by a private group, the Indah Water Consortium (IWK). Initially, it had been awarded to companies controlled by local businessman Vincent Tan, but he later sold on the project. In 2000, the government decided to buy it back. The consortium's listed parent, Prime Utilities Bhd, then demanded compensation for what it had already spent on upgrading and extending the sewerage system. Intrinsically, the failure had nothing to do with the virtues (or lack thereof) of privatisation, but rather with the fact that the government, in the face of public pressure, had forced the company to reduce its charges to consumers twice in a three-year period. With the price reduction, the project was no longer commercially viable. Daim says that his predecessor, Anwar, had given the scheme a soft loan of M$900 million, but even this did not allow the scheme to run profitably.

Government guarantees for projects had been a mistake, too. 'Our privatisation policy will remain. However in the past, when companies applied for privatisation projects, in most cases, they would ask for a Government guarantee. In reviewing this, future projects must be bankable and the Government must not provide guarantees. It is not the role of the Government to bail out the private sector. This was an error before and therefore mistakes were made.'[16] Daim reaffirmed

---

15 Speech by Daim to the Washington SyCip Policy Forum, Asian Institute of Management, Manila, 4 March 1999.

16 Remarks made by Daim at the 'Towards the Next Millennium' seminar, Kuala Lumpur, 8 February 1999.

this during our conversations. He was adamant that while he remained finance minister, there would be no more government guarantees for privatised projects. Those who were awarded projects, too, needed closer scrutiny. In early 1998, after his appointment as special functions minister, Daim was quoted as saying, 'A lot of fellows get privatised projects and they have no experience ... They're only interested in getting a project and pumping it into a listed company, see those shares fly. And then they borrow against the scrip. They want to get rich quickly and they forget about management. This must stop.'[17]

The lack of tenders for many projects was something else in need of revision. 'Everyone wants a project without tender, and I allowed it before because of the recession. But from now on, everything must be tendered for,' Daim said to me. Indeed, the government announced that from 16 October 2000 all projects would be decided on a tender basis, except in exceptional circumstances. Those circumstances might be if the government wanted something done quickly, suggested Daim.

Some of the privatised entities did not prove themselves to be models of prudence. Intria Bhd, for example, a construction and tollroad company that was awarded a 25-year concession to collect tolls on the bridge that connects Penang with the mainland, over-reached itself with some expensive forays abroad. Ultimately controlled by Halim Saad through UEM, in mid-1996 it bought the Costain Group PLC, an ailing UK construction company, for £41.4 million, or M$162 million at the time. It borrowed offshore for the purchase, so that by the time Malaysia's currency peg was introduced in 1998 at a new, lower ringgit exchange rate, Costain's purchase price in ringgit terms had blown out to M$253.8 million. Intria thus faced heavy debts and light cash earnings and was unable to fully service its debts. On top of that, Costain only made a profit in 1999, after having recorded successive losses since 1993. Intria's controlling shareholder, Mekar Idaman Sdn Bhd, went into receivership in July 1999 after defaulting on a M$550 million loan. (UEM had previously owned a 45% stake in Mekar before it went into receivership.) Bank restructuring agency Danaharta seized Mekar Idaman's 42% stake in Intria, as it had been offered as collateral for the loan. Intria's creditors (who were owed M$650 million) convinced Danaharta to invite bids for the Intria stake.[18] UEM submitted a bid of M$371 million for the 45% stake in Intria and beat off two other contenders, the successful tender being announced in February 2000. UEM then planned to divest Intria's stake in Costain, but for the successful bidder to have been its formerly controlling shareholder surprised many analysts who had perhaps hoped for a completely new ownership structure.

Malaysia's private sector was still too small to cope with all the privatisations

17 'Calling Doctor Daim', *Far Eastern Economic Review*, 19 February 1998.

18 'Intria battle shows flaws in Malaysian restructuring', *Asian Wall Street Journal*, 16 November 1999.

that were offered to it. Some assets passed from state control to the private sector and then, in the aftermath of the 1997-98 economic crisis when many Malay-controlled companies were highly indebted and in serious trouble, back to the state sector. The national oil company, Petroliam Nasional Bhd, or Petronas, became one means of supporting distressed Malay companies by agreeing to buy from them some of their assets. It also participated in projects where private sector participants could not be found.

Petronas was founded in 1974. It is Malaysia's largest company and had revenues of around US$10 billion a year by 2000 and almost $100 billion by 2013. Its taxes and dividend payments accounted for almost one-sixth of government revenues in 1999. It expanded beyond the oil and gas sector at the government's behest. In August 1997, it reportedly paid M$1.8 billion to a state pension fund for a 29% controlling stake in Malaysian International Shipping Corp (MISC), Malaysia's largest shipping company. The seller was Mirzan Mahathir's Konsortium Perkapalan – but rather than being an obvious bail-out for the prime minister's son who at the time had been hit by the Southeast Asian economic crisis, the sale price was at the bottom end of analysts' expectations. In 1999, Petronas commenced negotiations with HICOM to acquire a 27.2% stake in car manufacturer Proton. Both Petronas and Proton claimed they would be able to realise 'synergies' from the move, but analysts were sceptical. Negotiations were concluded in March the following year. The agreed price for the stake was M$1.03 billion.

I asked Daim if he had ordered Petronas to acquire the stake in Proton, to help bail out the parent HICOM. He was adamant that he had not done so. Instead, he says that Petronas's management initiated the deal and then briefed him on their intentions. Petronas's management believed that there would be synergies between automobiles and gasoline, particularly in respect of the many gasoline stations that Petronas operates around Malaysia. Daim said he gave the deal his blessing, but suggested to the Petronas officials that they move quickly because, in his view, Proton shares at the time were very cheap. Rather than controlling decision making in Petronas, Daim said he was dismayed at how long the oil company took to buy the Proton stake, claiming that from the time they decided to buy until the time they actually did so, Proton's shares 'tripled'. Petronas is big and bureaucratic. Daim complained to me that he felt that its decisions were not finalised until everything had been verified by consultants, by which time it was often too late. Rather than exert the kind of close control over this and other government enterprises that often was assumed, Daim laughingly suggested that if he had his way he would go through and sack everyone for allowing the price of a stock to triple before finally moving in to seal the deal. Daim also mentioned that Petronas had initially also wanted to buy a 32% stake in Eon from HICOM, Proton's profitable main distributor. But as it turned out, Petronas could not agree with HICOM on a price and so the government's Khazanah Holdings, which is chaired by the prime minister, decided to buy the stake instead. Daim mentioned to me that the first that he had heard that Khazanah wanted to buy the stake was when he read about it in the press despite the fact that he was the finance minister. Again, the episode emphasised that government in Malaysia at the time was not the neat autocracy that often was supposed, but something much messier and more complex.

Petronas was also one of the three shareholders in Putrajaya Holdings, which developed the administrative township of Putrajaya outside Kuala Lumpur. It was also instrumental in bailing out Bank Bumiputera from time to time, including M$2.3 billion that was injected into the bank in September 1984 to stave of its collapse, and another M$982 million injected in October 1989 when the bank was again in financial trouble.[19] Notwithstanding these sorts of potentially diversionary investments, Petronas's management has long been seen as highly professional and devoid of the corruption culture that completely pervaded Indonesia's state-run oil company, Pertamina for example.

Malaysia's Petronas announced a record net profit in mid-2000 of more than US$3.3 billion and routinely is rated as one of Asia's best-run companies. Indonesia's Pertamina, on the other hand, was a corrupt, perennial loss maker that might have done more for the Indonesian economy if it simply closed down. A recently completed external audit calculated that it lost around US$5 billion during two years alone in the mid-1990s because of corruption and poor management. The two oil giants nicely encapsulate the differences between Malaysia and Indonesia. In 2005, I asked former prime minister Mahathir during a conversation we had at his house outside Kuala Lumpur why he thought that Petronas had been so successful, especially when compared with Pertamina. In his view, it was because the company was placed under the direct control of the prime minister's office (his office for the large part), rather than being under an oil minister who might have used it to dispense patronage to his own political supporters and relatives. Mahathir saw Petronas as very much the jewel in the Malaysian economic crown.

Debatable Means but Good Ends

The Malaysian government's privatisation program might have proceeded more prudently and transparently to head off much of the criticism that it attracted. Even Daim ultimately conceded that mistakes had been made. But what is clear is that, taken as a whole, the program overall has been unambiguously good for the Malaysian economy, and that is to Daim's credit.

Lee Kuan Yew has been quoted as saying, 'Daim's most significant contribution to Malaysia's economy is to shift its policy away from state-owned and state supported ventures to private enterprise … Tun Daim pushed the privatisation program and made CEOs answerable to private shareholders who will concentrate on and want profits.'[20] This is high praise indeed from Lee, but

19 'Saviour complex', *Far Eastern Economic Review*, 12 August 1999.

20 M.S. Cheong and Adibah Amin, op. cit., p. 162.

curious, perhaps, given the extent to which government-linked companies came to dominate the Singaporean economy. Perhaps this is an area where Singapore can learn from Malaysia. Daim boasted to me in 2000 that he felt Malaysia now had more 'real' entrepreneurs than Singapore.

The World Bank, in its influential *The East Asian Miracle* report (1993), was similarly laudatory of Malaysia's privatisation drive. It concluded that Malaysia had recognised 'a mistake' with its rapid expansion of the state-owned sector in the early 1980s, and embarked on its privatisation plan. By 1984, the combined deficit of Malaysia's public enterprises amounted to 3.7% of GNP. Of more than 800 state firms that existed in the mid-1980s, about 100 had been sold by 1990. Many were small, commercial operations, but some were very large, such as Malaysia Airlines and HICOM. The World Bank concluded that 'a detailed analysis of the companies that were privatised shows consistent gains in social welfare'. Managers had been able to gain control over investment decisions, and formerly loss-making operations that represented a drain on the public purse had been turned around to be profitable and pay taxes.[21]

The privatisation program had reduced the size of government, reduced the numbers of civil servants and generally transferred the risk of losses from the government to the private sector; that is, from ordinary taxpayers to the shareholders of large companies – a move that is progressive in its redistributive impact. It also greatly expanded the number of shareholders in Malaysia and massively increased the market capitalisation of the KLSE. But perhaps most importantly, Malaysia's privatisation program meant that the term 'private sector' no longer was synonymous with non-Malay businesses. Singling out promising Malay entrepreneurs and awarding them large privatisation projects meant that, for the first time, there were a significant number of Bumiputera business people in the upper echelons of the private sector. It achieved what the NEP had been designed to achieve but which it had failed to do. The link between race and business had been broken. The break was not a clean one by any means. Plenty of Malay entrepreneurs messed up. But the transition had to be made and Daim was utterly key to its achievement.

Mega-projects

Daim's first stint as finance minister earned him a reputation for being prudent, even stingy. So, how did he feel about the various costly mega-projects that were promoted by the government and became a hallmark of government in Malaysia in the late 1990s? His first reaction is to say that most of the projects were decided upon while he was out of the cabinet. Whether they were good decisions or bad, he claims no responsibility for them. Which project impressed him most? Without hesitation, he nominated the Kuala Lumpur International Airport, which was

---

21 World Bank, *The East Asian Miracle*, Oxford University Press, 1993, p. 311.

opened in 1998. When it opened, it was the second-largest airport in Asia. Many commented, though, on its location so far from Kuala Lumpur. Some even cynically suggested that the rationale for this was to allow a few well-connected companies to make money from the necessary tollroad that now connects it to the capital. Daim rejects this. Instead, he suggests the location was chosen to help foster development in nearby Negri Sembilan and Melaka states. That seems true enough. MAS flight crews no longer needed to be based in Kuala Lumpur – many now live in Negri Sembilan, for example. The trip to the airport takes less time than if they lived in Kuala Lumpur.

Daim was less enthusiastic about Putrajaya, the administrative capital that was developed from scratch about 25 kilometres south of Kuala Lumpur. Its estimated cost at the time was M$20 billion. The project commenced in 1996 and was intended to be completed in 2012. When finished, it will have a residential population of 300,000 people, including 76,000 civil servants. The prime minister's residence in the new centre has been completed and attracted enormous criticism in Malaysia for its dimensions and extravagance. Much of the criticism was aimed at Mahathir, who, in his defence, argued that he would only be a temporary resident and that all future prime ministers would live in it. Funding for Putrajaya, including the prime minister's residence was under the control of the then finance minister Anwar. 'I don't know how Anwar agreed to it,' Daim said to me in 2000 in relation to the residence. But then, maybe Anwar expected that he would be the residence's next occupant and so, as finance minister, did not have too many qualms about approving the expenditure. Certainly, it had many bedrooms and Anwar had many children.

The Petronas Towers that rise above central Kuala Lumpur and are the world's tallest buildings are another mega-project that attracted criticism. It is hard to see how, on purely economic grounds, their enormous cost was justified. Buildings beyond a certain height are usually not economic, simply because the lifts and the attendant lift shafts required to service so many floors mean that many of the lower floors comprise little more than an aggregation of lift shafts which, of course, cannot be leased out. Furthermore, Kuala Lumpur is not a land-scarce capital city by Asian standards and there was not the shortfall in office space that other cities had experienced. The towers ended up being a joint venture between the government-controlled oil company Petronas and companies associated with the well-connected Malaysian businessman Ananda Krishnan after the project proved too ambitious for Ananda to complete alone. In my discussions with him, Daim refused to concede that the towers were wasteful. He mentioned that the grounds on which they now stand belonged to the Selangor Turf Club. The cars of club patrons caused enormous traffic and parking problems in the area. Ananda Krishnan arranged and offered to swap some land outside Kuala Lumpur for the land on which the club stood. The club agreed, as did the government, which was keen to solve the traffic problems. That might be a reasonable justification for the land swap and for using the site for something other than a well-patronised club with poor parking facilities, but it is no justification for then building not just one but what was the world's two tallest towers on the site. When I pressed Daim on this, he finally offered, 'Malaysians are proud of the towers. Who am I to say they are wrong?' Daim is correct on that point. Regardless of the economic arguments, ordinary Malaysians everywhere are very proud of the Petronas Towers, and if economic arguments alone are used as the sole criterion for such projects, then perhaps many of the world's finest and most recognised buildings would never have been built, the Sydney Opera House and the somewhat functionless Eiffel Tower in Paris among them. Economists have a great deal to offer when it comes to adjudicating on efficiency, but they have no monopoly on aesthetics. Ultimately, and as a businessman said to me in Kuala Lumpur in late 2000, whatever the merits of Malaysia's mega-projects, the thing that is most impressive about them is that they do actually get done. In Malaysia, he argued, dreams tend to have a habit of becoming reality, be they excessively extravagant or not.

I asked Professor Mahani who had worked with Daim as a key economics advisor during the 1997-98 economic crisis about her view of Malaysia's mega projects. She was equivocal. She sees a role for government in facilitating such projects 'but investment allocation must be more efficient.' The government must take charge of the bigger picture which business cannot, but, at the micro level, Professor Mahani believed that market signals must still be a prime determinant as to which projects go ahead, and which do not. It was a polite way of saying she thought there had been a lot of waste, but also that Malaysia had something to show for it.

The Bakun Dam

Among the mega-projects, the US$5.7 billion Bakun Dam project became something of a fiasco. It was to be a massive hydroelectric project in Sarawak that would supply Sarawak's power needs, as well as providing power to peninsular Malaysia and Singapore via enormous undersea transmission cables. Technically, the project was highly speculative and it was certainly very costly. Daim supported it (Anwar later claimed that he did not, although the first approvals for the project were granted by him), notwithstanding his tendency toward prudence. He was, it seems, convinced that it would prove to be a sound investment in the long run, and besides, as he was quick to point out, the Sarawak government strongly pushed for the project. Local construction company Ekran secured much of the entire privatised project.[22]

Ekran was the flagship company of Sarawak-born Ting Pek Khiing, who had impressed Daim and Mahathir with his ability to build resorts in Langkawi in record time. He acquired the company in 1991 and listed it on the KLSE the following year. Ting started out in business with little more than an audacious propensity for getting things done. Ting's 'can do' attitude attracted Mahathir's

---

22 E.T. Gomez, *Chinese Business in Malaysia*, Curzon, 1999, p. 172.

attention. Government contracts flowed aplenty to Ting – not because there was anything improper in his relationship with the government, but because Mahathir believed that Ting would deliver infrastructure and other development projects on budget and on time.

The Malaysian government entrusted the building of the Bakun Dam to Ting and Ekran in January 1994 (when Anwar was finance minister) and it did so without a public tender. Ekran then contracted out the project to a consortium headed by the giant Swedish-Swiss engineering company Asea Brown Boveri AG (ABB). In turn, ABB was required to accept firms linked to Ting as its main sub-contractors.

The project was highly controversial. Controversies over how Ekran was awarded the contract, environmental problems that attracted protests from around the world, and social problems in that the dam was to displace scores of tribespeople, all served to undermine Ekran's fortunes. In addition, an important feature of the project was to be the 650-kilometre submarine power transmission cable from Sarawak to peninsular Malaysia. The cable would have been by far the longest ever attempted. At the time, the longest such cable in the world was a 100-kilometre cable that connects Denmark with Sweden, so there were enormous doubts as to whether the plan was even feasible.

Ting insisted that ABB should bear full responsibility for all cost over-runs, despite a signed contract between the two parties that appeared to allow for the contrary. A bitter and drawn-out dispute over the awarding of the sub-contracts developed, and progress on the site was delayed. In early August 1997, Ekran dismissed ABB as the prime contractor for the Bakun project and it did so with the Malaysian government's blessing. The end-result was that Ekran was left with the rights to a project it could not complete on its own.

The following month, the Malaysian government announced that the Bakun project had been delayed indefinitely, and in November stated that it had taken over the project and Ekran's involvement was cancelled. The Treasury then embarked on a due diligence study of the project to see what work had been undertaken to date and what the government should pay Ekran as compensation for having acquired the project.[23] Eventually, Ekran and the government reached a settlement and Ekran was compensated for its efforts. Daim, on becoming finance minister again, reviewed the Bakun project. The project had been privatised under Anwar but Anwar was well known for not being too particular with all the details of his brief. Daim started by asking for projections of Sarawak industries' power needs – it was unclear whether this had previously been done. By early 2001, Ekran was out of the picture and the government was reconsidering the project. As for Ting Pek Khiing, Daim said to me in mid-2000 that he couldn't understand why he 'just doesn't retire!'

---

23 'Govt takes over Bakun hydro-electric project', *The Star*, 20 November 1997.

Success and Excess

The Malaysian government's zeal for the privatisation of state-owned utilities and for mega projects had a tremendous impact on the economy. The attitude of 'do later' was replaced by one of 'can do' and 'do now.' The economy boomed and not only did it grow, but it also transformed. The economic pie was expanding and so to was the proportion of the population who had a hand in making it. However there was a hurdle in the fast lane to development which nobody saw coming. Mixed in with all the success was some excess. Mega projects and privatisations meant entrusting a significant proportion of the national economy to entrepreneurs who were still novices. And many of these had borrowed heavily. The party couldn't go on and indeed it did not.

XII

MELTDOWN!

Daim was out of the cabinet between 1991 and 1998 but nonetheless remained highly influential. Informally his influence derived from his personal contacts and relationships within the government, and with those business people he had helped and nurtured at Peremba and while finance minister. More formally, he was chairman of the Northern Growth Triangle (with ministerial status); chairman of the Labuan Development Authority, whereby he headed the government's attempts to turn Labuan, off the coast of Sabah, into an offshore banking centre; co-chairman of the Langkawi Development Authority; and Malaysia's representative in the East ASEAN Growth Area (EAGA). His office was in the Economic Planning Unit of the Prime Minister's Department and he was given ministerial rank. He was also appointed the vice chairman of the Malaysian Business Council in February 1991, adjunct professor of Universiti Utara Malaysia in April 1993, and pro-chancellor of Universiti Sains Malaysia in February 1994. On top of that, Daim helped to run his various private businesses and continued as UMNO's treasurer. Daim might have withdrawn from active politics, but clearly he had not retired. He enrolled in some courses at the John F. Kennedy School of Government at Harvard University – partly to be away from Kuala Lumpur so that talk of disagreements between him and his successor Anwar or the appearance that he might be influencing Anwar could be avoided. The truth though was that even while he was in the United States, often Daim was contacted for assistance by Anwar in both government and UMNO party matters.

Daim enjoys power or at least the intellectual stimulus of it, but not the associated trappings. So, his period out of the cabinet was an enjoyable one. He was able to exert influence, but he did not have to attend all the meetings, or bother with all the protocol and paperwork, required of a cabinet minister. It was ideal. But it was not to last.

The economic climate proved benevolent for Malaysia during much of the 1990s. Commodity prices generally stayed high, Malaysia saw increasing foreign investment, particularly in its electronics and computer-component related sectors, and the economies of its major trading partners generally stayed in good shape. Captaining a ship in calm seas is no difficult task and wins easy credit, as Daim's successor Anwar Ibrahim, like Razaleigh Hamzah, was to discover. It was a good time to be finance minister. But all that changed in mid-1997.

The Thai economy, which had been labouring under high foreign debts for some time, suddenly went into free fall. The Thai baht plunged. Thai companies with borrowings denominated in US dollars but with baht earnings found that their debts in baht terms had exploded. Their rush to buy dollars by selling baht only exacerbated the problem, and the baht and the Thai economy spiralled down with even greater speed. It was not long before the economies of Indonesia, South Korea and the Philippines followed. Indonesia and South Korea, particularly, also had high levels of foreign debt denominated in foreign currencies, mostly US dollars and Japanese yen. The Indonesian economy also wasn't helped by political instability as the 32-year regime of President Soeharto drew to a close amid street protests and violence.

Malaysia differed from the others in that its companies were highly indebted, but generally to local banks and in ringgit rather than US dollars. Before the economic crisis, Malaysia also had one of the region's most diversified financial sectors. Bank finance dominated lending, but domestic debt markets raised about 33% of net financing. Furthermore, Malaysia's economy had other strengths. It had high national savings, large fiscal surpluses, low external debt and low inflation.

After Singapore, Malaysia's banks were the strongest in Southeast Asia. Non-performing loans (NPLs) were low and banking supervision generally exceeded average regional standards. Pre-crisis NPLs officially were 3.6% of total bank loans, while the banks' average risk-weighted capital adequacy ratio was 11.8% – well above the Bank for International Settlements' 8% minimum. Malaysia's current account deficit was high at 5.8% of GDP, but it had a relatively good match of foreign liabilities and assets, and foreign reserves exceeded short-term debt by a comfortable margin.

However, like Indonesia, Thailand and South Korea, Malaysia had high pre-crisis rates of private sector credit growth, a rapidly growing economy with increasing real estate and equity price inflation, real exchange rate appreciation and slowing exports. New credit expanded by more than 25% a year between 1995 and 1997, mostly for property and business services sectors. As a result, Malaysia's corporate sector became highly leveraged. By 1997, bank loans were around 170% of GDP – similar to levels in Korea and Thailand.

There were similarities, but Malaysia was not a Thailand, an Indonesia or a South Korea. Nonetheless, when the Asian economic crisis came, the ringgit was caught up in the region-wide maelstrom and currency traders dumped it too, causing its value to plummet along with the region's other currencies. Initially, Bank Negara attempted to defend the ringgit. It sold US dollars and other currencies to buy ringgit in a bid to force up its price (the ringgit's exchange rate). The strategy proved unsustainable and costly. Universiti Malaya Professor K.S. Jomo has asserted that the Malaysian government spent M$9 billion in 1997 and 1998 to defend the ringgit's value.[1] He offers no evidence to support this claim, and his colleague at the university, Professor Mahani Zainal Abidin, a key economic adviser to the government during the crisis, felt that the figure was more like M$1 billion. 'Bank Negara officials realised that they couldn't keep

1 Jomo, K.S. (ed.), *Malaysian Eclipse: Economic Crisis and Recovery*, Zed Books, 2001, p. 42.

fighting the pressure on the ringgit and had the sense to stop after having spent around M$1 billion', she told me in late 2000. On 14 July 1997, the ringgit was allowed to depreciate after years of having been tied to the US dollar. On that day it fell from M$2.50 to the US dollar to M$2.61. By 12 August, one US dollar bought M$2.83 and on 2 September it bought M$3.00. The ringgit sank to an intraday low of M$4.88 on 7 January 1998 before rallying and then weakening again. On 8 July 1998, it stood at $M4.16.

Seemingly, 'ringgit' sounded like 'rupiah' and 'Malaysia' sounded like 'Indonesia' to foreign currency traders in New York who might not have ever travelled to either country but nonetheless still traded in both countries' currencies and debt. The media, too, lacked sufficient understanding that Malaysia was not another Indonesia or Thailand. 'The foreign media should not be so preoccupied with trumpeting so many clichés as the cause of the Asian woes. Instead, the Western media should get to know the differences between Malaysia and other Asian countries. The political, economic and population make-up of Malaysia and our Asian neighbours are poles apart,' complained Daim in mid-1998.[2] Ultimately, the punishment meted out to Malaysia by the markets seemed to be in excess of its sins. The markets seem to have over-reacted, as they so often do. At the height of the crisis, crashing currencies and asset prices meant that Indonesia, with its political instability and particularly poor systems of corporate governance, was fairly priced. Malaysia, on the other hand, was a relative bargain. It meant that when Malaysia recovered, the bounce back was especially quick.

The 1997-98 recession was the most severe that Malaysia had experienced since the Second World War. In 1998, the economy contracted by a severe 7.5%. The economic contraction in 1985 had been much smaller, at just 1.1%. Daim claims that he predicted the 1997-98 recession two years before it happened, but what he did not predict was its depth.

There has been a lot of debate about what triggered the events of 1997-98. Speculators have been targeted by many, and Mahathir was even more specific when he blamed speculator George Soros and his Quantum Fund, in particular. Of course, the view that speculators alone 'caused' the economic crisis is simplistic. Daim acknowledged this. He said at a seminar in Manila in early 1999, 'The weaknesses in East Asia's corporate and financial sectors had been one of the factors contributing to the collapse of the equity and capital markets. When the crisis deepened, investors became worried about the strength and resilience of banks and corporations, which were masked by poor standards of disclosure and accountability. Shares were dumped with the collapse of investor confidence. The massive outflow of funds that ensued fueled the contagion nature of the crisis … The causes of the Asian crisis are complex.'[3] It was a thoughtful and

---

2   Speech by Daim at the AIDCOM Seminar on 'The Economic Crisis in Malaysia and the Role of the Media', Malaysia, 22 July 1998.

3   Speech by Daim to the Washington SyCip Policy Forum, Asian Institute of Management, Manila, 4 March 1999.

constructive assessment.

Daim was happy that the Malaysian government should share at least some of the blame. In a speech delivered a month later in Kuala Lumpur, he said '[T] he unfolding of events since July 1997 indicated there were some flaws in our macro-economy. The private sector became over-confident, engaging in external borrowing and over-investing in properties. Share prices were unrealistic. The banks too were happily giving out loans to the property sector beyond prudential proportions and the higher the share price, the more the banks lent to borrowers. State governments too had to share the blame as they were too ready to convert land for property development and in some cases these ran into thousands of acres. The party did not seem to be ending and we began to lose control of the need for prudence in the excitement of high performance.'[4] Before a problem can be fixed it must first be defined, and Daim, on behalf of the government, set about doing that.

I asked Daim whether he felt that Soros had been singled out for unfair attention, that too much blame had been laid at his door. 'He was the leader of the pack,' Daim responded. Plus, he had been very critical of Malaysia and Mahathir. As far as Daim is concerned, Soros had it coming, which of course is how Soros felt about Malaysia. Why Soros was so vehement in his attacks on Malaysia puzzles Daim, though. Soros had invested in Malaysia and also had invested with Wan Azmi Wan Hamzah in several joint ventures outside Malaysia.

Mahathir's tirade against speculators, however, was not as self-serving as many depicted. Certainly, corporate governance and the country's institutions were not as sound as they could have been, which undoubtedly led to a loss of confidence in Malaysia's ability to withstand a region-wide downturn. But by the same token, Malaysia did not score as badly on these indicators as some of the other Asian economies struck down by the economic crisis – most particularly Thailand, Indonesia and South Korea – yet Malaysia's currency and stock market were sold down as if they were. Speculators did appear to be toying with the ringgit. Much of the trading was not on the basis of the fundamentals of the Malaysian economy but more on the basis of what Malaysia's central bank was likely to do next and to what extent it could continue to afford to support the value of the ringgit. Daim claims that the Malaysian government had evidence that the Tiger Fund was routinely trading US$200 million a day against the ringgit in the lead-up to the crisis. Mahathir's strategy of pinning so much of the blame on George Soros gave Malaysians an external focus for their anger over the economic crisis. They could be united in their anger at a usefully distant though common foe. Over in Indonesia, no such external scapegoat was found. Instead, Indonesian Chinese bore the brunt of much of the frustration and had to endure seemingly state-sponsored rape, rioting and property damage.

---

4   Speech by Daim on 'Managing the National Economy During Crisis', Kuala Lumpur, 24 April 1999.

The International Monetary Fund

The economic crisis rolled through Asia in mid-1997 and the International Monetary Fund (IMF) turned up shortly after. The economic doctor arrived with a one-size-fits-all, cure-all remedy. Thailand, Indonesia and South Korea had little choice but to swallow the bitter pill on offer, but Malaysia had other ideas. First, Malaysia simply did not need the IMF's money. The Malaysian government estimated that M$62 billion was needed during 1998-2000 for its economic recovery program. The main requirement for funds was for the bank restructuring and recapitalisation program, as well as additional allocations for the Seventh Malaysia Plan. The government estimated that two-thirds of the requirements, or around M$40 billion, would come from domestic sources, such as savings and annual inflow of provident funds, pensions and insurance funds, and oil revenue from Petronas. One-third would come from foreign sources. Daim even suggested in a speech that the amount of resources that Malaysia could potentially tap was close to twice the government's requirements.[5] On top of that, the government was able to approach private debt markets itself to raise funds. This it did in 1999 when it issued global sovereign bonds worth at least US$1 billion.

If Malaysia didn't need the IMF's money, then perhaps it could take its advice. Finance minister Anwar was sympathetic to the IMF's policy prescriptions. His policy response to the economic crisis was higher interest rates and a tougher stance on NPLs, two measures that form the bedrock of the IMF's standard, 'one size fits all' policy prescription for economies undergoing a monetary crisis. Increased interest rates were to attract foreign money and thus restore the ringgit to higher levels. The prime lending rate (the rate that banks offer their best customers) rose from about 9% in mid-1997 to a high of 12.27% in June 1998. However, because funds were scarce and banks' assessment of the risks of lending rose dramatically, some borrowers faced rates as high as 24%.

In April 1997, Anwar introduced measures to restrain excessive bank lending to real estate, shares and units in unit trusts. The following September, loan classifications were tightened so that loans that had not been serviced after three months were classified as non-performing instead of after six months. The government's new rules required provisioning of at least 1.5% of total loans and 20% of the uncollateralised portion of sub-standard loans; it strengthened bank disclosure requirements and introduced a monthly stress test of bank credit positions. Bank Negara also instructed all banking institutions to establish loan rehabilitation units to separate the management of NPLs from daily credit management and administration. These measures were prudent and were precisely the sort that were introduced in the economies of Europe and North America in the wake of their banking crises in 2009.

Thailand, South Korea and Indonesia had to accept significant increases in domestic interest rates (designed to support the exchange rate), cuts to

---

5   Speech by Daim to APEC Finance Ministers Meeting, Langkawi, 15 May 1999.

government spending and banking reform, including the closure of financial institutions, as conditions for accepting IMF bail-out packages. But ultimately, such remedies were not appropriate for Malaysia. Its problem was not one of external indebtedness so much as high domestic debt. With domestic debt at 150% of GDP, the problem was not Malaysia's ability to service its external borrowings, but rather that of companies and individuals being able to maintain their local debt commitments. Given this, it made little sense to increase interest rates to support the ringgit. That would have exacerbated, rather than alleviated, the problem of the bulk of Malaysia's debtors.

Although the IMF remedy didn't seem right for Malaysia, Anwar was veering towards it. Amid the policy confusion, there were accusations that Anwar was excessively concerned with playing to the interests of foreign markets and foreign players. Some in Malaysia felt that he had become too concerned with building his international profile, rather than paying sufficient attention to the needs of his domestic audience.

The Malaysian government was in shock by the latter half of 1997. It was wracked by internal divisions about what to do. The policy differences were not minor – there were dramatically different ideas about which way the government should turn. Anwar was edging towards adopting an IMF-style set of policies. Mahathir opposed them, but was unsure of what other options should be considered. Part of the problem was that communications between Anwar and the prime minister appeared to be breaking down. Increasingly, seemingly contradictory messages emanated from the government. In early 1998, for example, Mahathir told journalists that a pillar of its NEP/NDP policies, the rule that prohibits Bumiputeras from selling equity stakes to non-Bumiputeras, would be suspended, as many Bumiputeras faced bankruptcy unless they could sell their stakes. Mahathir said the move would be temporary, but Anwar (who was still finance minister) said that the suspension had yet to be decided.[6]

According to Daim, Mahathir considered announcing a state of emergency. Most probably this would have involved establishing a National Action Council along the lines of that which was established in the aftermath of the 1969 race riots in Kuala Lumpur. Daim was vehemently opposed to the idea of imposing a state of emergency. 'One was imposed in 1969 [in the aftermath of the 1969 riots] and it was a mistake then too.' A similar declaration in 1997 would have 'more or less allowed Mahathir to rule by decree'. Daim believes that it would have been a disaster for Malaysia. All those foreigners who were convinced that Mahathir was a totalitarian dictator would have been correct after such an imposition, thought Daim, for the state of emergency would at last have given Mahathir the powers that many foreigners had always presumed he had. However, Mahathir was also interested in seeing some alternative options.

Daim called a meeting of nine members of the UMNO Supreme Council,

6 'Ethnic economics thrown overboard as depth of financial crisis hits home', *South China Morning Post*, 2 March 1998.

UMNO's key policy-making body, in late 1997 to attempt to avert Mahathir's plan. The nine members were each of the chief ministers of the UMNO-ruled states. The fact that Daim held no cabinet post at that stage was immaterial – the nine chief ministers attended anyway. The meeting provided testament to Daim's power, even if any formal position was lacking. Daim briefed them on the state of emergency option, which found little favour.

Mahathir subsequently denied that he was considering imposing a state of emergency. He told me in 2005 that he didn't know why Daim persists in claiming that he was. But Daim is adamant that his recollection is correct. 'Why would all the chief ministers have come for a meeting on the matter had Mahathir not been considering it?', he said to me in London in 2015. Most probably it is a case of two different perceptions and recollections of the same event on the part of two individuals who were involved. It serves to underscore the confusion at the time and the fast pace at which events were moving.

In any event, what Daim proposed to the meeting of chief ministers was what became the National Economic Recovery Plan (discussed in Chapter 14), which was then taken to Mahathir, with the broad backing of the UMNO Supreme Council. The plan was cogent and integrated. Mahathir agreed to it. With that, it was a *fait accompli*. Effectively, Anwar, whose proposals seemed piecemeal and were yet to be fully enunciated, had been sidelined. In any event Mahathir's frustration at the direction of economic policy was growing daily. Mahathir later squarely put the blame on Anwar for the worsening situation. 'As the financial crisis continued, it became apparent that the Minister of Finance [Anwar], aided by the central bank, was implementing policies which were making a bad situation worse,' Mahathir said in his book, *The Malaysian Currency Crisis*.[7]

Communication between Anwar and Mahathir continued to falter. Daim claims that Anwar, as finance minister, was close to allowing Bank Bumiputera to fail. Anwar was on the verge of announcing that the bank had gone into liquidation and would not be given further support by the government. The bank's senior management were in a panic and approached Daim for help, telling him of Anwar's intentions. Daim was incredulous. He felt that while it was arguable whether private sector banks should be bailed out by the government, a government-owned bank should be saved. He went to Mahathir to plead Bank Bumiputera's case and claims, to his surprise, that Mahathir did not know what Anwar was planning. Mahathir agreed with Daim's basic proposition that the government should not allow a government bank to fail. Accordingly, a plan was devised to save Bank Bumiputera.

Daim Returns to the Cabinet

In June 1998, Mahathir formalised Daim's role by appointing him as special functions minister charged with getting Malaysia out of recession. Anwar was

---

7   Mahathir Mohamad, *The Malaysian Currency Crisis: How and Why it Happened*, Pelanduk Publications, 2000, p. 23.

to stay on as finance minister. It was inevitable that the two would step on each other's toes. Although Daim is widely credited with getting Malaysia out of recession in 1985-86, and he was the one person connected to the administration that the markets felt had an intimate understanding of the economy, the KLSE fell on news of his appointment. The markets suspected that Daim planned to use public money to bail out well-connected companies, and also that he supported capital controls.[8] On the latter, he was still to make up his mind. And on the former, the evidence was equivocal. He had not bailed out his friends such as banker (and politician) Alex Lee, Ibrahim Mohammad of Promet, or Sabah-based businessman Syed Kechik in 1985 when he was finance minister and they were in trouble. Nonetheless, there was suspicion that the NEAC had been created to organise bail-outs for well-connected business people. It was another example that, despite Daim's record on economic management, the worst was always assumed of him. In early 1998, Daim had said in an interview with the *Far Eastern Economic Review*, 'You don't draw a line about who sinks and swims … It's not politically acceptable to use public funds to bailout businessmen who've made mistakes in judgment. If you bail people out, they'll never learn.'[9] The markets, though, were yet to be convinced.

Universiti Malaya Professor Jomo said that while Daim's appointment was not greeted favourably by the markets, the response would have been more enthusiastic among Malaysia's business community. 'He has been seen to be broadly consultative, meeting all kinds of people in the last few months through the [National Economic Action] Council. He is generally perceived to be much more sensitive to the needs and sensitivities and perceptions of the business community.'[10] There was one company, in particular, whose needs many expected Daim to be particularly sensitive to.

The most spectacular near-death experience among the major Malaysian corporates was that of Renong and Halim Saad. Halim had been mentored by Daim, so many expected that a government-sponsored bail-out for Renong would occur as a matter of course. In January 1998, the NEAC issued a statement in relation to the Renong case to say that companies of 'national or strategic importance' had a right to seek assistance from the government. However, a week prior to the statement, Daim had said publicly that it was the government's policy not to bail out any company. 'The decision of the Malaysian Government not to issue government guarantees for Renong illustrates this stance,' Daim said.[11] Daim did acknowledge in conversations with me that if Renong had failed, the government almost certainly would have stepped in, most likely by having the government's business arm, Khazanah, take a stake in the company. He had

8 'Asia Pacific' program, Radio National, Australian Broadcasting Corporation, 29 June 1998.

9 'Calling Doctor Daim', *Far Eastern Economic Review*, 19 February 1998.

10 'Asia Pacific' program, op. cit.

11 'Renong case shows Malaysia is learning', *Bangkok Post*, 18 March 1999.

discussed the plan with Halim, and Halim had put it to his creditors. Daim did say, though, that he was 'too busy' at the time trying to save the banks to become too involved in the highly complex problems that had engulfed Renong.

The message on bail-outs remained mixed, however. Daim was later to say, 'One of the measures undertaken by the Government was to assist viable companies facing financial problems. However, critics only viewed these measures as bail-outs for the large companies. This is certainly not true. On the contrary, there are also thousands of small companies that benefited from this policy. These measures were undertaken to save thousands of jobs and in recognition of the significant contribution of these companies to the nation. This action is not peculiar to Malaysia, as many other countries have done it before, including the United States, France and Australia. This is another proof of the double standards of developed countries for whatever agenda they may have.'[12] This has a ring of truth. Western governments routinely face political pressure to bail out this company or that industry. However, it is the efficacy of such bail-outs *per se* that is open to question. The fact that a bail-out might occur in France or in Australia does not make such bail-outs in Malaysia any more prudent or less expedient. Daim's concern with double standards, though, is understandable. In any event, what is now clear is that the markets had expected Daim to intervene heavily in the economy to provide government assistance to well-connected companies. On that score, they were to be disappointed. He was prepared to if he had to, but ultimately he didn't.

Daim, Minister of Finance, Mark II

By mid-1998, Daim was already functioning as de facto finance minister and Anwar had become hopelessly estranged from Mahathir. On September 1, the government introduced capital controls. Anwar was fired the next day, and Mahathir assumed responsibility for the Finance Ministry (Daim was made Finance Minister later). Daim maintained, however, that rejoining the government was never his intention. 'I hate coming to work at 8 o'clock,' he was quoted as saying to reporters. 'Help me revive the economy and I'll be the first to exit.'[13] He probably meant it. Becoming finance minister again may not have greatly added to his power, but it did greatly increase the bother.

The manner of Daim's departure the first time he served as finance minister allowed for the possibility of him returning. Politicians worldwide have a tendency to stay on until forced out. The inevitable life-cycle of most successful political careers is to go into politics, make a significant contribution, and then to see that legacy eroded due to a decision not to retire when all is going well but to stay on until one either is forced out by one's colleagues or loses office via an election loss. Politicians tend to stay until it is no longer tenable, or possible, to hold on

---

12 Budget 2000 speech given to Parliament by Daim on 29 October 1999.

13 'Malaysia's players debate capital controls', *Asian Wall Street Journal*, 1 September 1999.

any longer, ensuring that even the most brilliant political careers tend to end in disappointment or acrimony. These inevitably unpleasant departures usually make a comeback awkward, if not impossible. Rather than the last thing in the public's mind being the high point of a politician's career, the usual memory is of the unpleasant events that led to the eventual departure. Daim, however, left of his own volition and when his political career was still on a high. This allowed him, as a politician, the rare luxury of a successful comeback. Ismail Noor and Muhammad Azaham in their book *The Malays*, compare Daim's return to the helm of the economy with the 'call back for duty' in the aftermath of the 1969 riots to Tun Dr Ismail Rahman, who returned from retirement to become Minister for Home Affairs to help return the nation to stability.

The depth of the 1985-87 recession can be attributed to the macroeconomic management of Malaysia during the preceding years. Profligate government spending and insufficient attention to building a strong and prudent financial sector meant that when commodity prices fell, the Malaysian economy was not in a sufficiently robust state to absorb the shock and carry on. Arguably, conditions might have been worse. Had the economy continued on the trajectory that it had been on prior to Daim's first appointment as finance minister – budget deficits, a high degree of state ownership of enterprises, and so on – then clearly the depth of the 1997-98 recession would have been much greater. Malaysia did not perform as well as Singapore in the crisis, but its performance was not nearly as bad as that of Indonesia and Thailand. To a degree, this was a product of the groundwork laid by Daim between 1984 and 1991.

One crucial measure was the reduction in Malaysia's foreign borrowings. During the latter part of Daim's first period as finance minister in the 1980s, the government took advantage of the liquidity of Malaysia's domestic finance system to raise borrowings locally and then use these to prepay foreign debt. Daim instructed Bank Negara to withhold approval for domestic companies wanting offshore loans. This single act, perhaps more than any other, saved Malaysia from a fate similar to that of Thailand and Indonesia during the 1997-98 economic crisis. Malaysia's relatively low foreign currency debts meant that it barely mattered what happened to the ringgit when it came to servicing and repaying their debts – Malaysian companies were more or less insulated from the currency crisis and the rapid fall of the ringgit. Thai and Indonesian companies, on the other hand, had been allowed to borrow heavily in US dollars and yen and saw the value of these loans in their domestic currencies skyrocket as those currencies plummeted. Many could not then service the loans and went bankrupt, or at least should have had bankruptcy laws been properly enforced in those countries.

In late 1997, liquidity concerns in relation to smaller banks caused a flight to larger and overseas banks as depositors sought out quality rather than high interest rates. The situation stabilised somewhat in January 1998 after Bank Negara issued a statement saying that it guaranteed to pay principal and accrued interest on deposits at the financial institutions that it supervised. Throughout 1998 and 1999, NPLs grew to levels where, without external assistance, some banks' capital adequacy ratios would have fallen below the mandated 8%. By the end of 1998, the banking system's gross NPLs reached 20% of total loans. So, Malaysia's banks were in trouble, especially compared with where they had been in previous years, but by regional standards their position was not so bad. The cost of recapitalising banks post the economic crisis in Indonesia was 50-60% of GDP, in Thailand it was 40%, in South Korea it was 15% and in Malaysia it was 12%, according to Bank for International Settlements data. Nonetheless, rescuing Malaysia's banks became a priority for Daim.

One of Daim's first steps as finance minister was to temporarily relax the NPL classification system in September 1998 to six months again (Anwar had tightened it to three months one year earlier) and allow restructured and rescheduled loans to be reclassified as performing loans. This measure met with some criticism, but given that it represented a return to what had prevailed little more than a year earlier, and also given the unexpected severity of the recession, the change was not unreasonable. The government felt that the tighter provisioning rules were deterring banks from lending, which ran counter to the government's desire to reflate the economy.[14] Many finance companies also experienced severe difficulties during the economic crisis. The government significantly raised their minimum capital requirements to stimulate mergers between them and to raise public confidence. It also increased the risk-weighted capital adequacy ratio for finance companies from 8% to 9% by December 1998 and to 10% by December 1999.

The groundwork for Daim's tenure as finance minister was already laid however. For months he had been working with the National Economic Action Council and particularly the Council's working group on devising a plan to restructure and revive the economy. Daim's arrival at the finance ministry this time was in marked contrast to the first time. This time he arrived with a comprehensive blueprint – one that he had been instrumental in creating.

14 East Asia Analytical Unit, *Asia's Financial Markets: Capitalising on Reform*, Commonwealth of Australia, Canberra, 1999, p. 197.

DAIM ZAINUDDIN

With Dr Mahathir bin Mohamad.

With Narayan Dutt Tiwari, India's Finance Minister (1987 to 1988).

With Margaret Thatcher, Prime Minister for Great Britain (1979 to 1990).

With Warren Christopher, US Secretary of State, (1993 to 1997).

With P.V. Narasimha Rao, India's Prime Minister (1991 to 1996).

With Blaise Compaoré president of Burkina Faso (1987 to 2014).

With Hassanal Bolkiah, Sultan of Brunei (since 1967).

With Prem Tinsulanonda, President of the Privy Council of Thailand, and former prime minister.

With Shah Rukh Khan, Bollywood actor.

With Soeharto, President of Indonesia (1968 to 1998).

With Lee Kuan Yew, Prime Minister of Singapore (1959 to 1990).

With Nelson Mandela, President of South Africa (1994-1999).

With Ismail Omar Guelleh, President of Djibouti (since 1999).

With Paul Keating, Prime Minister of Australia (1991 to 1996).

With Nawaz Sharif, Prime Minister of Pakistan (1990 to 1993; 1997 to 1999; since 2013).

With Susilo Bambang Yudhoyono, President of Indonesia (2004 to 2014).

XIII

POLITICAL CRISIS ANEW

The economic crisis of 1985-87 triggered a political crisis the impact of which was to last for several years. The 1997-98 crisis produced some political fallout of its own. Former deputy prime minister and finance minister Anwar Ibrahim's sacking and subsequent arrest on sexual impropriety and corruption charges in the wake of the introduction of capital and currency controls attracted publicity around the world. Much of the international media coverage assumed that Anwar was innocent of all charges. (Whether the alleged sexual offences should be criminal acts is a separate matter, although again, some of the international media seemed to have difficulty in distinguishing between Anwar's possible guilt and the appropriateness of the criminality of the acts.) It also assumed that he was the voice of reason in the Malaysian government and that in the midst of the economic crisis he was being removed. There were, of course, other points of view, but these received little airing at the time.

New Times and New Skills

Deputy director of the Institute of Strategic and International Studies (ISIS) Malaysia, Zainal Aznam Yusof, told me that in his view a good finance minister needs three qualities. He should have a good grounding in the macro-economy. He should understand how business people operate. And he should have a good and well-developed relationship with the media. He said that Daim is strongest in the middle criterion. All three are important but during the economic crisis when business people were hurting badly it was an understanding of business that was essential. Dr Zainal's NEAC colleague Professor Mahani Zainal Abidin mentioned to me that in her view Daim was able to bring something to the table that Anwar could not in this context. 'Anwar was not a businessman, unlike Daim. Daim could bring background and experience to the task that Anwar could not.' Such is a practical view of the virtues of Daim compared with Anwar as finance minister from two of Malaysia's more prominent economics professionals. Others cited Anwar's relatively chaotic manner of running the finance portfolio as a reason for why he should not have been missed from the office during crisis times. He was, as mentioned earlier, very good at handling the international media, but on a day-to-day basis was unimpressive with the hum-drum nature of administrative matters.

A political view is that Daim was unencumbered by political considerations. Not aspiring to higher office, he was more likely to do what needed to be done. 'If a person is too political, he can't run the economy in a crisis. Tun was the right person for the crisis', the then head of the Back Benchers' Club, Jamaludin Jarjis told me. It was a sentiment echoed by then defence minister Najib Tun Razak for whom Daim's disinterest in building a power base within UMNO added to rather than detracted from his claim on the job. 'Finance ministers should not use their positions to build up their own base, rewarding their supporters here and buying additional support', Najib said to me. 'Daim doesn't have an agenda of his own – this is his great strength.' For Jamaludin, there was another consideration too. The mere presence of Daim working as hard as he does and thus demonstrating by example would have a calming effect on the markets. 'Tun's long hours and hard work encourages confidence in the financial sector, among others. This is a very important angle', argued Jamaludin.

Quite apart from these measured comments, the disappointment with and even dislike of Anwar among the Kuala Lumpur elite in the wake of his arrest and imprisonment was startling. The gap between perceptions of Anwar within senior levels of Kuala Lumpur and the esteem with which he is regarded outside Malaysia seemed to be especially wide. It was not simply a question of Anwar wanting to take over from Mahathir and possibly attempting to subvert Mahathir's position as prime minister in the process. Others have done that and yet were not regarded with nearly as much acrimony as was Anwar. Tunku Razaleigh is a case in point. He very nearly succeeded in knocking off Mahathir as prime minister in 1987 and at least wanted to try for an UMNO vice presidency, if not the presidency, in 2000 but for a lack of party support. And yet Razaleigh remained fondly regarded by many in the government, including by Daim himself. Not for Razaleigh the innuendo and accusations that surrounded Anwar, and yet there might have been plenty of material for such claims given Razaleigh's substantial private wealth (Razaleigh had large real estate holdings in Kelantan's capital, Kota Bahru, for example, although he is believed to have sold many of his assets to fund his political ambitions) and descriptions of him in his earlier years, particularly in the foreign press, as a *bon vivant*.

Indeed, at the time of Anwar's rumoured firing and ultimate arrest, relatively few senior figures in Malaysia expressed any overt displays of support for him. One of the few senior members of the government to call on Anwar at his house was Domestic Trade and Consumer Affairs Minister, Muhyiddin Yassin (who was elected an UMNO vice president at the 2000 UMNO elections after having last held the position in 1993).

I asked Daim if he felt that Anwar was guilty of corruption whereby he had attempted to have witnesses change their statements, and sodomy, which was the specific sexual impropriety charge against him. He replied that after having read the evidence and witnesses' affidavits, he did feel that Anwar was guilty, but the question was something for the courts to decide. I asked him if he felt that it was appropriate in a modern country such as Malaysia for sodomy to be a criminal offence. After some hesitation, he replied that sodomy was both 'sinful and criminal', so yes, it should remain a criminal offence in Malaysia. Aside from the apparent criminal aspects of Anwar's behaviour, to Daim, Anwar's main transgression was 'hypocrisy' – he had held himself up as a pious Muslim but had behaved quite differently.

The Turmoil Intensifies

According to Daim, prior to Mahathir's decision to fire Anwar, Mahathir called a meeting of the various UMNO Menteri Besars and briefed them on the sodomy allegations. The consensus apparently was that Anwar should be fired and charged. But Daim felt that the order was wrong. Anwar should be charged and then fired, and he told Mahathir so. He argued that it would be better if Anwar was arrested immediately, which he felt would destroy Anwar's credibility. But Mahathir ignored the advice and instead – according to Daim – precious time was lost. Partly, Daim says, the delay in Anwar's arrest was due to the police, who had decided that Anwar should not be arrested while the Commonwealth Games were still being staged in Kuala Lumpur. To do so then would have provoked serious civil disobedience and security problems. When the police did detain Anwar, they initially did so under the Internal Security Act (ISA). It was another misstep. That, alone, provoked howls of outrage. Mahathir later said that the decision to use the ISA was the police chief's alone and certainly not his or the government's. The charges against Anwar after all were simple criminal charges; they were not political. Not surprisingly, many wondered, including many in the Cabinet, how someone could go from being deputy prime minister one day to a threat to national security the next? Plainly, it was ridiculous.

Anwar, on hearing that Mahathir was about to move against him, confronted Mahathir, who told him that he should resign. Anwar asked for a week to think about it. Then, having decided that he would not resign, Mahathir fired him. The time between Anwar's sacking and his eventual arrest allowed him to galvanise support – the very thing that Daim had feared would happen. Daim said to me that, in his view, the whole affair of Anwar's dismissal from the government was 'mishandled'. The delay in arresting Anwar cost 'Mahathir, the government and Malaysia' dearly, Daim believes. It allowed Anwar to state his case before the international media and to organise his supporters. Lee Kuan Yew, on his first visit to Malaysia in ten years in August 2000, echoed Daim's views during a media conference in Kuala Lumpur that the Malaysian government had mishandled the Anwar episode. 'It was an unmitigated disaster, and I felt more sorry for Dr Mahathir than I felt for Anwar,' Lee said.[1]

I wondered if the police might not have been too hard on protesters during the so-called *Reformasi* protests in Kuala Lumpur of 1998 and 1999. Certainly the protests and the police aggression did not look good on television and inevitably led to the false impression that all of Kuala Lumpur was in uproar. But no, to Daim, the protesters were engaging in unlawful and aggressive behaviour and the treatment meted out to them was appropriate.

---

1   'Singapore's Lee, on Malaysia visit, criticizes blunders in Anwar case', *Asian Wall Street Journal*, 18 August 2000.

Additionally, he believed that Indonesian supporters of Anwar played a role in stirring up the protests. He claims that supporters of Indonesian Islamic politician Amien Rais went to Malaysia and trained some of Anwar's supporters in civil disobedience methods. There is no doubt of Rais's support for Anwar. He was quoted in the media as saying that 'the Malaysian Government should treat Anwar Ibrahim as a political detainee and no longer as a common criminal'.[2] (Today, Daim wonders whether the support Anwar has received from the Indonesians is misplaced. He claims that when the IMF refused to pay Indonesia its first installment of emergency loans during the economic crisis, senior members of the Indonesian government telephoned Anwar and asked him to intervene with the IMF on Indonesia's behalf. Daim says that Anwar refused to help, but that Mahathir later spoke with the IMF on Indonesia's behalf instead.)

The Indonesia link has some measure of truth. Anwar did have close links to the Indonesian Association of Intellectuals (ICMI) prior to his arrest. After his arrest, several of his close aides left Malaysia and went into hiding in Indonesia. The main Islamic party in Indonesia, the PPP, and one of its cadre, Nasir Tamara, (a personal acquaintance of Anwar's), organised street protests in Jakarta in support of Anwar. On 13 May 2000, Wan Azizah, Anwar's wife who by then had taken his seat in the Malaysian Parliament, had a breakfast meeting with President Abdurraman Wahid while she was in Jakarta to give a speech at a conference organised by the Council of Asian Liberals and Democrats (a conference that I also spoke at). Wan Azizah's meeting with Wahid was evidently a good one. She returned to the conference looking particularly triumphant. While in Jakarta, Wan Azizah also met with Amien Rais, who by then was the chairman of Indonesia's People's Consultative Assembly.

Perhaps the most traumatic event of the whole Anwar saga was when he appeared in court with a black eye. Daim said that the beating that Anwar was given by the inspector general of police, Abdul Rahim Noor, while in custody, which led to the black eye, was 'terrible'. He was appalled, as were other senior members of the government. Anwar 'should not have been treated in that way', but it also did 'enormous damage' to Malaysia's reputation overseas and gave the *Reformasi* campaign in Malaysia a rallying point. Daim remains incredulous that the police chief behaved as he did and then compounded it by taking so long to admit that it was he who was the perpetrator. 'Why did the fellow take so long to admit that it was he who had done it?' Daim asked rhetorically when we discussed the case. (The assault occurred on 20 September 1998 and Abdul Rahim did not own up to it until late February 1999. The opposition claimed the beating was all part of a conspiracy ordered by Mahathir. Daim, at least, genuinely didn't know who was responsible until Abdul Rahim eventually confessed. The beating was cetainly not ordered by Mahathir who was as surprised as anyone when he saw the results.) The black eye was a 'disaster', said Daim. In March 2000, the police

---

2   'Forced smiles in Southeast Asia, as relations turn sour', *International Herald Tribune*, 23 May 2000.

chief was given a two-month sentence and released on bail pending appeal. 'Was this too light?', I asked Daim. He merely replied that it was under appeal. 'Was Anwar's six-year sentence for using his position to have witnesses withdraw their statements too harsh?' Daim hesitated slightly – the look on his face seemed to suggest that he thought that it might be – but he simply said that it, too, was under appeal.

I asked then defence minister Najib Tun Razak if he agreed with Daim's observation that the Anwar episode had been mishandled, and he too was unequivocal. 'We all would agree with that; that we wouldn't get an "A" mark for the handling of the Anwar issue.' Najib, as had been Daim, was critical of the infamous mattress episode whereby the prosecution had an allegedly soiled mattress dragged into the court room to tender as evidence. 'The PR was appalling and the black eye was an unmitigated disaster,' said Najib.

Daim and Anwar

Daim and Anwar were close once. The latter was among a small group of confidantes that Daim consulted when Mahathir offered Daim the post of finance minister the first time. In turn, when Daim left the position, he recommended to Mahathir that Anwar take his place. Anwar also launched the book *Daim: The Man Behind the Enigma* when it was published in Kuala Lumpur in 1995. There are plenty of photographs of the two sharing jokes, talking and even hugging. It seems astonishing to see how far the relationship fell considering where it once was. What went wrong?

The problems between Daim and Anwar had their genesis when Daim was no longer in cabinet and was concentrating on his private businesses and Anwar was finance minister. The first matter of major contention was the sale of Hock Hua Bank in Sabah. It had only eight branches, a tiny customer base and a small assets base. Nonetheless, Daim had to pay M$90 million for it. The transfer price of all banking licences is set in conjunction with the Finance Ministry in Malaysia, and hence the finance minister, namely Anwar. Daim wanted a banking licence, but they were hard to come by. He was not particularly interested in Hock Hua's Sabah operations but more in the licence. As he says, M$90 million was 'far too much' to have to pay, but he had little choice. He complained to Anwar, but his response simply was that Daim could afford it. Why Anwar had any interest in the amount being so large is not clear – after all, the sum that was paid did not go to the Treasury but to the Sarawak-based Chinese owners of Hock Hua Bank. There is little doubt that the price Daim had to pay was high given the assets. I had a chance meeting with John Ting, Hock Hua's CEO in Sibu, a few weeks after the sale went though in 1997. He was clearly delighted with the price. A further aggravation for Daim would have come from the fact that the sale was completed just prior to the onset of the Asian economic crisis, which saw the already over-inflated price of Hock Hua Sabah plummet along with the value of other banks in Malaysia.

Another sticking point between the two men is much pettier, but seems to have been a source of annoyance to Daim. Anwar's official residence in Kuala Lumpur actually happened to be owned by Daim. Despite extensive renovations to the house paid for by Daim and requested by Anwar, apparently the rent paid for the house each month was just M$7,000. This was far below the commercial rate for the house, something verified in 2000 when Daim was able to rent it out to a businessman for M$25,000 per month. Daim says that he asked Anwar to pay more for the house, but he refused, saying that Daim was rich and didn't need the money. To add insult to injury, Daim claims that Anwar had another house in Kuala Lumpur that he privately owned, but which was rented out for M$15,000 per month by virtue of his occupation of Daim's house. To Daim, Anwar was simply profiting at his expense. Relatively trivial though the story might seem, irritations such as these can undo something much mightier.

There was an important policy difference between Daim and Anwar as well. Malaysia has tight provisions on who can buy a bank. Applicants must be practically free of debt, for instance. The broad rationale behind such restrictions is to prevent non-banking conglomerates from owning and operating banks. This contrasts with Indonesia, where, prior to the 1997-98 economic crisis, practically every one of the country's more than 200 banks was part of some wider, diversified non-banking conglomerate. Such a structure is a recipe for disaster, because such banks are then typically used to channel loans to their owners' non-banking interests.

Malaysia's banking regulations have tended to mean that its banks generally belong to owners whose main interest is in banking. The finance minister is empowered to grant exemptions, however, and that is what Anwar did as finance minister. The most obvious example of this was his allowing Hong Leong Group to acquire Hong Leong Bank (formerly owned by Khoo Kay Peng when it was known as MUI Bank). Hong Leong is Malaysia's largest conglomerate and had not been permitted by Daim to buy a banking licence when he was finance minister in the 1980s. (Similarly, Hong Leong Group in Singapore, which is related by family relations and some cross shareholdings to Hong Leong Group in Malaysia, has not been permitted a banking licence by the Singapore government despite its once strong desire to have one.) Other members of the Hong Leong Group in Malaysia included some of Malaysia's bigger companies, such as Hume Industries, Nanyang Press, Hong Leong Properties and Hong Leong Industries. Daim was completely opposed to Hong Leong acquiring a banking licence. He attempted to take it away in 1999 with his original bank merger plan that was ultimately overturned by Mahathir. Indeed, his first attempt at banking reform can be seen as an attempt to unwind some of what Anwar did to the banking system during his time as finance minister.

Anwar struck back at Daim after his sacking and imprisonment. In a police report lodged by Anwar in July 1999, and in his testimony of October 1999, Anwar claimed that Mahathir had fired him shortly after he had presented Mahathir with 'evidence' of 'corruption' of several senior ministers. In an affidavit made in 1999, Anwar accused Daim of receiving shares and cash worth as much as M$600 million during or prior to 1990 from Halim Saad, Tajudin Ramli and Wan Azmi Wan Hamzah. Anwar sought to imply that the money was an improper payment to Daim. Daim countered that the funds were simply donations to UMNO given to him in his capacity as UMNO treasurer. When I asked him about the payments, he claimed that the total amount was not M$600 million but a sum far less, and in any event the amount was pledges of shares rather than hard cash. He claims he told the three businessmen that UMNO did not want shares and if they wanted to donate them, then the shares should be sold and the cash proceeds be donated instead. This Tajudin Ramli and Wan Azmi did. But not Halim. Daim says that Anwar, while finance minister, forced Halim to give up several of his key assets, and claims that, consequently, an annoyed Halim decided to withdraw his offer of shares or cash for UMNO. Anwar, Daim says, knew this – in fact, the letters were all copied to Anwar – but he still went ahead with a later affidavit that included details that Daim says are completely erroneous.[3]

Partly, the accusations backfired. Many wondered why Anwar chose to raise them only after he had been put on trial for corruption, which, in the case of those that related to Daim, was at least nine years after the transactions were supposed to have taken place. Also, Anwar had been chairman of the Cabinet Committee on Corruption since the time he had been Minister of Education. Surely a prudent finance minister and conscientious cabinet minister would have dealt with the perceived impropriety earlier? Furthermore, the allegations seemed to be easily rebutted by Daim. Daim, particularly, had been the target of rumour and innuendo over the years. The fact that Anwar was unable to come up with anything more substantial was telling, when he himself had been at the centre of things and thus in a position to know. Perhaps the upper echelons of Malaysia's government were more rotten with rumour than with corruption? Anwar seemed unable to demonstrate otherwise, despite the very powerful incentive for him to do so.

Notwithstanding the personal enmity between them, Daim is loath to directly criticise Anwar's performance as finance minister. While he is critical of Anwar's granting of licences and benefits to business groups that had not been favoured by Daim when he was finance minister, he has little comment on the policy direction and initiatives that Anwar took in office. He claims that he took little interest in what Anwar did as finance minister; the job was his and Daim felt no proprietorial interest. He did say to me, however, that had he been finance minister during the Anwar years, he would have taken advantage of the growing economy to embark on extensive corporate and personal tax reform. But he was at pains to point out that this is not a criticism of Anwar; he was simply stating what he would have done had he still been finance minister, rather than what necessarily should have been done.

---

3   'Financiers of the century: Daim Zainuddin', *Finance Asia*, December 1999/January 2000; 'Malaysia's Anwar alleges graft among top officials in Cabinet', *Asian Wall Street Journal*, 25 October 1999.

XIV

THE NATIONAL ECONOMIC ACTION COUNCIL – A MODEL FOR THE WORLD

The creation of the National Economic Action Committee (NEAC) was the principal reason for Daim being tempted back into the cabinet. He felt that a well-crafted and highly professional response was needed to solve the economic crisis that had engulfed Malaysia. The usual politicking and compromise had to be suspended while a comprehensive recovery plan was devised and put in place. The NEAC allowed for that. The professionalism and the power to do what Daim felt was required was vested in it, so he was content to assume the role first of special functions minister and then once more, of finance minister.

Plans for the NEAC's creation were first publicly mooted in November 1997. It was then established in early January 1998. It was tasked with identifying the most appropriate strategies to mitigate the impact of the regional economic crisis and of finding ways to revive the economy. Daim recommended to Mahathir that the NEAC be of finding empowered to act quickly and have special powers. But the cabinet felt that this might encroach on its authority, so the NEAC was made subordinate to cabinet. Daim believes that in reality this did not matter, as the NEAC was to be headed by the prime minister and if the NEAC felt that something should be done, this would be taken as the prime minister's wishes too. Accordingly, the cabinet would then provide quick endorsement of the NEAC's wishes. Formally, the NEAC was to be a 'consultative body to the cabinet to deal with the economic problems' and comprised representatives from various sectors. But informally, it gave Mahathir and Daim the firepower they needed to override the usual complexities of shepherding change though the government and the bureaucracy.

The creation of the NEAC allowed things to move much faster than was possible under the existing structure of government bureaucracy. Problems and suggestions were presented directly to the NEAC through the executive director (a position held by Daim), without passing through the normal government channels and lengthy approval process. If there were merits to the ideas presented, they could then be acted upon quickly with the full backing of the government.

The NEAC's formal objectives were to:
* restore public and investor confidence;
* ensure that the economy did not go into a recession following the decline in the value of the ringgit and the fall in the share market;

- revive the national economy and make it competitive globally; and
- strengthen the economic base of the country so as to achieve developed nation status through rapid and sustainable economic growth.

It comprised the council itself and several subsidiary bodies. The council had 26 members, including senior ministers, the heads of various peak business chambers, the consumer association and the public sector employees' union, as well as the Director General of the Economic Planning Unit (EPU) in the Prime Minister's Department and (the now late) Dr Noordin Sopiee, the chairman of the government-allied economic think tank, the Institute of Strategic and International Studies (ISIS) Malaysia.

Next, there was the NEAC Executive Committee, which comprised Mahathir, the deputy prime minister (Anwar and then Abdullah Badawi), Daim, the governor of Bank Negara (although according to Mahathir, 'for some reason' the governor did not attend a single meeting and instead sent the deputy governor[1]), Noordin Sopiee, the EPU director general, a senior businessman, and Dr Sulaiman Mahbob, the head of the NEAC Secretariat.

After the executive committee came the NEAC Working Group which was headed by Daim and comprised the former head of the finance ministry and later chairman of Public Bank Thong Yaw Hong, businessman Wan Azmi Wan Hamzah, ISIS deputy director Dr Zainal Aznam Yusof, and Professor Mahani Zainal Abidin of the Universiti Malaya. There were several other members, but their membership was nominal and it was this group that comprised the real core. Administrative and research back-up was provided by an eight member NEAC Secretariat. A communications team was also established to provide daily briefings to the media, and to respond to press queries and incorrect or misleading articles.

The real power resided with the NEAC executive committee and much of the work and decisions regarding policy initiatives was determined by the NEAC working group whose core was utterly professional and had Daim's trust. The Council itself met only occasionally to discuss general issues that required deliberation and support from the top. The executive committee and the working group met much more frequently. Indeed, the executive committee met almost every morning during the crisis to review the latest leading economic indicators. Data on trade performance, external reserves, interest rates, bank lending, retail sales, motor vehicle and housing sales, freight figures, imports, new business start-ups and bankruptcies, unemployment, job vacancies, electricity consumption and so on, were all examined. Formally, the Working Group met once a week, although meetings occurred nearly every day in the midst of the crisis and particularly when its consultative process was at its most active. Nominally, Daim was a member of the working group and he tended to chair meetings.

---

1 Mahathir Mohamad, *The Malaysian Currency Crisis: How and Why it Happened*, Pelanduk Publications, 2000, p. 28.

Apart from the decision to adopt currency controls (discussed in the next chapter), the rest of the top leadership, except Mahathir, was not intensely involved in the day-to-day process of economic crisis management. Mostly it was Daim, the executive committee and particularly the Working Group that monitored the situation and made recommendations.

The Practicalities of the Creation of the NEAC

According to NEAC working group member Zainal Aznam Yusof, the NEAC was established because Daim 'wanted a non-bureaucratic, independent viewpoint that he could tap during the crisis.' Daim, it seems felt that he could not get that from the existing bureaucracy, which, after all, is there to provide careful and prudent management in times of a steady economic environment. Daim wanted to be able to count on a body that was pragmatic, professional and concerned more with outcomes and less with the niceties of due process. There was no time to waste.

But how did Daim go about staffing the Working Group – his hand-picked economic swot team? Some candidates were obvious. Thong Yaw Hong had risen to head the ministry of finance in the 1970s and 1980s. He had worked with Daim before and the two had a good working relationship. Daim wanted Thong for his experience in dealing with Malaysia's last economic recession. Thong is an extraordinary figure, who has risen to the very upper echelons of the Malay-dominated civil service but also commands substantial respect from within the Chinese Malaysian business community, as evidenced by his chairmanship upon retirement of the Chinese Malaysian-controlled Public Bank. As a Malaysian who commands respect from both the Malay and the Chinese communities, he was, in the words of fellow working group member Mahani Zainal Abidin, 'an inspiration'.

Wan Azmi Wan Hamzah was also an obvious candidate because his business experience could provide a valuable perspective. His companies were not as badly affected by the economic crisis as were others and thus he would have more time to spend on working group matters compared with some of his business colleagues. At the same time he would be seen to have less at stake when it came to making recommendations on corporate debt work-outs and the like.

Mahani Zainal Abidin and Zainal Aznam Yusof were approached to join for their professional economic expertise. Zainal Aznam Yusof was a natural choice. He was well known to the government from both his role at ISIS and a tenure of almost 20 years at the EPU. He had also served as Southeast Asia regional economist at Kleinwort Benson Research (Malaysia) Sdn Bhd. When Daim was casting around, looking for suitable people to be appointed to the working group, he called Dr Zainal and asked him if he would like to help out. Dr Zainal later told me that Daim warned him: 'You won't be paid or anything like that'. Nevertheless, he agreed and saw it as part of his 'national service'.

But how did Professor Mahani come to join the team? She told me at her

Universiti Malaya office in December 2000 that she was approached for a role on the working group in early January 1998 and was called in for an interview with Daim. She had not even met him prior to that and didn't know quite what to expect. Having no idea how to prepare for the meeting, she decided to take along her résumé, which Daim glanced at with some bemusement. It seemed he already had a clear idea of her experience and expertise. Obviously, she was not part of Daim's inner circle, but with her appointment to the working group she suddenly found herself in the position of being a key adviser. It underscores Daim's desire for advice that was professional and which he could therefore trust.

The NEAC was given no formal budget. It relied on people who were seconded or who provided their services voluntarily. Professor Mahani, for example, was seconded to the working group full time from January 1998 to the end of 2000, and the Universiti Malaya continued to pay her salary during that time.

Bureaucracies everywhere like to protect their turf and those in Malaysia are no different. The NEAC was physically set up in the EPU within the prime minister's department. Separate rooms and offices were made by erecting new room dividers and so on. As might be expected, relations between the NEAC and the EPU required careful management. Initially, some of the staff of the EPU felt threatened by the creation of the new and seemingly alternative body. I asked Dr Zainal if there had been any significant problems between the two bodies. 'We were working to a very tight schedule…In that sense I guess we ruffled some feathers', he conceded.

Daim for his part kept the Working Group and the ministry of finance quite separate by providing each with specific and separate tasking. There does not appear to have been any great overlap or obvious rivalry between these two bodies. Often Daim gave the working group proposals that had typically been suggested or submitted to him. He would then ask them for their advice and comments. The suggestions came from all sections. Some were way out and others were useful, but everything was considered. Meanwhile, the ministry got on with the everyday tasks of keeping the government funded and running.

The National Economic Recovery Plan

The NEAC saw clear signals early on in its deliberations that Malaysia was heading for a deep recession. The preparation of a comprehensive national recovery plan thus became its top priority. The creation of the National Economic Recovery Plan (NERP) was an extraordinary feat. Although the Malaysian economy was in a rapid downward spiral, from January to July 1998, the NEAC working group managed to have consultations with representatives from 238 organisations and companies across Malaysia and with a further 24 individuals such as retired Bank Negara governors, prominent retired journalists, former cabinet ministers and important serving back benchers. The consultations with organisations and companies cut across a wide spectrum and included those from the agriculture sector, the automobile industry, the capital market, the real estate sector, entertainment associations, the foreign and local media, the higher education sector, labour unions, the hotel and tourism sector, retiree organisations and state economic development corporations. The pressure and the hours for those working on the NEAC, particularly in the lead-up to the creation of the NERP were enormous. Dr Zainal told me, 'For that period, it was very intense. There were meetings every day – we met hundreds and hundreds of people day in and day out, and all the while the economy was exploding around us.' Daim attended many of the consultations. According to Zainal, when Daim travelled as part of his NEAC work, he 'used to come back from consultations from around the states upset – many people did not seem to feel that there was a crisis.' The mood though was different in Kuala Lumpur. Many senior business figures were utterly shell-shocked.

The writing of the NERP was a combined effort by the working group and the EPU. EPU officials attended the working group's meetings and recorded its deliberations. They then went away and wrote the minutes up, and submitted them to the working group for comment and amendment. The NEAC secretariat provided typical secretariat services, but also was involved in note taking and drafting papers. The notes and the records of the consultations were developed into a series of some 30 working papers that were submitted, through Daim, to the NEAC executive committee. Committee members commented and made suggestions as they saw fit. Only one, a paper on financial markets liberalisation, was rejected in its entirety. The others were accepted, albeit with comments and some revision, and incorporated into the NERP.

The NERP was released in August 1998 and it contained six key objectives. They were:
- stabilising the ringgit;
- restoring market confidence;
- maintaining financial market stability;
- strengthening economic fundamentals;
- continuing the government's equity and socioeconomic agenda; and
- restoring adversely affected sectors.

Dozens of recommendations were made to support these objectives. They ranged from the broad and grandiose ('Recapitalise the banking system and in particular the domestic banks…') to the seemingly minute ('Increase non-aeronautical revenue by promoting retailing at airports…') No sector was left unanalysed and without suggestions for micro-economic reform. The NERP also recognised that Malaysia had an image problem overseas and said, 'There is the need to improve the image of the country both domestically and overseas. The government should consider using professional image and public relations consultants to project the country's image both domestically and overseas.' It is a consideration with which various interviewees with whom I spoke concurred.

The NERP was also critical of the performance of several sectors of industry (petroleum, for example) and public administration (particularly, state governments). It contained proposals for increasing the openness and transparency of government and regulatory agencies. It argued for the more timely release of economic information and for better tracking of the economic performance within and outside the government. It also called for improvements in the consistency of government policies through consultations and coordination.

Arising from these recommendations, the Securities Commission and the KLSE adopted measures to improve the regulatory environment. These are discussed in a later chapter. Other committees were established to explore further and implement NERP recommendations. Overall, the NERP meant that Daim now had a blueprint for reform – a road map for what needed to be done. No longer would the government's response to the crisis be reactionary, piecemeal or ad hoc. There was now a comprehensive framework. But first there was another matter. The NEAC had just delivered its NERP, but the working group was in for a surprise. While it was developing the NERP, the executive committee had been debating a policy initiative of its own: currency and capital controls.

XV

RADICAL ECONOMICS – CAPITAL & CURRENCY CONTROLS

Daim oversaw the floating of the ringgit during his first stint as finance minister and its fixing during his second. And he was happy on both occasions. Nothing could be more pragmatic than that. Senior members of Mahathir's administration debated the appropriateness of capital controls for more than six months, according to Daim, until they were finally introduced. Those involved in the debate included Mahathir, Daim, Anwar and NEAC Executive Committee member Noordin Sopiee. None of the discussants favoured the move at first, says Daim. 'We were all anti-currency controls.' According to Mahathir, one member of the committee came up with no less than 32 reasons why Malaysia should not attempt to control its exchange rate in the way that was being proposed.[1]

But as the economy deteriorated and the ringgit languished, one by one they became convinced that the controls were the right way to go. Mahathir was the first to decide that they should be tried; Daim fell into line shortly after and Anwar, according to Daim, also eventually agreed. His view was that they might as well be tried – he was happy to be convinced that they might work and he said that if they did, he would personally go to Indonesia to convince the Indonesians that they should impose similar controls. Capital controls had also been formally placed on the agenda of the executive committee, and for eight weeks, or more than 26 meetings, the committee debated the pros and cons. All the meetings and deliberations of the executive committee were tape-recorded, according to Daim, so that there could be no argument about who adopted what position and when. (Daim subsequently gave the recordings of those meetings to Malaysia's Islamic University to be part of the university's archival material.) At the daily morning meeting of the committee on 6 August 1998, it was finally decided that strong but selective currency controls should be put in place, but the implementation date was left open.

Discussion on capital controls was confined to the NEAC Executive Committee. The working group was not privy to the debates and discussions. Working group member Dr Zainal Aznam Yusof says that once the group heard that the capital controls were coming, the members' immediate position was that while they might well be useful, they should not be applied for too long.

---

1 Mahathir Mohamad, *The Malaysian Currency Crisis: How and Why it Happened*, Pelanduk Publications, 2000, p. 37.

Accordingly, they set about devising plans to modify the controls, to make them more workable, less administratively cumbersome and less intrusive. Zainal felt that the capital controls should have been implemented a little sooner, but as he told me, 'I feel that the pegging of the ringgit was at the right level'. The issue of repatriation tax was of the biggest concern to the working group members. It was especially clumsy to administer for fund managers. In due course, the exit tax was modified and ultimately abolished for funds kept in Malaysia for longer than 12 months.

I asked Professor Mahani if she felt that the capital controls had been implemented too late and that their effect was largely ambiguous as some had suggested. She replied that from her perspective, the capital controls were important for two reasons. First of all, they restored confidence in the economy – Malaysians could see that very significant action had been taken and that the government was re-asserting control. Secondly, the capital controls shielded the economy from the political unrest that was around the corner. The latter factor was a fortunate coincidence rather than the rationale for the prime minister's desire to introduce the controls. But like many economists, Professor Mahani did not give capital controls her full support. They were useful – Malaysia's economy was just too small for the ringgit to float complete freely she believed – but there needed to be a way to incorporate market signals into the exchange rate mechanism. Certainly tying the ringgit to the US dollar might bring more stability, but it also meant that its value would be determined in part by events in the US economy, which bore little relation to the Malaysian economy. For his part, Dr Zainal told me in December 2000 that he 'would maintain the peg for some time yet', which was indeed what happened.

The NEAC Executive Council and the Working Group were not the only ones that needed to be convinced about the capital and currency controls. According to the then Defence Minister Najib Tun Razak, the currency peg had almost no support among Malaysia's senior figures when it was first mooted by Mahathir. 'Most cabinet members were taken aback, when they first heard that the controls were to be introduced … It took us a while to come to terms with it.' But on the positive side, Najib told me that the view quickly became, 'Well, at least there is a decision, at least there is a policy'. Malaysia was facing a crisis like it had never faced before – any policy was better than no policy. It was like a life raft in a dangerous sea – grab ahold of it first and then examine the contents more closely after.

Off the Deep End

The controls were introduced less than a month later on 1 September 1998. As mentioned, Anwar was fired from his position as finance minister the following day and Central bank governor, Ahmad Mohamed Don, had resigned from his post four days earlier. It was widely assumed that he disagreed with the policy approach that was to be taken. Anwar had been brought around on the issue, but his relationship with Mahathir had by then deteriorated to such an extent that it was unworkable. In any event, he was soon to be charged with corruption and sexual misconduct offences.

From 1 September 1998, the ringgit was made non-tradable outside Malaysia and was pegged to the US dollar at the rate of 3.80 per US dollar. Ringgit held outside Malaysia had one month to be either converted to another currency or repatriated to Malaysia. Foreign investments were locked into Malaysia for a 12-month period. In February 1999, the government replaced that measure with an exit-levy system which was refined in a series of moves in 1999, culminating in September 1999 in a flat 10% exit tax on all portfolio investment profit, regardless of the duration of the investment. Malaysians were also only permitted to carry no more than M$10,000 out of the country. Reaction on the KLSE to the currency and capital controls was immediate. The KLSE Composite Index fell 40.21 points, or 13%, the day the announcements were made, a drop compounded by an overnight fall on Wall Street. However, after the markets had more time to digest the news, the KLSE turned around the next day with a 31.89 point gain that wiped out most of the preceding day's loss.

The government's move to demonetise the ringgit outside Malaysia was as much to target Malaysians as foreign investors. Daim claimed that Malaysians had moved as much as M$32 billion into Singapore at the height of the economic crisis, a clear indication of the lack of confidence that Malaysians had in their own country's financial sector. However, to a degree, such sentiments become a self-fulfilling prophecy. The more that money poured out of Malaysia, the more unstable the financial sector became and the greater the chance of the collapse of individual institutions.

That Malaysia's currency had been buffeted by speculators, and even short-sold to force down its value, there can be no doubt. It is a problem not unique to Malaysia nor to Asia. Australia, too, has experienced similar problems. Indeed, Malaysia and Australia share some important similarities. Both have roughly equivalent populations, and both have export bases that are heavily reliant on commodities and primary products. This was true in 2000 as much as it is still the case today. As such, the currencies of both in their free state are highly sensitive to international commodity prices and to the activities of speculators. The Australian dollar, as one of the most heavily traded currencies in the world, should be more impervious to wild swings in its value compared with the less-traded ringgit. However, even the Australian dollar is subject to swings that have little to do with the Australian economy's fundamentals. A case in point was what happened over the weekend at the end of January 2000. The Australian Bureau of Statistics announced on the Friday that Australia's main measure of inflation, the Consumer Price Index (CPI), had shown unexpectedly low growth for the quarter. This, of course, was good news. All governments and all central banks want low inflation. Coupled with a strongly growing economy, rising commodity prices and falling unemployment, the Australian economy had not been in such a healthy state for many years. However, that night, the Australian dollar recorded its biggest fall on international currency markets in three years, dropping US$0.03, or almost 5%, from US$0.6550 to US$0.6235. This when many analysts argued that a more appropriate value for the Australian dollar was US$0.665 trending to US$0.700, given that it was backed by such strong economic fundamentals. So, what had gone wrong? Simply, currency traders had sold off the Australian dollar on the expectation that Australia's central bank would be less likely to raise interest rates because of the good inflation result. Consequently, the expected interest rate differential between deposits in Australia and overseas would grow, meaning that fewer short-term funds would be attracted to Australia to take advantage of Australian interest rates. With fewer funds coming in, traders were betting that the Australian dollar would fall, so they sold off their holdings to beat the fall thereby ensuring that the prophecy would be self-fulfilling.

Thus, perversely, despite the Australian economy demonstrating its strength and status as a 'safe haven' for foreign funds by producing another low inflation result, the Australian dollar had not risen but had fallen substantially. Instead of a reward for its sound economic performance, the markets delivered Australia some punishment. It is a good example of how speculation-driven short-term capital flows can lead to some very peculiar outcomes. And for Daim, the worst case outcome was what Malaysia experienced in 1997 and 1998. 'We are of the view that we have been unduly and overly punished for opening our economies to capital flows. We have been punished for being market-friendly,' he said.[2] The question was whether the cure for this, such as the capital controls that Mahathir and Daim introduced in 1998, would lead to an outcome that was worse than the disease. Malaysia was about to find out.

Winners and Losers

Malaysia was universally condemned when it introduced its capital controls. Economists worldwide were appalled. Eventually, when the disaster that had been predicted did not transpire, many economists sat back and took a renewed interest in what Malaysia had done. In fact, what Malaysia had given the economics profession was a first class opportunity to observe an economic experiment from its inception to its end. Rather than collapse, the Malaysian economy fared rather well. World Bank economist Richard Newfarmer told an Asian Development Forum in June 2000, 'The current policy regime governing capital flows including interest payments is not distortionary and has been quite favourable to economic growth as the recovery has demonstrated.' It was quite a turn-around compared with the doom and gloom that the economists had predicted.

Within a short period of the introduction of the controls:
- exports continued to outstrip imports by a growing factor;
- foreign reserves ballooned;

---

2 Speech by Daim to APEC Finance Ministers Meeting, Langkawi, 15 May 1999.

- the manufacturing and the agricultural sectors, particularly, were boosted;
- domestic demand, particularly from private consumption, rebounded, as did consumer confidence; and
- Malaysian interest rates fell appreciably.

A mid-1999 survey of 151 manufacturers by the Federation of Malaysian Manufacturers found that 62% of respondents wanted the currency peg of 3.80 to remain. Not everyone was happy, however. 19.2% – mostly manufacturers who imported a large proportion of their inputs – said that they preferred a stronger ringgit, while 6.6% wanted the peg removed altogether.[3] The currency controls did not see direct foreign investment dry up. In 1999, among the prominent investors was Hewlett-Packard, which announced a decision to invest a further M$700 million into its Penang electronics operations, and Siemens, which announced another M$600 million investment for its semiconductor and electronics plants in Melaka and Penang.

Some of these positives might have occurred anyway. It is difficult to tell the extent to which the capital controls led to these outcomes. What is certain, however, was that the disaster that many had predicted did not emerge. From Daim's perspective, the most important and immediate result was that capital controls meant that Malaysian interest rates were effectively decoupled from international rates and could thus be manipulated at will without the risk that capital outflows would then bring about further falls in the ringgit. Thus the central bank was able to immediately lower prime rates. The new head of Bank Negara, Ali Abul Hassan Sulaiman, also favoured lowering rates. He had been appointed by Mahathir a week after the capital controls were introduced and had been the director-general of the Economic Planning Unit within the Prime Minister's Department from where he had overseen Malaysia's privatisation program in the 1990s, among other responsibilities. He subsequently blamed his predecessor's tight monetary policy in late 1997 and 1998 for restricting business activity excessively and causing the escalation in NPLs that led to the economy's sharper than expected contraction in 1998.

The flow of foreign funds from Malaysia after the 12-month period elapsed, during which time funds had to stay in Malaysia or face punitive taxes, was also much smaller than most had been expecting. Even Daim privately had expected more to leave than actually did. On the first day, just US$328 million left Malaysia. Mahathir was publicly triumphant. Daim, in his office attending to paperwork, was more sanguine. He felt that it was still early days. Nonetheless, on day two just US$78 million left and only US$50 million on day three. The cumulative total was much less than the US$10 billion that some had forecast and even less than the US$3–4 billion that Mahathir had been prepared to concede was a possibility. (Even the NEAC had publicly declared that US$5–7 billion would flow out of the

---

3 'Capital controls are boon to Malaysian manufacturer', *Asian Wall Street Journal*, 30 August 1999.

country.[4])

The ringgit peg allowed Malaysia to accumulate a large current account surplus, which saw foreign reserves increase to US$30 billion by October 1999 from US$23 billion a year earlier. In some respects, such a growth in foreign reserves was seen as a major plus of having a peg, but actually it was more limited than that. Such growth was due only to the ringgit being pegged at a level which saw it undervalued. Not every buyer of ringgit could find a seller, so the government was forced to step into the marketplace to supply the difference. It sold ringgit and, in so doing, accumulated foreign currency in exchange. By continually selling ringgit, the government in effect was creating new ringgit that otherwise would not exist. The risk was that this would lead to a rapid growth in the money supply and possible inflationary pressures. Inflation, though, did not seem to be a problem for Malaysia in the wake of the introduction of the currency controls. The January 2000 year-on-year consumer inflation figures showed an annual increase in inflation of just 1.6%. (Approximately 40% of the CPI was accounted for by prices of foods such as rice, flour, sugar and milk powder that the government deemed as 'essential' and thus regulated; but nonetheless, there was not a noticeable increase in consumer prices in Malaysia.[5])

There were other risks, too. An undervalued currency might mean that Malaysian wages become too low in terms of other currencies, leading to a skilled labour flight. Another risk was the crowding out of higher value-added industries with lower value-added ones, as the latter sought to take advantage of cheaper overhead and labour costs. But such problems would only become apparent in the longer term. The controls were removed in 2005.

It is difficult to say conclusively whether Malaysia's capital controls were successful or not, largely because we don't know what would have happened had they not been imposed. The main difficulty is that, with the benefit of hindsight, they were imposed as the regional economic crisis was close to bottoming out. But what the controls did do was to give the Malaysian government some breathing space in which to address economic problems and implement much needed reforms. Without them, the government would have had to continue to respond to the ever-changing external environment, which was beyond its control, rather than attempting to fix the problems in the domestic economy in isolation and with no external distractions. Daim's view is that irrespective of whether Malaysia's recovery was due to the capital controls or due to the region's recovery, and thus would have occurred anyway, the important thing was that Malaysia's recovery entailed 'minimal social costs'. This was the case especially when compared with the high social costs borne by the IMF-assisted economies due to the strict conditions imposed on them.[6] Indonesia is an obvious example where the social costs were horrendous.

---

4 'Clearing the air on capital flows, ringgit', *The Star*, 23 August 1999.

5 'Malaysian consumer prices rise less than expected', *Asian Wall Street Journal*, 18 February 2000.

6 'Daim on the health of the economy', *The Star*, 22 October 1999.

Debate and Analysis

MIT professor Paul Krugman argued that the controls were appropriate as a short-term measure, but that they should be lifted as the economy stabilised and recovered. The controls would then be kept in reserve if needed again. Said the *Asian Wall Street Journal*'s (largely critical) editorial of 2 September 1999, '… while most analysts are quick to agree that the controls had little to do with Malaysia's recovery, the fact that the measures have not wreaked immediate havoc with that country's economy seems to have put a dampener on any serious criticism of them.'

The reactions of the IMF and the World Bank to the introduction of Malaysia's capital controls were muted, but most suspected that officials of the two international bodies were privately aghast. Their reactions became more tempered with time.

The IMF conceded in its 1999 annual review of Malaysia's economy that IMF board members 'broadly agreed that the regime of capital controls – which was intended by the authorities to be temporary – had produced more positive results than many observers had initially expected'. The IMF directors 'commended the authorities for using the breathing space well, to push ahead with a well designed and effectively implemented strategy for financial sector restructuring'.[7] In August 2000, the IMF's new managing director, Horst Kohler, even went so far as to concede in a speech to the National Press Club in Washington that the policy was 'not so bad and in fact, was not a disaster to the economy'. The measures, though, should not be used 'indefinitely'.[8] There was a sense that the IMF was able to learn from Malaysia's experiment.

The controls exposed a significant policy divide between the World Bank and the IMF – two bodies that hitherto had always appeared to work in tandem with one another. The bank's senior vice president, Joseph Stiglitz, urged Asian leaders to shrug off 'the Washington consensus' and praised Malaysia for doing so.[9] Stiglitz said that the greatest 'wrong lesson' to draw from the region's emerging recovery was that the IMF's policies had worked. 'People say, "Look at the recovery that has occurred, that means that the policies that were put in place were the correct policies." Nothing could be further from the truth,' Stiglitz told a World Economic Forum East Asian Summit in Singapore in October 1999. He said the region had not been well served by the advice it had received during the economic crisis. The region's leaders, by and large, had not stood up strongly enough for their own interests. 'Many within the region know that the policies pursued entailed

---

7 'IMF says Malaysia may have been right', *Asian Wall Street Journal*, 9 September 1999.

8 As reported in 'Malaysia's control measures not a disaster, says new IMF chief', *The Star*, 9 August 2000.

9 'World Bank backs Mahathir', *The Australian*, 20 October 1999.

excessively contractionary macro-policy but their voices were not heard … I hope that the recovery … will bring with it a renewal of self-confidence that allowed the region to forge three decades of unprecedented growth, stability and poverty reduction, based not on the dictums of the Washington consensus but a deeper understanding of their own economies and societies.'

Stiglitz pointed to Malaysia's economic policies after it chose to ignore the IMF's advice and imposed capital controls. Malaysia 'deliberately tried to keep interest rates low. It imposed certain kinds of capital controls and yet its recovery is among the fastest of the countries in the region.' In an interview at the same time, Stiglitz said: 'Malaysia has done very well … These capital controls, these exit taxes, seem to not have had the adverse effects that critics have worried about.' Stiglitz said it was difficult to simultaneously reform the corporate and financial sectors. 'If you have a large number of firms that are in very bad economic shape, it's very hard to restructure the financial system because as those firms go bankrupt the banks get into [further] trouble.' This had been the experience of Thailand, which had largely followed the IMF's policy prescriptions. Stiglitz was not alone in his praise. Journalist Peter Alford, writing in *The Australian* newspaper, said: '… if any central bankers of any developing country with an economy open to the wash of hot capital haven't earnestly consulted Bank Negara about the mechanics of imposing capital controls in a crisis, they aren't on the ball. Not necessarily because they should do it, but because if they ever feel the overwhelming need, they should know how to do it properly.'[10] It had taken the audacity of Daim and Mahathir to impose the capital controls in the face of international opinion, but it took the professionalism of Malaysia's federal civil servants to implement them. And in so doing, Malaysia was able to provide the world's policy makers with a very valuable case study.

---

10 'Mahathir does it his way', *The Australian*, 22 October 1999.

XVI

IMPLEMENTING THE WORK
OF THE NEAC

M alaysia's reaction to the economic crisis contrasted with, say, that of Thailand. In Thailand the public relations were excellent, but there was too little action. Reform and restructuring stalled due to politics and vested interests. In Malaysia, the PR was terrible, but there was a lot of action. Many analysts had argued that the capital controls would be like a wall around the economy, that the Malaysian government would no longer need to bother with reform, and that the abuses of the past could continue unchecked. But they were wrong. Instead, the government used the breathing space afforded by the controls to undertake reforms that would not have been possible had the ringgit been freely traded. The shutters had come down, but the shopkeepers did not take a siesta. Instead, they set about refurbishing the shop. Very quickly, Malaysia leapt ahead of its neighbours in dealing with bad loans, writing down assets, recapitalising the banks, and so on. Daim used the crisis to push for a variety of reforms, and in this task he was assisted by the professionalism of the federal civil service. The East Asia Analytical Unit in the Australian government's Department of Foreign Affairs and Trade said in its 1999 report, *Asia's Financial Markets: Capitalising on Reform*, for example, that 'Bank Negara is considered one of the best regulators in Asia, renowned for its strict interpretation of rules and transparency'.[1] It was strong praise by one government's agency of another. These reforms made at the time have been of benefit to Malaysia even fifteen years on.

Danaharta, Danamodal and the CDRC

The foot soldiers in the government's fight to mend the economy were three agencies that were established in 1998. They were Danamodal, Danaharta and the Corporate Debt Restructuring Committee (CDRC). Danamodal was established to recapitalise financial institutions, as many of them experienced reductions in their capital adequacy ratios as a result of rising NPLs and withdrawals by depositors. Danaharta was created as a special purpose vehicle to acquire NPLs from financial institutions so that banks could be free to concentrate on banking operations. And the purpose of the CDRC was to help solve corporate debt problems through negotiations with creditors and debtors.

---

1   East Asia Analytical Unit, *Asia's Financial Markets: Capitalising on Reform*, Commonwealth of Australia, Canberra, 1999, p. 197.

The NEAC working group had been asked to examine the proposals, submitted by officials at Bank Negara, to set up the three bodies. After the restructuring agencies that had been established in the United States in the wake of the Savings & Loan debacle and similar agencies in Sweden were examined, the working group recommended in the NERP that similar agencies be established in Malaysia.

According to Professor Mahani, 'Dr Mahathir and Tun [Daim] were very good with Danaharta, Danamodal and the CDRC. They did not interfere. They wanted professional institutions with international best practice and they achieved this. Not once did they attempt to influence the workings of these bodies. Professional staff were selected and they were allowed to get on with their jobs and that is to Dr Mahathir's and Tun's great credit.'

At the time, Malaysia had some of Asia's most comprehensive insolvency rules, but they were rarely fully utilised. Even at the height of the 1997-98 economic crisis, the number of failed companies brought before the courts was comparatively low and certainly not commensurate with the numbers of companies in trouble. One reason why there were so few formal bankruptcies in Malaysia was because many troubled companies sought court protection under section 176 of the Companies Act, which allowed managers to retain control of their companies and to be protected from liquidation proceedings brought by creditors.

In January 1999, section 176 was tightened but still remained relatively sympathetic to debtors. The government introduced changes to stop companies from applying for restraining orders against creditors without the creditor's knowledge, for example. New rules required borrowers to submit a statement of financial condition, so that they could not acquire additional debts or dispose of assets during the period of the restraining order. In addition, to protect creditors' rights, restructuring companies were required to appoint independent directors to their boards, nominated by a majority of creditors, to oversee the restructuring process.

Rather than further tightening bankruptcy procedures, the Malaysian government chose to rely on the newly established CDRC and Danaharta. The CDRC was run by Bank Negara, and the then head of the Rating Agency of Malaysia, C. Rajandram, was appointed as its chairman. Companies in trouble could largely voluntarily apply to the CDRC for assistance, which would then develop a debt restructuring deal that had to be approved by the creditors.

Importantly, the debt restructuring agreements were voluntary and out-of-court. By mid-2000, it had resolved the situation of some 22 companies that had total debts of M$16.966 billion, and had another 23 companies with M$13.495 billion in debts still on its books that were in the final stages of being restructured. The majority of the 22 were companies listed on the main board of the KLSE. Approximately 65% of total debts were converted into bonds, while swapping debt for equity accounted for 14%.

Anwar had appeared more prone to allow major corporate collapses in the wake of the crisis than Daim, whose approach was, as usual, more pragmatic. Big bankruptcies by big companies might have been an appropriate punishment for bad management and provided a useful demonstration effect for other corporate debtors, but Daim felt it was a benefit that was not outweighed by the costs of unemployment and other social dislocation that would result. 'There is no doubt that businesses that are badly managed should be allowed to fail. However, there may be some grounds for government assistance for troubled industries and companies that fall under the criteria of national and strategic interests. This is also the practice in Western countries ... However, in seeking for a solution, the government is now taking a tougher stance to ensure that a well-considered market approach is adopted. There should be no "bailing out" of these corporations using public funds, while private investors and lenders must take their appropriate "hair-cuts". The decision of the Malaysian government not to issue government guarantees for Renong and the Central Bank's takeover of MBf Finance illustrate this stance,' explained Daim.[2]

The CDRC was designed to employ methods that the government felt were relatively painless to both shareholders and creditors. Some analysts predicted, though, that it would become the means by which the government would bail out its friends in the corporate sector. 'This accusation is completely baseless,' said Daim. 'Are we prepared to have these companies with growth potential fail and become bankrupt? Perhaps that is what some would like to see happen; bloodshed, suicides, thousands unemployed or forced to sleep on the side walk, as what has happened in a number of other countries affected by the same economic crisis.'[3] The CDRC thus formed part of the government's armoury to fight the economic crisis, while striking a balance between corporate and social responsibility. The IMF, Daim felt, erred too much on the side of corporate responsibility, an emphasis that was inappropriate for multi-racial Malaysia. It was a view that was later to be supported by the World Bank.

The CDRC worked swiftly and efficiently. By March 2000, it was targeting self-liquidation by the end of the year, signalling that Malaysia's economic recovery was well under way and that the CDRC had largely completed its work. It had received around 70 applications for debt workouts, mostly in 1998. Creditors were generally happy with the workings of the CDRC – largely because they were simply happy to get some money back. Without it, there was a strong possibility that in many cases they would have finished up with nothing.

The second vehicle for dealing with delinquent debtors was Danaharta, set up by the government to buy non-performing loans from Malaysia's banking sector. It purchased, with government-guaranteed bonds, loans from institutions whose non-performing loans (NPLs) exceeded 10% and were valued at more than M$5 million. It then developed debt restructuring deals with the debtors

---

2   Speech by Daim to the Washington SyCip Policy Forum, Asian Institute of Management, Manila, 4 March 1999.

3   Budget 2000 speech given to Parliament by Daim on 29 October 1999.

whose loans it acquired. To do this, the government gave the agency very extensive powers for dealing with debtors. If Danaharta recovered more than it paid for an NPL, it paid 80% of the surplus back to the financial institution. Sales of NPLs to Danaharta were technically voluntary, but banks that rejected a Danaharta NPL bid were required to write down the NPL's value to just 80% of Danaharta's offer. Another incentive for banks to sell their NPLs was that they could amortise the losses over five years.

Danaharta was given broad powers, making it, on the whole, more effective at restructuring loans and realising capital than banks. For example, ordinarily a bank was required to go to court to begin foreclosure proceedings, but Danaharta only needed to give 30 days' notice that it intended to foreclose if it considered that a defaulting company was beyond saving. Its legislative powers allowed it to sell properties after 30 days, thus preserving their value and it was also able to impose conditions on defaulting debtors to facilitate asset restructuring and rehabilitation, and to appoint special administrators to manage the affairs of distressed companies and develop a workout proposal to settle the debt problems of the company. The appointment of a special administrator came with a 12-month moratorium on the assets of the company in order to preserve their value. If Danaharta approved the workout proposal of the special administrator, the administrator could then call a meeting of the secured creditors to consider and vote on the proposal. A majority in value terms of the secured creditors was required for approval, along with the assent of the relevant regulatory agencies. The special administrator provided an option for maximising value through the use of skilled specialists to turn around distressed enterprises. Without that option, lenders would increasingly look to liquidation and holders of security would rush to enforce their security, which would bring down already weakened enterprises and erase their value. Overall, Danaharta's strategy worked extremely well and won much praise.

Its approach to asset management fell somewhere between that of a rapid disposal agency such as Thailand's Financial Restructuring Agency (FRA), which had also been established in response to the economic crisis, and a warehousing agency, which stores assets until prices recover, similar to what had been established in Mexico. Danaharta's approach of rehabilitating assets before selling them meant that it was able to achieve significantly higher recovery rates than the FRA. The Thai agency seized assets and sold them quickly in what was akin to a fire sale – something that was both traumatic and led to selling assets while they were still distressed and thus at low prices. Danaharta, on the other hand, was prepared to wait until the market had recovered before selling assets and, in the meantime, restructured them to improve their resale value. The management of more than 20 debtor companies, for example – many listed – including nine stockbroking firms, was taken over by Danaharta, which then set about restructuring them and selling their assets.

Like the CDRC, Danaharta moved quickly and efficiently. By June 1999 – six months ahead of schedule – Danaharta had largely completed its NPL acquisition plan, and had carved out a total of M$39.3 billion in gross NPLs – M$31.5 billion of this was from the domestic banking system. That represented around 35% of the banking system's NPLs, acquired at an average discount on face value of 57%. It had under its control almost M$10 billion from 66 financial institutions. By the end of 1999, the gross NPLs acquired by Danaharta had risen to over M$45.521 billion from 68 financial institutions. M$26.394 billion of the gross NPLs came from just two institutions – the Sime Bank Group and Bank Bumiputera.[4] Danaharta's mopping up of NPLs more than halved the NPL ratio to 7.9% of loans, which at the time was less than Singapore's rate.

The next task was to dispose of the loans. Part of Danaharta's function was simply to collect the debts of delinquent debtors and then sell them on to other financial institutions, leaving the debt recovery up to the buyer. By late 1999, Danaharta had restructured or disposed of M$17.6 billion, or 35%, of the total assets it had acquired. The sales included two tranches of foreign loans. The average recovery rates on those were quite high – 71% on the second tender and 55.3% on the first. Even the lower figure of the two was considered quite high by regional standards. Danaharta announced that it was 'extremely pleased' with the rate.[5] In March 2000, Danaharta held one of several property tenders. The property, held as collateral for NPLs acquired by Danaharta from financial institutions, involved 123 separate pieces of real estate valued by the agency at M$276 million. This and other such sales would eventually allow Danaharta to dispose of all its assets and recover as much as it could on the bad loans that it had purchased.

The third agency in Daim's recovery plan was Danamodal. Its job was to recapitalise Malaysia's financial institutions, by injecting capital into ten banking institutions in the form of Exchangeable Subordinated Capital Loans. These totalled M$6.9 billion, or 14% of the banking sector's total 1998 tier-1 capital, boosting the average risk-adjusted capital ratio to 12.7%, well above the then internationally accepted standard of 8%. The systematic purchase of large volumes of NPLs and the injection of capital into under-capitalised banks significantly reduced the potential for systematic bank failure. It allowed the banks to resume lending, which was an important part of Daim's strategy.

Among the institutions that had to be bailed out by Danamodal was Rashid Hussain Capital. Rashid Hussain had been one of the NEP's brightest stars. During the late 1980s and 1990s, he was awarded the brokering and financial advisory roles for many of the government's massive privatisations, allowing his company to become Malaysia's largest brokerage firm. Although he owed much to the government's patronage, he also brought a lot of skills and entrepreneurship to the table. Nonetheless, he had grown too big too quickly. As Malaysia's economy was enveloped by the region-wide economic crisis, Rashid attempted to save, and

4   'Danaharta hopes to restructure RM30b gross loans by June', *New Straits Times*, 1 March 2000.

5   'Danaharta recovery rate 71%', *Asian Wall Street Journal*, 25 February 2000.

thereby acquire, Sime Bank. Had it worked, Rashid's group would have emerged as one of the largest finance groups in the country. Instead, the deal went wrong, and ultimately Rashid had to be saved with an injection of capital of around M$1.5 billion from Danamodal.

Arab-Malaysian Bank, too, needed an injection of around M$1.5 billion to stay solvent. And in mid-1999, Danamodal took effective control of MBf Finance by subscribing to new shares offered by MBf, giving it a 77.9% stake in the company. The capital injection allowed MBf to meet capital adequacy requirements as well as staving off the collapse of Malaysia's largest finance company.

Although the banks were given ten years to repay Bank Negara, two of the recapitalised institutions – Sabah Bank and United Merchant Finance – were quick to repay their capital injections and had done so by October 1999.

Praise for Malaysia's three economic crisis agencies – Danamodal, Danaharta and CDRC – was plentiful and fulsome. A director of Dresdner Kleinwort Benson, one of the successful bidders for the loans sold by Danaharta, commented that he was impressed with Danaharta's handling of the auction in which his company participated and that 'Danaharta was professional and has a clear idea of its role in ultimately maximising recovery of the assets'.[6] A principal of Morgan Stanley was quoted in the media as describing Malaysia's bank restructuring program, involving Danaharta and Danamodal, as 'very elegant and well crafted, and has the potential to deliver the goods'.[7] Singapore-based Lim Say Boon of Crosby Corporate Advisory wrote in the *Far Eastern Economic Review*, '[Malaysia] has followed the textbook prescriptions – setting up a bad debt agency, a bank recapitalisation agency, and a corporate restructuring committee. Run by thorough professionals, the processes have been transparent and unrelenting.'[8] Daim, too, was happy. He said of Danaharta and Danamodal that 'their progress has been very commendable. Even foreign analysts and international agencies have acknowledged the speed and effectiveness of their operations, which had helped to stabilise the banking sector.'[9] Impressing Daim is probably even more difficult than impressing foreign analysts, so the performance of the agencies must have indeed been impressive. By late 1999, Daim was able to report to Parliament, 'The establishment of Danaharta, Danamodal and the Corporate Debt Restructuring Committee (CDRC) has successfully addressed the NPL problems, enhanced the capital base of the banking system and encouraged corporate restructuring.'[10] There had been no to-ing and fro-ing as in Thailand,

---

6 'Danaharta sells US$94.5mil foreign loan assets to 5 parties', *The Star*, 17 August 1999.

7 'KL's bank cleanup on track, but more must be done: S&P', *Business Times*, 18 March 1999.

8 S.B. Lim, 'Real change in Asia', Rethinking Asia column, *Far Eastern Economic Review*, 22 June 1999.

9 'Pace of financial reform has not slowed, says Daim', *The Star*, 23 October 1999.

10 Budget 2000 speech given to Parliament by Daim on 29 October 1999.

and nothing like the debacle of Indonesia's efforts to recover from the economic crisis. Instead, the efforts of the agencies under Daim had been clinically efficient.

Spending Up

From October 1997, Malaysia already had adopted a 'virtual IMF' policy for close to eight months. Public expenditure was cut by almost 20% and monetary policy was tightened repeatedly so that interest rates rose from single digits to more than 12%. Included was a drastic reduction of loans growth and the shortening of the default period for the classification of non-performing loans from six to three months. The central bank also imposed a maximum margin of 70% for consumer financing for the purchase of passenger motor vehicles, the maximum repayment period for hire purchase loans for vehicles was restricted to five years, and lending for new construction was severely curtailed. But these measures had worsened, rather than improved, the economy.

While examining the economic prospects of the country, the NEAC raised questions about the suitability of such measures. The reversal in fiscal and monetary policy came while the NERP was being prepared. Given the collapse in private demand and the onset of a credit squeeze, it was decided that the public sector should increase spending and ease monetary policy so that businesses could be sustained. It was the opposite of the standard IMF panacea, and many predicted that Malaysia was courting disaster. But NEAC working group member Professor Mahani told me that she believed that the NEAC's biggest success was to encourage the shift in the government's thinking from the IMF-type restrictionary policy to an expansionary policy. When the NERP was finally published it made the government's intent explicit. 'High interest rates are damaging for business and would not necessarily attract inflows of funds', it said. 'However, it is necessary to keep the nominal interest rate above the inflation rate so that real interest is still positive, and savers receive a positive return for their deposits so that funds do not go offshore in search of higher returns.' Accordingly, Bank Negara eased the three-month intervention interest rate three times in August 1998 from 11.0% to 9.5%. The hire purchase financing ceiling was also raised to 85%.

Daim took up the challenge to spend with relish. Having delivered seven budgets from 1984 to 1990, he had the opportunity to deliver the 1999 and 2000 budgets in the wake of the region-wide economic crisis. Those expecting cost cutting and even the stingy Daim of old were in for a surprise.

Budgets in Malaysia are formed by a budget 'dialogue'. The government and particularly the finance minister and his officials invite the private sector and other interested parties to make suggestions and proposals for what they feel should be included in the budget. The minister and his officials then sit down and do the sums to see what is feasible and what is not, given the government's own objectives. Additionally, each ministry submits its proposals for the year to the Finance Ministry, which then assesses what is possible or where cuts might be made. A draft plan is then developed and presented to the prime minister for his input. Daim, as finance minister, said he typically had two consultative sessions with Mahathir at this stage. In attendance would be Mahathir, Daim, the deputy prime minister and various government officials. The broad principles of the budget were then presented to the cabinet. On the day that the finance minister was to present the budget to the Parliament, the minister went to the Istana to brief the king on the budget's contents. Once the king had agreed in principle, the cabinet was then informed on the detail. For most ministers, it was only then that they had final confirmation of what cuts or expenditure increases their ministries were to receive. Then, at 4pm, the budget was ready to be presented to Parliament. Daim said the cabinet briefing on the morning of the budget's presentation was not always the mere formality it might appear. Occasionally, cabinet ministers objected to some of the contents, requiring that last-minute refinements be made before the budget was delivered to Parliament. It was a stressful time, as expectations had to be managed, and cabinet was not the rubber stamp dominated by the personality of Mahathir that many erroneously assumed. It was a complex forum of often competing interests. Ministers have constituencies of interests, not just their home electorates, that must be listened to and appeased.

The 1999 Budget announced in October 1998 was overtly expansionary. The centrepiece was a switch from prior year tax assessments to current year assessments for corporate tax, which effectively gave all Malaysian companies a tax-free year in 1999. The move allowed many Malaysian companies to enjoy unexpectedly high net profits so soon after the economic crisis, although no doubt some companies deliberately withheld profits from 1998 and booked them in 1999 to access the tax-free period. It was a marked contrast to the 'crisis' budgets Daim had brought down during his first stint as finance minister. Then, he had furiously cut back on spending, preferring to give little away. But as Daim has remarked, the problems then were different from the problems that Malaysia now faced.

If Daim's 1999 Budget was generous, then the one the following year was more so. His 2000 Budget, brought down in October 1999, forecast a 4.3% growth in GDP (after a 7.5% decline the previous year); cut personal income taxes across the board by 1%; raised the personal income tax-free threshold to remove 213,000 taxpayers, or 15% of the total, from the tax system; reduced import duties on 305 items; and gave civil servants a 10% salary rise. The move to lift the income tax-free threshold meant that a single person with a monthly income of about M$1,400 and a married person with two children with a monthly income of about M$2,100 would no longer pay income tax.

Overall, the budget incorporated a dramatic increase in government outlays of 28%, to M$78 billion.[11] M$53.4 billion was for operating expenditure and M$24.67 billion was for development expenditure. With revenue estimated at

---

11 By the time the 2000 Budget was retabled in early 2000 (on account of the national elections having been called, which meant that the budget could not be passed when it otherwise would), the growth forecast for 2000 was lifted from 4.3% to 5.8%. The revised budget figures also projected a government budget deficit of 4.5% of GNP.

M$59.9 billion, the budget allowed for a budget deficit of M$13.0 billion, or 4.4% of anticipated gross national product (GNP).

Not surprisingly, civil servants welcomed their 10% across-the-board pay rise. This and other benefits for civil servants led Siva Subramaniam, president of the Congress of Unionised Employees in the Public Services (Cuepacs), to proclaim, 'We never expected the budget to be so good. We are rather surprised.'[12] (The retabled budget of early 2000 extended the 10% rise to Malaysia's 400,000 pensioners as well.) Subramaniam's surprise was understandable. The last time Daim had been finance minister, he had called for a freeze on civil service employment and their salaries. Daim also mentioned in his budget speech the need to curb bribery. (The pay rises for civil servants would help with this.) Many thought it was unusual for the finance minister to so overtly mention such a topic in a budget speech, but it was interpreted as a sign of the government's seriousness on the issue.

As mentioned, Daim's apparent new-found generosity surprised many. Last time, he had cut spending and privatised. His policy prescriptions were a Thatcherite's dream. This time, he oversaw an enormous increase in government spending. The apparent fiscal conservative had become an overt Keynesian. Had Daim swapped sides? The one common thread running between Daim's approach in fixing the two crises was his insistence that interest rates be lowered and then be kept low. Credit is the lifeblood of an economy, and Daim simply could not see how any economy could be brought back to life by squeezing out its blood. The IMF begged to differ. But Daim hadn't swapped sides. He was simply being what he had always been – a pragmatist. He has never been one for ideology, being only interested in what works and what doesn't. As he explained to me, 'The recession this time was different because the private sector was in a much poorer shape. Companies had huge debts and the banks then refused to lend despite the fact that they had been bailed out [by the government] … After years of lending too much, the banks had gone to the other extreme.' Different times called for different policies and Daim, as ever, was satisfied to do what he felt was needed. The problem Daim encountered was mirrored in Europe in 2010 after its banking crisis. The banks were pumped up with government money but still they refused to lend after years of profligacy.

Tighter and Better-enforced Regulations

'Tun is a very strict disciplinarian. Rules are there to be followed and if they are not then they must be enforced', so said KLSE chairman Mohammed Azlan Hashim when I spoke with him in December 2000. The economic crisis also provided an opportunity to review the rules that governed corporate Malaysia. The crisis had exposed two problems: rules that were inadequate, and rules that

---

12 'Best deal for civil servants in 15 years', *The Star*, 29 October 1999.

were insufficiently enforced. Daim's reappointment as finance minister coincided with a tightening of the rules and their more stringent application. According to Dr Zainal Aznam Yusof, Daim was absolutely instrumental in shaking up Malaysia's Securities Commission so that it would be more effective and have more bite.

Accordingly, the commission decided to get tough in 1999 and in that year charged more than ten prominent corporate players with various securities infringements. Some of the alleged misdeeds had occurred as far back as three years ago and it was not clear why charges had not been laid before. Some alleged that those who had been charged were associates of Anwar and they were being punished for that. This was a ridiculous allegation. If crimes had been committed, then charges should be laid. The real question should have been why no-one had been charged earlier, when Anwar was finance minister. In any event, some charges were against people who had no links to Anwar whatsoever, and even a former Member of Parliament who had been a candidate to head the Gerakan party was accused of corporate offences.

Businessman Ishak Ismail of Idris Hydraulic and KFC Holdings Malaysia was among those charged. He was Anwar's former divisional secretary, and some suggested that that was the real reason why he was charged. Ishak had allegedly submitted a letter to the Securities Commission in 1996 saying that he had no equity in KFC Holdings between January and May 1996, a statement disputed by the Commission. In fact, Ishak was believed to be among KFC Holdings' biggest shareholders and when KFC Holdings transferred the ownership of an office building to another company, Idris Hydraulic, which Ishak controlled, not only was the transaction not at arm's length but KFC Malaysia received no payment for the building whatsoever. Clearly, the transaction seriously disadvantaged KFC Holdings' minority shareholders. The uproar that greeted the news pushed KFC Malaysia's share price down by more than 40% over the next month when the broader market fell by just 1%. KFC and Idris agreed to reverse the transaction, but there was one problem – Idris had already pledged the building as collateral for a loan.[13] The episode was a good example of the type of sloppy corporate governance that had played such a large role in promoting the Asian economic crisis. Arguably, Anwar's departure might have made charging Ishak easier. But that is not to say that the charges were politically motivated. Ishak quite simply had been associated with some of the most outrageous corporate manoeuvres seen in Malaysia. Not to have charged him would have been absurd.

The newly appointed chairman of the Securities Commission, Ali Abdul Kadir, responded to suggestions that the commission's newfound teeth were primarily aimed at former Anwar associates. 'As the regulatory authority for the capital market, we investigate people in the due course of our business program … If we find something that anybody has done in contravention of the acts,

---

13 'KFC Malaysia faces struggle to revive stock', *Asian Wall Street Journal*, 11 July 1998.

whether they are corporate figures or market players, we still have to charge them.'[14]

Other prominent business people charged in the crack-down included:

- Ong Weng Seng, the managing director of Associated Kaolin Industries. He had allegedly stated that M$26 million of the company's bond issue proceeds had been temporarily placed with a financial institution when M$5 million had already been utilised.
- Wan Muhamad Hasni Wan Sulaiman of Abrar Group. He allegedly defrauded investors in 1997 through an investment scheme called the Raya Fund from which he improperly channelled M$5 million to a citizen of the Sultanate of Oman.
- Soh Chee Wen, formerly of Promet Group. He was charged with defrauding Shah Alam-based Omega Securities in 1997.
- Tony Tiah Thee Kian of TA Securities. He was charged with abetting Soh.
- Low Thian Hock, executive chairman of Repco Holdings. He allegedly manipulated Repco's share price in December 1997.
- Benny Ng Wu Hong of Sarawak Securities. He allegedly devised a scheme to defraud Sarawak Securities that used phantom shares and false collateral so that the trading margins were wrongly boosted in 42 of his clients' accounts, thus avoiding margin calls. (He had been a member of the Kuala Lumpur Stock Exchange Committee.)
- Ismail Zakaria, the former CEO of Sime Bank. He was charged with four counts of breaching banking laws, in relation to loans of M$175 million, without appropriate authorisation from the bank's board.
- Joseph Chong, managing director of Westmont Industries. He was charged in February 2000 with abetting Westmont Industries to furnish a misleading report to the KLSE in March 1997 and was subsequently fined M$400,000. (Chong was a former government MP for the Batu constituency.)

Soh Chee Wen was among several Malaysian businessmen who disappeared overseas at the time that the Securities Commission sought to charge them and was placed on Interpol's alert list. He remained a fugitive until returning to Malaysia in 2002.

Others were charged, too. Abdul Murad Khalid, assistant governor of the central bank who had been responsible for banking regulation and supervision, was charged in September 1999 for breaching Malaysia's banking regulations when he failed to declare shares in 51 properties valued at M$24 million that he allegedly owned. A company called Ben Harta Sdn Bhd, whose shareholders were allegedly nominees acting for the former central banker, held the assets.[15] And in March 2000, Daim's parliamentary secretary, Hashim Ismai, told the

---

14 'Exchange crackdown hits Anwar-linked duo', *South China Morning Post*, 26 July 1999.

Dewan Rakyat that 16 companies listed on the KLSE had been given public warnings by the Securities Commission, and another company had been charged under the Securities Industry Act for producing a misleading statement. Hashim also said that a total of 622 remisiers had been 'suspended from service' on account of 'inappropriate' conduct in dealing with their clients.[16] The Securities Commission had a new head, and the finance ministry a new minister. Conspiracy or no conspiracy, it's a new broom that sweeps clean and, at the end of the day, those who had not done anything wrong had nothing to fear.

Was Daim happy with the number of people who faced Securities Commission-related charges during his second appointment as finance minister (especially given that very few were charged while Anwar was finance minister)? Not really. He said to me that he would have preferred the commission to take preventive measures, arguing that the fact that the commission had to press charges showed that it had failed in its job in the first place. While Daim acknowledged their professionalism, he would have preferred commission staff, and other civil servants as well, including those in his own Finance Ministry, Bank Negara and at the KLSE, to have had greater private sector experience. Because of this lack, Daim believes that they had insufficient direct knowledge of how business operates and how laws can be flouted. Thus they were hampered when it came to constructing preventive measures. Furthermore, the lack of business background meant that they had no network of personal contacts in the private sector to feed them information about what was happening and when laws had been, or were about to be, broken.

Daim argued that a big problem with charges laid by the Securities Commission was that trials were delayed and evidence was destroyed in the process. It is a view that was completely endorsed by Dr Zainal Aznam Yusof, whom Daim appointed to the commission in March 1999. Dr Zainal's main criticism of the commission was that its deliberations and reaction time were too slow. (Dr Zainal's appointment was a flow-on from recommendations of the NERP, which detailed the need for strengthening the commission's role.)

Daim also complained that the courts were not fully educated in the technical aspects of business and often failed to understand the nature of the alleged breaches. (I can vouch for this. I attended Malaysia's first insider trading trial in Kuching in 1997 at which the presiding judge consistently misheard 'call option' as 'cold option' before asking the court, 'What is the "cold" option?' Notwithstanding the judge's ignorance of basic stock market terms, she was empowered to find the defendant guilty and even to send him to prison.) Daim believed that these problems rendered charging and court trials inadequate. More resources needed to be devoted to preventive measures, he argued.

---

15 'New allegations could damage Anwar's image', *Asian Wall Street Journal*, 29 October 1999.

16 'Action taken against 17 companies under Securities Industry Act', *Business Times*, 14 March 2000.

Interestingly, during our discussions in London in 2015, Daim said that one of the jobs that he was never offered but which he would have liked in government was the position of Attorney General. 'Why?' I asked. 'So I could have brought charges against all those who should have been charged – all those guilty of corruption and other crimes.' It is a regret of Daim's that too many got away with too much in Malaysia.

Evolving Corporate Governance

Although Daim had said in speeches that poor corporate governance was not the only reason for the Asian economic crisis, a desite to improve the situation was sparked by the crisis. At the time, Deputy Prime Minister Abdullah Badawi said, 'Good governance and transparency are two prerequisites if Malaysia is to improve its competitiveness and inspire confidence.'[17] Daim concurred, saying: 'One can go to great lengths describing the damage caused by the East Asian crisis. But if there is any good coming out from the crisis, it is the sense of urgency to address the issues of corporate governance.'[18] As KLSE chairman Azlan Hashim said to me, 'Corporate governance is an evolving process. It's an issue for all countries not just Malaysia. Even in the UK reports have been issued aimed at enhancing corporate governance.'

Malaysia's laws to promote sound corporate governance were among the best in Southeast Asia, but that did not mean that they were near best practice by world standards. Furthermore, while the laws might have been relatively good, many directors appeared to be unaware of all their responsibilities. A joint 1999 study by international accounting firm PricewaterhouseCoopers and the KLSE that was released by the Securities Commission chairman found that only 13% percentage of firms knew that the prevention and detection of fraud were part of a director's fiduciary duty. A massive 89% of respondents were unaware that the whole board is ultimately responsible for the establishment of proper controls within the company. Another 43% of respondent companies did not have a formal channel where investor complaints could be directed and addressed.[19]

Arising from recommendations contained in the NERP, Daim established the Finance Committee on Corporate Governance to recommend best practices. Its report came out in February 1999 and must be among the most impressive of such documents to have been issued anywhere up to that time. The work of the committee and its 270-odd page report significantly raised the profile of the need for better corporate governance in Malaysia. The report contained 70 key findings

---

17 G. Roden, 'Free press missing from Malaysia transparency plan', *Australian Financial Review*, 27 January 2000.

18 Speech by Daim to the Washington SyCip Policy Forum, Asian Institute of Management, Manila, 4 March 1999.

19 ''Most of Malaysia's listed firms unaware of directors' duties', *The Edge*, 26 March 1999.

to raise standards, and to better protect the rights of minority shareholders. Said Daim, '… as we come out of this economic quagmire we should emphasise good corporate governance at the firm level. In the recent past, there have been many cases where "corners were cut" and rules were bent and there were other abuses, such as asset shifting, transactions with conflict of interest, and poor-financial monitoring. Increased concern of responsibility and accountability as well as transparency in the running of the business organizations as envisaged under our corporate laws and procedures have to be further adopted.'[20]

The economic crisis sparked a flurry of regulatory reforms, spearheaded by Daim, that would promote better corporate governance, transparency and disclosure. A new Securities Act with tougher penalties for breaches of securities laws, including a maximum of ten years and a fine of not less than M$1 million, or both, was introduced. Disclosure rules for banks were tightened as well. Also, despite Malaysia's repudiation of the IMF and its panacea, the country was among the first to commit to the IMF's Special Data Dissemination Standards System.

In January 1999, the government announced new rules that a person may be a director of a maximum of five listed companies and ten privately held companies. However, after some intense lobbying from business people, the government eased the rules in March 1999 to allow individuals to be a director of a maximum of ten listed companies and 15 privately held companies. The move was designed to:

- enhance corporate governance by enabling directors in listed companies to focus more on a smaller number of companies;
- help directors become more knowledgeable about the companies they serve while promoting a greater degree of professionalism; and
- minimise and subsequently eliminate the practice of directors sitting on numerous boards merely to lend their names and reputation to the companies without being accountable for and actively involved in running them.

During that same month, the KLSE announced new provisions for listed companies. Effective from 31 July that year, listed companies would be required to issue quarterly financial results rather than half-yearly results. The quarterly results were required to include a balance sheet, income statement and explanatory notes detailing the borrowings and shares purchased, and the status of corporate proposals that had been announced. Annual results would also have to be issued along with auditors' reports within four months of a company's financial year end.

The Securities Commission announced a month later, in late April 1999, sweeping new revisions to the listing rules:

---

20 Speech by Daim to the National and International Chamber of Commerce and Industry (NICCI) Luncheon, Malaysia, 8 July 1999.

- requiring companies that seek main board listing to have a minimum paid-up capital of M$60 million instead of M$50 million;
- tightening the rules on backdoor listing or reverse takeovers;
- new rules on profit projections for companies that want to list; and
- the listing of construction companies and trading/retailing companies to be restricted to the main board only.

In September 1999, Daim appointed a Capital Market Strategic Committee (CMSC) to assist him in developing a capital market masterplan. The Securities Commission chairman, Ali Abdul Kadir, was appointed to head the committee. The other committee members to be appointed were KLSE chairman Azlan Hashim, Francis Yeoh of YTL Corp, Federation of Public Listed Companies chairman Megat Najmuddin Khas, Mohaiyani Securities managing director Mohaiyani Shamsudin, Amanah Merchant Bank chief Yeyaratnam Tarmotharam, and Stephen Taran of Salomon Smith Barney. The objective of the plan was to address weaknesses in Malaysia's capital markets that were highlighted during the economic crisis.

The capital market masterplan was especially important, as Daim was eager to see the development of an active bond market in Malaysia and the plan would lay down the framework for that to occur. A bond market would provide an alternative to debt financing and lead to greater diversity in Malaysia's financial sector. Danamodal's large issues of bonds to recapitalise the banks helped to deepen Malaysia's capital markets, but more needed to be done.

One of the main impediments to the development of the bond market had been the lengthy approval process for the issuance of private debt securities. To speed up the approval process, the Securities Commission was appointed as the one-stop agency for the approval of private debt securities; this was an explicit recommendation of the NEAC working group. Until then, supervision of the bond market had been dispersed across several government agencies. A financial guarantee insurer was also established to help provide private bond issuers with an avenue to credit to enhance their bonds. Daim announced in his Budget 2000 address to Parliament in October 1999 the abolition of stamp duty and real property gains tax on instruments used in the securitisation of assets. He said, 'The development of the bond market will continue to be undertaken to complement the role of the bank as a traditional provider of loans in addition to reducing the dependence on the banking system. This reliance on the banking system can expose it to systemic risks. As long-term financing of the corporate sector is met through short-term loans, the corporate sector has faced problems of financing mismatches.'[21] The rules were changed to allow insurance companies to also purchase corporate bonds.

---

21 Budget 2000 speech given to Parliament by Daim on 29 October 1999.

Daim's view that Malaysia needed to develop a private bond market received support from Dr Zainal Aznam Yusof. 'The development of a private debt market is essential to corporate Malaysia's further development and modernisation', he told me.

Corporate Restructuring – Daim Lends a Hand

Refining the framework was not the only activity to occupy Daim in the wake of the economic crisis. The Malaysian government was well known for occasionally playing a highly intrusive role in the private sector, particularly when it involved large companies with big privatised projects or projects deemed to be of strategic interest. It was as if taking on such projects also meant being prepared to allow the government to step in if it felt that all was not going well. The economic crisis meant that Daim found himself directly involved in several high-profile interventions within the corporate sector.

After Daim became finance minister again, he had a hand in facilitating the restructuring of two large groups, Malaysian Resources (MRCB) and Multi-Purpose Holdings (MPHB). Both interventions were portrayed in the regional media as a purging of business people who were seen as having been close to Anwar. However, it was also the case that both groups were in serious financial difficulty and needed urgent restructuring.

The management of MRCB was reorganised so that it passed into what was seen as Daim-friendly hands. (MRCB owned at the time 48% of the New Straits Times Group, 43% of Sistem Televisyen Malaysia or TV3, 39% of Malakoff Bhd, 27% of Rashid Hussain Bhd and 64% of KL Sentral project.) Several Anwar-linked directors resigned, and Abdul Rahman Maidin, a businessman known to Daim, was appointed to the board. Next, he was appointed chairman and then it transpired that he had purchased 95% of the equity in MRCB's largest single shareholder. Abdul Rahman Maidin had been a member of the council of the Indonesia-Malaysia-Thailand Growth Triangle (IMT-GT) that was chaired by Daim. He was also a deputy president of the Malay Chamber of Commerce at the time and chairman of the Penang chapter, and a director of Medan Mas, a company that was awarded a licence in 1997 to broadcast television over the northern Malaysian peninsula.[22]

The government-facilitated takeover of MPHB also demonstrated the centrality of Daim's manoeuvring in the corporate sector. Lim Thian Kiat (or T.K. Lim, as he is better known) had acquired the company from the MCA in 1989 through his family company, Kamunting Corp. He developed it into a sprawling conglomerate, building it up in such a way that he personally owned very little of most of its subsidiaries. Using the classic pyramid structure of holding companies and cascading subsidiaries, he was able to control a great deal with relatively little

---

22 'No more delays', *The Edge*, 8 March 1999.

equity. In addition, a high proportion of the equity that he did have was borrowed. This did not stop him from having all the trappings of corporate wealth. There were chauffeured black Mercedes, corporate jets and speedboats. Ultimately, the group suffered from poor management and high indebtedness.

By the time of the Asian economic crisis, MPHB and Lim were in deep trouble. Shortly after Anwar was fired as finance minister (Lim and Anwar had grown close; notwithstanding this, Lim and Daim had once been close and their families had undertaken business projects jointly), it was announced that Lim was out of MPHB. Some sections of the media opined that his departure was on account of his links to Anwar. More plausible, though less sensational, was the fact that Lim had been given substantial favours by the Malaysian government, but had ultimately allowed his corporate position to deteriorate and thereby had not fully acquitted his end of the bargain. Faced with the choice of bankruptcy and possibly losing everything, or going quietly with some of his personal assets left intact, he opted for the latter, and a new management was installed at MPHB, one that was felt might do a better job.

Daim's account of Lim's departure provides a good example of how business can be done in Malaysia, with a lot of behind-the-scenes activity to secure a good result, but little transparency, thereby allowing outsiders to presume the worst.

Daim claims that in the middle of the economic recession, Lim 'fled' Malaysia although to where Daim isn't sure. Multi-Purpose was heavily indebted and Lim could not see a way out. Lim subsequently contacted Daim to say that he would return to Malaysia if he could be 'protected' from arrest and that he would tell Daim 'everything' he knew about Anwar. Daim claims he told Lim that he was not aware that he faced arrest, nor was there any evidence of Lim having done anything wrong, so he therefore could not see why he shouldn't return to Malaysia. As for Lim's allegations regarding Anwar, Daim says he told Lim that if he knew of anything that Anwar had done wrong, then he should tell the police and not him. Lim subsequently returned to Malaysia and gave the police a statement in relation to Anwar. Daim told me that he had no idea what information Lim had provided to the police, only that he had indeed made a statement.

Daim claims that Lim made it clear that he wanted to sell out of Multi-Purpose – he was tired of running the group – and that his departure was at his instigation rather than brought about by pressure from Daim. It transpired later that one of Lim's motives was that the group was sinking under chronic debt. Daim says he did not know at the time just how indebted MPHB was and that Lim certainly did not let on. Daim rang his contacts to let them know that Multi-Purpose was for sale. Lim wanted to sell the group to Quek Leng Chan of Hong Leong Group, but Daim vetoed this and said that Quek was not appropriate. (It is no secret that Daim is not an admirer of Quek.) Southern Bank, Genting and Ananda Krishnan, among others, were all interested in buying control of Multi-Purpose, according to Daim, as was local businessman Dr Chan Chin Cheung, so Daim advised Lim to talk to Chan. Having been so directed, Lim negotiated with Chan, the two agreed on a price and the deal was sealed. (Chan headed a group of seven investors.) Daim believes that Lim, suitably cashed up, then left Malaysia.

Daim gave Chan permission to take over Multi-Purpose. (Permission was required from the finance minister because the group encompassed a bank.) Analysts widely interpreted Lim's departure in terms of him being an Anwar 'ally' and thus no longer welcome on the Kuala Lumpur business scene, but equally, the indebtedness of Multi-Purpose meant that Lim's departure was inevitable anyway. Furthermore, a company owned by Daim's family had gone into a joint venture in 1984 with Lim and his family and some other interests. It was not as though Daim and Lim did not have any past connections.

Chan, a low-profile businessman in Kuala Lumpur, had been a director of Renong and was close to Daim. (Chan had controlled Renong and been its executive director until 1990. He was instrumental in the reverse takeover of UMNO's former key Fleet Group assets by Renong in late April 1990 – the assets were injected into what had been Chan's Renong.) But how did Chan obtain so much cash (rumoured to be as much as M$750 million) to buy out Lim's equity in Multi-Purpose? The regional media portrayed Chan as apparently having come from nowhere – apart from his connection with Daim. In fact, Chan is from a wealthy, old-moneyed family. The Istana in Kuala Lumpur, the official residence of Malaysia's kings, had at one stage belonged to Chan's family until they sold it to the state. And in any event, Daim says that he believes that most or all of the money to fund the purchase of the MPHB stake was borrowed from a foreign bank.

Chan, his fellow investors and their advisers then set about restructuring MPHB, which under Lim had grown into an unwieldy mess with little transparency, a confused tangle of cross shareholdings and chronic indebtedness. They broke the company into three groups: one that focused on stockbroking, another that was in banking, and a third that was involved in infrastructure. Chan then relinquished his posts at the group and other investors bought in.

So, the takeover of MPHB was not nearly as conspiratorial as some in the regional media supposed. Lim's departure was not so much because of his presumed Anwar links, but because he had run out of money, he was highly indebted and his business interests were on the verge of blowing apart. Lim had shown himself to be more an assembler of assets than a builder of them. His management was poor, and to ensure the survival of the assets in the group, it was best that he left. The group's involvement in strategic activities such as banking and infrastructure development guaranteed the government a role in deciding who would be permitted to take control. That allowed an entrée for Daim, who ensured that MPHB fell into hands that were not only capable but also politically friendly and would resurrect the assets to ensure their survival. It might not have always been obvious to outsiders what was happening at MPHB, but ultimately the group evolved into three more streamlined and focused mini-groups. As far as Daim was concerned, the end justified the means and, on this occasion, the end was a particularly good one. Daim did not force Lim out because he had been close to Anwar. Rather, he saved him from bankruptcy.

Another area in which Daim was accused of intervening but where the accusation was perhaps less fair was the Employees Provident Fund (EPF). It is Malaysia's sole pension fund and by 2000 represented 90% of the pension fund assets in the country. It was established in 1951 to provide pensions for most Malaysian workers and by 2000 had 8.2 million members (about half of whom were salaried workers who had to contribute 11% of their salaries with a 12% top-up from their employers; the other half were retirees). As at mid-1999, it had assets of M$145 billion. It was enormous – so much so that it had practically run out of blue chip investments within Malaysia. All investments were decided by a seven-member panel selected by the minister of finance which reported directly to him. Through this mechanism, the EPF had been used to bolster the stock market, and to buy bonds in controversial national infrastructure projects. The fund argued that this was sound, because most of the projects were backed by a government guarantee. Daim, however, claimed that, although he as finance minister appointed the panel, he did not seek to influence its investment decisions and was only interested in the bottom line at year's end.

Nevertheless, the *Asian Wall Street Journal* reported that the EPF deliberately sought to support the KLSE in 1998. Daim was unequivocal in his discussions with me that he had not instructed the EPF to use its funds in this way. Perhaps the officials were anticipating what the government would like to see happen (as officials in Malaysia so often do). He stated that his main point of disagreement with the EPF's management was over its policy of giving relatively high dividends. Daim said to me that he felt that the EPF should not announce dividends that were any higher than interest paid on deposits held with banks. Otherwise, excessive speculation would be encouraged on the part of EPF management as it sought to chase growth to fund the high rates of return.

In Recovery

By the end of 2000, the NEAC was still to be dismantled, although some parts had been wound down. The NEAC Executive Committee, for example, still met occasionally, but nothing like as frequently as when the crisis was in full swing. The NEAC Secretariat had been re-tasked to look at the issue of globalisation. Nor was the working group as active as it had been and largely busied itself monitoring the effects of capital controls and responding to media criticism of the government's economic policies. But, by and large, they had done the job they had been established to do.

Banking recapitalisation, said the Switzerland-based Bank for International Settlements (BIS) in its annual report for 2000, appeared to be gaining ground faster in Malaysia and South Korea than in the other Asian economies affected by the Asian economic crisis.[23] Both the South Korean and Malaysian recovery plans called for banks to sell their bad debts to government-owned asset management companies at large discounts and for public funds to be injected into under-capitalised financial institutions. The BIS also noted that Malaysia, rather than seizing assets and then selling them, took the time to restructure them so that when the time came to sell them, their value had increased. The government asset management agencies could thus achieve a higher cost recovery rate than otherwise, although the delay might mean the interest costs of the bonds issued to banks in exchange for the assets would be higher. But overall, the BIS was impressed.

Restoring Malaysia's banks to health was essential to restoring the economy. The currency controls had proved useful, too. Not perhaps because the ringgit's value was controlled *per se*, but because it was thereby maintained at a very competitive, if not under-valued, rate. Malaysian exports were well priced on world markets and correspondingly surged. They rose 30.9%, or M$8 billion, to M$33.9 billion, and imports rose 31.8%, or M$6.1 billion, to M$25.2 billion, in December 1999 from a year earlier. These figures were the highest monthly levels ever recorded up to that point. The strong export growth boosted the trade surplus by 28.5%, or by M$1.9 billion to M$8.6 billion comparel with the previous year. Malaysia's cumulative trade surplus for the full year was M$72.3 billion – the largest ever recorded. The economy also expanded by 5.4% in 1999 against a government budget forecast at the end of 1998 of 4.3%. Meanwhile, and perhaps most surprisingly, inflation declined from 5.3% in 1998 to 2.8% for 1999. The good news continued into the next year. Malaysia's GDP grew at an annualised rate of 11.7% in the first three months of 2000. It was the largest year-on-year gain since the first quarter of 1996, when annualised growth reached 12.2%. Manufacturing, which accounted for almost a third of the economy, led the growth, expanding at an annualised rate of 27.3% from a year earlier. The Malaysian economy was exceeding the already high expectations that had formed as the economy sprinted out of recession.

The promising economic outlook was reflected on the Kuala Lumpur Stock Exchange. The KLSE Composite Index hit 1,009.53 points on 24 February 2000, an increase of 284% compared with its lowest level of 262.7 points on 1 September 1998. The market capitalisation of the KLSE rose by M$551.18 billion, or 304%, for the period, from M$181.49 billion to M$732.67 billion. The market cooled in 2000 and into 2001, but it remained way above where it had been during the economic crisis.

The World Bank's chief economist, Joseph Stiglitz, claimed that Asia's recovery 'had to do with exports and not the [IMF] bailout'.[24] He claimed that those economies that fared best during the economic crisis were those that were most successful in retaining their credit systems. 'One cannot have a strong economy unless there is a flow of credit. The policies pursued in Korea and Malaysia to

---

23 'Bank for International Settlements applauds aggressive governments', *Wall Street Journal*, 6 June 2000.

24 'Banking official wary of crisis policies', *Asian Wall Street Journal*, 20 October 1999.

maintain the flow of credit rather than shutting them down were correct policies and played a strong role in the recovery.' He also defended Malaysia's capital controls. 'It was perfectly prudential for Malaysia to say, "How do we protect ourselves from this kind of volatility?" … In effect, [Malaysia] purchased some insurance. It turned out that there was no price for that insurance.' The controls also allowed Malaysia to keep interest rates low and thus keep credit flowing. They had not deterred direct foreign investment into Malaysia, because Malaysia had been careful to distinguish between short-term and long-term investments in how it applied its controls and taxes on repatriation. Stiglitz was not the only economist to support Malaysia's actions with the benefit of hindsight. It was easy to be wise after the fact, though; at the time that Mahathir and Daim introduced capital controls, practically no economist or analyst anywhere outside Malaysia openly supported their moves. It had been an enormous gamble, which had paid off.

Managing Malaysia's two economic crises was Daim's 'greatest achievement' according to then defence minister Najib Tun Razak. What was needed on both occasions was incisive and steady management and this Daim provided. I asked Najib whether it was possible that Daim had been given too much credit for getting Malaysia out of the morass it was in on both occasions. 'No', Najib said, 'I think he does deserve all the credit he is given'. Fine words from a man who himself was to become prime minister.

XVII

DAIM THE TUTOR

Each Thursday night, whilst minister, Daim held a prayer meeting in the *surau*, or small mosque, in the grounds of his Kuala Lumpur residence. Ostensibly, the meeting was open and anyone was welcome to attend. Certainly, security appeared to be minimal on one evening that I was there. The *surau* is small but impressive and has blue and green stained-glass windows with Arabic writing. I was in the company of about 35 others, several of Malaysia's most prominent Malay businessmen among them. Sometimes the crowd would be much larger. As one of the attendees mischievously observed, during the height of the economic crisis when many senior business people were labouring under heavy debts and wondering if they would survive, there seemed to be a marked increase in religious observance, as the crowd for Thursday night prayers at Daim's house swelled. At other times, the meeting would be dominated by worshippers from the surrounding residential area. After the 90-minute prayers finished, all the worshippers would file out of the *surau* and into its antechamber where a simple Malay-style meal would be served. A number of round tables were set up at which people ate, and a long trestle table held the various dishes from which people could serve themselves. The atmosphere was far from raucous. The diners would chat quietly and after perhaps half an hour bid each other farewell and leave. The Thursday night meetings brought together people with shared religious beliefs, but also there might be a heavy sprinkling of the Malay business elite, and among them, the Malay entrepreneurs that Daim helped to mentor, the entrepreneurs first described in Chapter 7.

High Profile Casualties

One of the most troubled business groups during the economic crisis was Halim Saad's Renong. It was hit hard by the crisis, having high debts and long-term investment pay-offs, which left it vulnerable to rising interest rates and a falling Malaysian ringgit. Its asset valuation slumped from approximately M$20 billion to around M$4 billion during the economic crisis, and total group debts blew out to M$20 billion – equivalent to around 5% of all the loans held in Malaysia's banking system. The group came very close to collapse and some analysts predicted its breakup. Its efforts to save itself required a lot of imagination. It stunned the market in 1998 when its cash-rich subsidiary, Malaysia's largest construction company, United Engineers Malaysia (UEM), announced that it had bought an almost one-third stake in Renong for the equivalent of US$700 million. Investors had come to tire of complex corporate manoeuvres on the KLSE that were often to the detriment of minority shareholders. Just when stock analysts thought that they had seen it all, a subsidiary listed on the stock market had turned around and bought control of its parent. It was not the sign of corporate rectitude that stock investors were looking for in such troubled times. Investors were further dismayed when they learned that UEM was going to have to borrow to make the purchase – and borrow heavily. The last straw was that the price UEM was going to pay for its Renong stake was 41.5% above the prevailing market price. UEM's minority shareholders were very unhappy. Renong's minority shareholders did not fare much better, because the government waived the rule that would have required UEM to make a general offer for all of Renong's outstanding shares, so they were unable to access the same high price that the sellers of the Renong stake were about to be paid.

Foreign fund managers – whose funds were among UEM's minority shareholders – were dismayed. They had noticed a decline in UEM's price prior to the announcement and had sought an assurance from the company that it was not about to be the target of asset injections from its parent, Renong, in a bid by the latter to raise cash. They were assured that this was not the case, so they raised their stakes in UEM, believing that at the then market price the company had been over-sold. But within a fortnight the Renong-UEM deal was announced. It was difficult to avoid the conclusion that UEM's share price decline had been due to insider trading by those who were aware of what was shortly to be announced.[1]

Amid much negative comment in the media, the government revoked the waiver that it had granted to UEM on being required to make a general offer for Renong's shares. It looked as if Renong's minority shareholders might be allowed to benefit in the same way as the large shareholders that had just sold out. The only trouble was that it would have potentially bankrupted UEM, which was hardly to the benefit of its minority shareholders. So, within a fortnight of the waiver being withdrawn, the government changed its mind again and reinstated it.

The impact of the Renong-UEM deal was cathartic. The KLSE, already hard hit by the Asian economic crisis, fell by almost 7% on the day the deal was announced and by another 3% the following day. Perversely, it was the good companies that were hit hardest. Many investors felt that they, too, might be cannibalised like UEM had been in an effort to bail out weaker firms. The securities chairman at the time, Munir Majid, said the deal 'rocked confidence in the KLSE as no other single corporate event did in the market crisis of 1997' and vowed to ensure that such an event would not happen again.[2]

Halim might have been one of those mentored by Daim, but that does not mean that Daim was impressed with all the manoeuvrings at UEM and Renong.

1   'KLSE suffers 6.8% blow as UEM deal draws flak', *Business Times*, 19 November 1997.

2   'Renong case shows Malaysia is learning', *Bangkok Post*, 18 March 1999.

That the KLSE fell so much in one day as a direct consequence of the proposed Renong-UEM deal was not lost on Daim. He made a point of describing the reaction on the KLSE during our discussions, his dismay clearly evident. The deal, it seems, was not Daim's idea – he was too busy attempting to save Malaysia's banks, which were in urgent need of recapitalisation to save them from collapse.

Daim told me that around that time, when it looked as if Renong might not receive the support of its creditors, he called Halim and told him that if the government was forced to bail out Renong (most probably via the government investment arm, Khazana National Bhd, buying a stake in the group), he would insist on Halim resigning from all positions at Renong and selling out his equity stake as well. Halim, says Daim, then took this option to Renong's creditors, but they insisted that Halim should not resign. Seemingly, they felt that one of Renong's prime assets was Halim's government connections. In their view, Renong would be worth even less without Halim. The irony of the market's assessment that Halim was both the cause of Renong's problems and indispensable to it because of his perceived connections gave Daim cause to chuckle during our discussions.

Renong finally applied to the newly established Corporate Debt Restructuring Committee (CDRC) for help and became its first high-profile case. A new plan was adopted whereby Plus Bhd, the wholly-owned subsidiary of Renong, would issue M$8.4 billion in bonds, without a government guarantee. The plan was not the government bail-out that it initially had promised to be, so it won praise from most analysts. Nonetheless, the state sector still played a heavy role. As much as 83% of the offer was taken up by local institutions, including the Employees Provident Fund and Petronas.

By the end of 1999, Halim announced that all Renong's non-core assets should be disposed of to reduce the almost M$20 billion in group debts, declaring that anything was for sale at the right price. After the sales, Renong hoped to concentrate on construction, engineering, highways, property development and transportation. UEM also announced a plan to raise M$4 billion from an initial offer of shares in its tollroad subsidiary, Plus Bhd.

Renong's telecommunications arm, Time Engineering, with M$4.5 billion in debts, was also placed under the guidance of the CDRC. The committee put the company's telecommunications assets up for sale, but Halim declared that the bids brokered by the CDRC were unacceptable. The assets were supposedly worth M$16 billion, but the highest bid was just M$1.48 billion. Halim decided on another plan. The assets, under the company's subsidiary, Time Telecommunications, were renamed Time dotCom and were separately listed on the KLSE. Time dotCom announced that it was to take on board Singapore Telecommunications as a strategic investor with a 20% stake. The deal was aborted after intervention by Mahathir (further discussed in Chapter 19).

Daim had invested a lot of political capital in Halim. And he seemed genuinely proud of him. Certainly, Halim had some spectacular early results. His completion of the North-South Highway defied many sceptics. Ultimately, the highway was one of the few assets in the Renong empire that earned significant money. But Renong was hit particularly hard during the 1997-98 economic crisis and provided the government with plenty of headaches. I asked Daim if he regarded Halim as a good manager. 'He used to be!' he joked. But on a more serious note, he conceded that after initial success Renong had grown too large making management control difficult. In the wake of the economic crisis, Halim himself acknowledged the need for paring down the scope of his activities – a move that met with Daim's approval. Halim was quoted as saying that Renong's expansion into telecommunications was hampered by his own lack of knowledge about the sector. 'I didn't know enough about this business,' he told reporters in April 2000.[3] I asked Daim if he was disappointed with Halim. 'He always comes and seeks my advice, but he doesn't always listen,' said Daim with the air of a proud but frustrated parent.

Another person mentioned by Daim as being hard hit by the crisis was Tajudin Ramli. Tajudin had acquired from the government a 32% controlling stake in Malaysian Airline System (MAS). With the arrival of the 1997-98 economic crisis his debt levels increased significantly, but the revenues fell for most of his companies. Tajudin sought to reorganise his companies to reduce the debt. One plan in 1998 to sell MAS aircraft to a new company and then to lease them back to the airline failed amid complaints from minority shareholders. The day the plan was announced, the price of MAS stock on the KLSE fell by almost 10%. Tajudin was forced to rethink his plans.

In May 2000, he announced new plans to restructure his private debts and those of his companies. Celcom would reschedule its loans, including M$1.75 billion owed to foreign creditors. Naluri Bhd, which by then had emerged as the new holding company for MAS, would retire at least 50% of its M$780 million in secured debts via asset sales over a two-year period. The remaining 50% of the secured debts would be paid through the conversion of Naluri warrants over the next five years. The Naluri deal was brokered by the CDRC. TRI owed US$532 million to its Eurobond holders, and MAS itself had debts of around M$10 billion. Tajudin was also in trouble with his personal debts of an estimated M$700 million and was forced to negotiate with the government asset management agencies in relation to these.[4] Daim encouraged MAS to find a strategic and equity partner. To ease MAS's plight, Daim raised the 30% limit on foreign ownership to 45%. Partly, he felt able to justify this measure because 9% of MAS was owned by the Brunei Investment Agency, which he felt was 'almost like' domestic equity.

Though proud of the achievements of those he mentored, Daim is happy to admit that they made mistakes. Tajudin had the ambition and the audacity that Daim wanted to cultivate among his fledgling Malay entrepreneurs, but as many commentators have pointed out, Tajudin, like Halim, expanded too fast,

---

3 'Changing lanes', *Far Eastern Economic Review*, 8 June 2000.

4 'Malaysia unveils corporate revamps', *Asian Wall Street Journal*, 16 May 2000.

which hampered management, and acquired too much debt. A lot happened in MAS that perhaps Tajudin was not aware of because he had to keep a watch on too many other business ventures. Managing both a major telecommunications company and a national airline – both extremely complex and fast-changing businesses – is something that few entrepreneurs anywhere have sought to do. By late 2000, Tajudin was willing to admit defeat and his controlling 29% stake in MAS was purchased by the government.

Daim agrees that Tajudin might have taken on too much too quickly, but he also points out that the saga of Tajudin's time at MAS is more complicated and less black and white than it might seem. Daim says that by the early 1990s, MAS under government ownership had become sluggish and moribund. Many of MAS' regional managers around the world had become comfortable in their adopted countries and some used political connections to avoid transfers. Year in and year out, the airline showed losses in its operations but managed to record profits from areas that had little to do with the actual business of carrying passengers. In 1992-93 for example, MAS recorded an operating loss of M$179.6 million but still managed to declare a pre-tax profit of M$157.5 million on the back of revenue from aircraft sales.

Mahathir particularly was tired of the airline's poor performance. It was decided that a buyer should be found for the government's stake in MAS. Tajudin was approached as a buyer because of his past experience in transportation. The existing share price was around M$3.50, but it was decided that the government's stake would be sold at a price of M$8 per share – the government wanted a big premium because its stake came with management control. Tajudin agreed and had to borrow massively to pay for the stake. However, according to Daim, Tajudin said that although he paid for management control of the airline, he did not enjoy full control. The government, and particularly the Prime Minister and the Minister of Transport, saw the airline as a 'national asset' and still reserved the right to impose on it all manner of non-commercial adjustments and changes. A prime example was the establishment of new international routes. The government would negotiate and request new routes to other countries for strategic and national prestige reasons and then expect MAS to fly those routes regardless of their profitability. Many routes were opened with the prime objective of making Kuala Lumpur's international airport the main hub in the region. That might have been a legitimate government objective, but it was not an appropriate role for MAS.

To help pay for all this, Tajudin sought an increase in domestic airfares but the request was knocked back for political reasons. Then, he wanted to cut staffing levels, but he was told he could not. The government had told Tajudin that it wanted a private-sector manager who would run the airline on commercial grounds but in reality he found himself regularly called into the Ministry of Transport to hear the cabinet's latest views and directives. Tajudin was the main shareholder in MAS, but the government effectively retained a 'golden share'.

Tajudin, however, was not blameless when it came to the governance and management of MAS. Certain transactions between MAS and companies later shown to be controlled by Tajudin's family did not appear to be to MAS' advantage. Nevertheless, it is definitely the case that Tajudin's hands were tied, and unfairly so, when it came to major management issues at the airline

When the Asian economic crisis struck, MAS and Tajudin were unable to withstand the sudden adverse turnaround in the business environment. Daim says he negotiated with Airbus, Swiss Air and KLM to see if they would buy stakes in MAS. But instead, the government decided that it would buy back the MAS stake from Tajudin. He was highly aggrieved that his hands had been tied from day one in his management of MAS and was now being blamed for all its problems. When it came time to agree on a buy-back price, Tajudin insisted that the government must pay a premium for control of the company in the same way that it had forced him to pay a premium. Daim says that he and Mahathir agreed that he would not be involved in cabinet discussions on the buy-back from Tajudin because he and Tajudin were friends. A price of M$8 per share was agreed. The Opposition and foreign media promptly portrayed this as a bailout for Tajudin. But Daim counters that independent advice from foreign investment houses suggested that MAS had an intrinsic value of at least M$8 a share. He is also critical of those in the government who said that M$8 a share was too high. 'If the government itself could not defend the M$8 price, then it cannot be expected that other possible buyers would agree on that price.' Thus Daim believed that elements in the government unwittingly or otherwise were damaging the potential value of MAS.

In the face of criticism of the buy-back from Tajudin, Mahathir gave the impression that he had not been fully briefed about the price and other terms of the deal. This annoyed Daim, who has retained correspondence between Mahathir and himself in the lead-up to the deal being announced in which both men refer to the terms involved. However, the buy-back was allowed to be portrayed as a bailout for Tajudin and Daim has remained adamant that it was not. 'How can it be a bailout when you end up losing the company?' Daim asked me rhetorically.

Cronies?

The economic crisis sparked off considerable debate about the efficacy of the government's policy of selecting Malay business people for fast tracking into the upper echelons of the corporate world. The foreign media particularly used the term 'cronies' to refer to the business people that the government had helped, a term that had in the past more commonly been associated with practices in Indonesia or the Philippines. At what point does a business figure cross the line from being well connected to being a crony? The term crony suggests impropriety on the part of individuals but should it be used to describe a situation that is a clear outcome of government policy?

Daim has endured considerable innuendo concerning his close friendships with prominent Bumiputera businessmen such as Halim Saad and Wan Azmi

Wan Hamzah. The insinuation is often that they hold shares in companies as nominees for Daim or his family. That same accusation has been made in relation to prominent Chinese Malaysian businessman Vincent Tan. Why a man who already happily acknowledges that he is privately very wealthy should want to use nominees is never explained. Daim does, however, acknowledge that he has been close to these and other figures and was important in their rise to prominence. In fact, when I asked him to nominate what he was most proud of during his time in public office, he replied that it was his identification and grooming of future Malay entrepreneurs.

Why was it necessary, though, to hand out so many contracts and privatisations without going to tender? Surely, if all such projects were tendered for, then the Malaysian government, and Daim in particular, might have avoided much of the criticism. Of course, one reason not to tender is to make sure that those who did end up with projects are friends of the government, or at least are not hostile. Furthermore, a completely open tender would not guarantee that the winners were Malay. Another reason for the tendency not to go to tender and perhaps a more benign view is that during the early stages of an economy's growth, there simply aren't enough local companies with a proven track record in infrastructure and other development to allow for a fully competitive tender. There might be plenty of capable foreign firms, but awarding contracts to foreigners is always fraught with potential political problems.

So, the rationale might be that it is not unreasonable to give contracts to local, but sometimes unproven, companies. How, then, to allocate contracts among local contenders? Again, there could be a competitive tender open only to locals, but if the criterion is only price, then many tenderers might be successful at winning the bid but might not actually have the capability to complete the task. So, then, price becomes only one of the necessary criteria. A proven track record would, of course, be desirable, but for a young, maturing economy, that might eliminate most, or even all, contenders. A tender could well be held in such circumstances, but it would not be competitive. At this point, the only viable way in which to select candidates for this or that project is to use subjective criteria. Personal connections then become important as a way to sort through possible candidates. People or companies are awarded projects because they are known to the government and, by virtue of that, the government has formed an opinion that they have the capacity (though perhaps not the track record) to carry out a particular project. And so it has been with the Malaysian government. Of course, this is only appropriate for as long as there remains insufficient local talent with a proven track record. Over time, as more tenders are let locally and more companies gain a track record, there is no reason why government cannot shift towards awarding more and more of its business on an open and fully competitive basis. Until then the government must tread a fine line between picking potentially capable contractors and engendering a culture of cronyism. There are no easy ways of determining when that fine line has been crossed.

Daim rejects the notion that his protégés are 'cronies', or that he has been entirely responsible for their careers as is sometimes alleged. During our discussions, he argued that his role has been over-stated. He concedes that most of those identified as his protégés had their start in business due to his intervention – perhaps they were awarded a contract or a privatisation deal – but after that Daim is adamant that they were left largely on their own. Any subsequent deals they might have done with the government were initiated by them. He says that after the initial project they might still come to him for advice and guidance, but that is as far as it goes. Many approached him during the 1997-98 economic crisis for assistance, but none can really be said to have been 'bailed out' by the government. Their proximity to Daim meant that they had the means to make the request, but not that it would be granted.

The entrepreneurs mentored by Daim maintained their friendships with him, but he did not structure their careers for them, nor did he tell them what project they should undertake next. As evidence, he proffers the number of times that Halim or others have made an important corporate move which he only heard of when reading the newspapers, or when he offered advice which was not taken. Certainly, there seem to have been numerous occasions when Daim has been privately disappointed or critical of a step that one or another of his mentees has has taken. Nonetheless, Daim conceded that it 'helped' to be close to him. He says that those who were, had the inside running for information about what the government was thinking and what it would like to see happen. This undoubtedly put them in a good position to bid for projects and contracts.

One Kuala Lumpur-based businessman offered an alternative view to me in late 2000. In the context of the problems at Renong and MAS, he compared the government's policy of offering projects and opportunities to a select group to the approach of a venture capitalist. In this instance, the investor picks perhaps ten new ventures in which to allocate his funds. The process is risky because the ventures are new and therefore untried. Of the ten perhaps only two will succeed. The fact that eight ventures might fail cannot be dismissed, but they must be seen in the context of the two that succeed and hopefully those two more than compensate for the rest.

For his part, Daim says that he was 'disappointed' with those Malay business people he had closely helped and nurtured, for their lack of anticipation of and preparation for the 1997-98 economic crisis. None made money during the economic crisis, he says, but more importantly, most had expanded 'too fast, borrowed too much and were over-confident'. Many did not acquire the management skills Daim feels they should have. Rather than consolidate their interests and manage, they were too busy expanding, so that the quality of the management of their existing assets suffered. Certainly, many Bumiputera business people had an unduly bad time in both the 1985 and 1998 recessions, which says something about their business acumen. But in their defence, it might also be the result of the types of businesses that well-connected Malays were typically given to run, businesses that tended to be capital- (and hence debt-) intensive infrastructure projects. They did not have the flexibility in costs that, say, simple goods or commodities trading have and, in which many Chinese entrepreneurs are involved. Then head of the Back Benchers' Club, Dato' Jamaludin Jarjis, went further. 'I'd rather not talk about Chinese and Malays so much as old and new entrepreneurs,' he said to me in late 2000. 'Many of the new ones happened to be Malay and because they were new, they lacked experience and capital so that when the crisis hit, it hit the new ones hardest and many them happened to be Malay. Being new, they had limited networking and experience to cope with the new conditions.'

Then Defence Minister Najib Tun Razak also supported the policy of selecting and promoting Malay entrepreneurs, but like Daim was critical of the conduct of some of those chosen. Najib told me in late 2000 that in his view, 'In a capitalist system you have to create wealth and wealth can only be created if you can find individuals who are business savvy...I think there's nothing wrong with the policy but if there is any specific criticism it is how the individuals have conducted themselves and how they've projected their public image...Perhaps some have not been as careful with public perception as they should have.' Projecting the right image is important to assuage public concern that the benefits and opportunities that they received might be unfair. Said Najib, 'It's easy to exploit such things because envy is a strong emotion.' Najib felt that a greater degree of humility among the selected Malay entrepreneurs might have been helpful.

Daim has also been critical of the attitude to business of many Malays that the government has helped, singling out the 'get rich quick' mentality for special criticism. In 1995, he said, 'The Government has done everything for them, even given them shares for investment. But as soon as the prices move up, these shares are sold. It is alleged that even before they get the shares or the licenses, some have already sold them to non-Bumiputeras'.[5] And, 'Too many went into business with the ambition of becoming politicians, though there seemed to be just as many who went into politics to be businessmen ... Those who know how to concentrate have been very successful. The opportunities are there. The Government has created an excellent environment for everybody, especially the Bumiputeras. It is up to them to accept the challenge given by the Government. No government in the world has done so much for its have-nots. If they fail they have only themselves to blame.'[6]

Five years on, Daim was still critical. He said to me that the 'get rich quick' mentality was no longer as apparent among the Malays, but only because the more difficult economic situation meant it was no longer as easy to get rich so quickly. He felt that the practice of awarding contracts to Malays who then sub-contract to non-Malays (the so-called Ali-Baba relationship) was still a problem in Malaysia. It was Malay women, he believed, who were the hands-on managers, whereas their male counterparts were more likely to want to 'act like real bosses,

5   M.S. Cheong and Adibah Amin, *Daim: The Man Behind the Enigma*, Pelanduk Publications, 1995, p. 123.

6   Ibid., pp. 123-4.

sitting around in air-conditioned offices and not getting their hands dirty'. It was also Malay women that Daim found more impressive and more entrepreneurial than many Malay men.

By 2000, there were rumblings in Malaysia that the NEP had been 'hijacked' by a small group of Bumiputera entrepreneurs, particularly those who were perceived as being close to Daim, such as Halim and Tajudin. The rumblings came mostly from young urban Malays who seemed to want more of a share of the spoils of the NEP. Daim's message to such young Malays is both simple and blunt. He believed their understanding of the NEP was 'shallow'. The NEP is not just about creating a few well-known Bumiputera entrepreneurs at the top, he told me. It is also about providing better hospitals, education and services in rural areas. 'If others are successful, you should try to emulate them and also be successful … For those who want to criticise, at the end of the day they can continue to criticise,' said Daim. Dato' Jamaludin, himself a successful Malay entrepreneur, said to me in late 2000 that he felt that too much attention and comment was being devoted to too few. 'Halim [Saad] attracts a lot of attention like a sore thumb but there are still eight more fingers after the two thumbs that get a helping hand…There are the success stories – it is those fingers that we have to remember to look at too.'

Daim's view that the NEP was about more than just the top echelon of Malay businessmen was supported by deputy director of ISIS Malaysia, Zainal Aznam Yusof. Dr Zainal cited some statistics that suggested that the economic gap between Malays and Chinese might have widened slightly in recent years. Twenty-five years ago, such a revelation would have caused enormous controversy. But today, such statistics are noted but do not cause the storm that they once would have. Dr Zainal saw this as evidence that regardless of this or that statistic, Malays do feel now that they have a far greater share of the economic cake. Thus, he believed that the NEP had been a success.

Nonetheless, no policy should be immune from critical analysis and some policies that might be optimum at one time might become less so as conditions change. Universiti Malaya Professor Mahani Zainal Abidin believed that the 'umbrella' concept whereby each Malay entrepreneur in turn created others relied on conglomerate business structures. Such structures, she contended, are now old fashioned and are no longer the most effective way of corporate organisation. She felt that it was now time for a wider group of Malays to be given opportunities to succeed in business. Dr Zainal Aznam Yusof also argued that, 'The nexus between government and business must go to the next phase…In the early stages, it was all about numbers, but now it needs to be about developing quality entrepreneurs.' The affirmative action program shouldn't be abandoned but, but more emphasis must go into developing quality entrepreneurs, believed Dr Zainal. 'Perhaps the policy has not been ideal but given the social needs it seems to have been the most practical solution', offered Azlan Hashim. 'The selection process needs to be based on merit – you must determine criteria for success and be careful in your selection process'. What each of these commentators suggested was not a wholesale tearing up of the government's affirmative action policies but changes in degree; shifts in emphasis.

But were the NEP and the government's other affirmative action policies a success in net terms? Daim believes so. There were some extraordinarily costly blunders, such as those that engulfed Bank Bumiputera with monotonous regularity. There was also a lot of waste, inefficiency and fraud, generally, which almost always occurs whenever governments take such a direct and intrusive role in the economy. But, as Daim argues, no country has ever tried such a degree of social restructuring in such a short period. There were bound to be errors and inefficiencies. The real issue is whether the costs of these exceeded the benefits of what was achieved. As far as Daim is concerned, the NEP led to some very obvious benefits. The significant rise in the numbers of Bumiputeras who graduated, the rise from 2% Bumiputera corporate equity to 20%, and the rise in the numbers of Bumiputeras who were genuinely involved in senior corporate management is beyond dispute. But the real success of the NEP and Daim's propulsion of a group of hand-picked Malay business people – and this is not to deny all the failures, the waste and the inefficiencies along the way – is that the policies gave Malaysians, especially those of Malay descent, a sense of self-confidence. They broke the nexus between race and entrepreneurialism and did so quickly. The perception remains that a top few, hand-picked Malay business people have been accorded enormous privileges. The privileges might seem 'unfair' by any standards. But what the government, and more particularly Daim and Mahathir, chose to do was to explicitly sacrifice fairness for expediency. Have the benefits outweighed the costs? The population of Malaysia is astonishingly splintered along ethnic lines and yet it is one of the most peaceful, multicultural nations on earth. Measured in terms of racial harmony, lifting Malay pride and enhancing social cohesion, most Malaysians might grumble about perceptions of fairness, but ultimately they answer in the affirmative.

XVIII

BANKING AND
STOCKBROKING REFORM

The reform of Malaysia's banking and stockbroking sectors was of great interest to Daim during both his periods as finance minister. The interest derive as much from his personal business experience, as from his position as minister. It is an area in which Daim achieved a great deal, but also one in which he failed to achieve all that he wanted. Some of the work that he undertook was reversed by Anwar Ibrahim while Anwar was finance minister, while some of what he wanted to achieve during his second time as finance minister was subverted by politics and vested interests. The economic crisis of 1997-98 gave Daim's zeal for stock market and banking reform greater immediacy. Reform in these areas was also an explicit concern of the NEAC.

Banking Reform

During the first few years of Daim's first stint as finance minister he had to rescue Bank Bumiputera after it lost more than M$2 billion, and deal with various crises at other prominent financial institutions such as Perwira Habib Bank, Supreme Finance, First Malaysia Finance, KL Finance, Kewangan Usaha Bersatu Bhd (KUBB) and Pekembarjaya. On top of all this was the failure of many of the deposit-taking cooperatives that serviced the Chinese community, particularly MCA members. Then there was the M$700 million collapse and bail-out of the Cooperative Central Bank, as well as constant problems among Malaysia's insurance companies. Undoubtedly, it was a searing experience. The country faced so many problems, and yet Daim found himself having to deal with one financial institution collapse or near collapse after another. Apart from mismanagement and occasional fraud, the problem was that Malaysia simply had too many financial institutions. By the time of Daim's second time as finance minister, that problem had little changed. If anything, it had worsened. New banking licences had been granted, and while the international banking sector had consolidated through massive banking mergers and acquisitions, Malaysia's had not. Thus, although Malaysia's banks and other financial institutions had grown, they were significantly smaller in relative terms than the giant American and European banks that had grown to become truly global.

By 1999, Malaysia's financial sector was in need of urgent consolidation. It had 21 commercial banks, 25 finance companies and 12 merchant banks. That so many banks and other financial institutions had to be bailed out during the economic crisis demonstrated why consolidation was needed. Bank Negara determined that there should be fewer and larger banks in Malaysia, so that the banking sector would be ready to withstand international competition in 2003, when financial markets were liberalised under a World Trade Organisation agreement. The government had spent more than M$60 billion propping up troubled financial institutions throughout the past decade, and Daim did not want to waste any more public funds on such bail-outs. 'We can't afford to save banks [only] every 10 years or so. That's why mergers are unavoidable,' he said.[1]

Bigger banks are generally safer. They have larger capital bases with which to withstand shocks. There are also significant economies of scale to be had in banking. It takes few or no extra staff or infrastructure to handle a US$1 billion transaction compared with a US$1 million transaction. So, larger banks tend to be much more profitable, in terms of return on net capital, than smaller banks. The other attraction of bigger banks is that they are more difficult for single individuals or families to control. This, too, makes them safer. It reduces the likelihood of a majority shareholder directing the bank to lend to his other businesses. Such related-party loans are dangerous because they are often done without appropriate risk analysis. (Bank managers might be simply ordered to make the loans for example.) If such loans become excessive, then the loan portfolio will become insufficiently diversified and more risky. As Bank Negara governor Ali Abul Hassan Sulaiman said in 1999, 'There is actually no more place for family-run banks to survive in the long run.'[2] He was right. Families tend neither to control nor to run banks in mature financial sectors, and the sectors are better for it.

The exception to the 'larger is safer' rule in the Malaysian context, though, was Bank Bumiputera. But then, Bank Bumiputera, with its government management and supposed social policy objectives, was a special case. It was one of Malaysia's largest banks but had a habit of stumbling from one crisis to another. By early 1999, it was technically insolvent for the fourth time in 13 years. The bail-out in February 1999 involved the government, via Danaharta, taking over almost M$6 billion in bad loans from the bank before merging it with the Bank of Commerce, a unit of the Renong Group. The merged entity became known as the Bumiputera-Commerce Bank. That latest bail-out brought the cumulative cost to the government of bailing out the bank to M$10.4 billion.

The government and the central bank had made it clear in the wake of the 1997-98 economic crisis that they expected to see mergers in the financial sector. However, almost none were forthcoming. Daim had become impatient and finally,

1 'Malaysia hurries bank mergers, raising discord', *Asian Wall Street Journal*, 6 September 1999.

2 'Rocky road to Malaysian bank reform', *The Australian*, 18 August 1999.

in 1999, he announced a plan whereby the country's 58 banks and other financial institutions would be forced to merge into a handful of large financial institutions.

Consolidation of the banking sector had been under way for some time around the world, so the Malaysian government was not out of step in wanting to see fewer and bigger banks. Most medium-sized, mature economies had only a small number of banks and these tended to be relatively large. And the trend is for further consolidation. By the end of 2000, Australia, for example, had just four major banks. Singapore too had four major banks and the Singapore government was known to be keen to encourage at least two of those to merge.

Six banks were hand-picked by the Malaysian government to be the 'anchor' banks. They were Malayan Banking, Multi-Purpose Bank, Bumiputera-Commerce Bank, Perwira Affin Bank, Public Bank and Southern Bank. The government then told the remaining institutions with which of the six they were required to merge.

There were sound public policy reasons why some of Malaysia's other major banks were not selected as anchor banks. The government, at huge public cost, had just bailed out RHB Bank and Arab-Malaysian Bank. To then reward the owners of those banks with anchor bank status would have made little sense. PhileoAllied Bank was under investigation in mid-1999 for possible breaches of legal lending limits to a single customer.[3] Thus it would have been difficult too make this bank an anchor bank in such circumstances.

An important policy consequence of the banks selected as anchor banks was that after the mergers had occurred, the association of Malaysia's major banks with conglomerates that had property and other non-banking interests would be significantly less. PhileoAllied Bank would be part of a larger bank and no longer associated with PhileoAllied Group's real estate and other interests, for example; and Hong Leong Bank would also be subsumed into a larger bank, and no longer be linked via common ownership to all the other members of the Hong Leong Group, such as its property, manufacturing and cement interests. Multi-Purpose Bank was no longer controlled by the Multi-Purpose Group but managed separately, and at the time of the original banking merger plan, it was expected that Renong Group's stake in Bumiputera-Commerce Bank would be sold – indeed, in March 2000, Renong announced that it planned to sell its entire stake in Commerce Asset-Holding Bhd, the parent company of Bumiputera-Commerce Bank.

The reduction of the exposure, and potential exposure, of Malaysia's major banks to non-banking affiliates would have significantly enhanced governance and prudence in the sector. Importantly, what Daim's bank merger plan would encourage would be the separation of shareholders from their institutions. Bigger banks mean that it is less likely that any given bank will be controlled by a single shareholder. Widening the spread of shareholders would encourage a greater

---

3   'PhileoAllied Bank under probe by Bank Negara', *Business Times*, 7 May 1999.

separation between ownership and control, which in turn would mean that banks more likely would be managed in a more professional and prudent way.

The merger plan was very bold. It upset the established order and, not surprisingly, attracted a lot of criticism. Some argued that Daim's original plan called for some of Malaysia's better managed and more dynamic banks to be subsumed by apparently less well-managed and smaller banks. There was some truth to this. But management personnel are transitory; the institutional and corporate arrangements within which banks sit are less so. The important thing was to further separate bank owners from management and to de-link Malaysia's banks from non-banking interests.

Despite the trend to banking consolidation around the world, Daim's plan became mired in speculation that banks with owners perceived to be close to former finance minister Anwar were not selected as anchor banks because of those links, and some of those that were selected were picked because of their alleged links to senior government figures. PhileoAllied Bank's owner Tong Kooi Ong, for example, was seen as close to Anwar and his bank was not selected as an anchor bank, but what was forgotten was that his bank was under investigation at the time for lending breaches.

The relatively small Multi-Purpose Bank, on the other hand, was under the control of business people who were seen as 'close' to Daim. Had the plan proceeded, then Multi-Purpose would have become Malaysia's second-largest bank after Malayan Banking. It was supposed to merge with RHB Bank (among ten others) which had an asset base five times the size of Multi-Purpose's assets. The small sizes of some of the designated anchor banks caused problems in that some of the owners of the banks to be merged were demanding cash for their equity. The banking arm of RHB Capital was possibly worth as much as M$5 billion and PhileoAllied was valued at M$1 billion. Both were expected to merge with Multi-Purpose, but the owners of both initially demanded cash from Multi-Purpose for their stakes. Multi-Purpose's assets base was less than M$8 billion and its cash on hand was just M$400 million.[4] Obviously cash payments would be out of the question.

Critics claimed that the plan would reduce the proportion of banks that are 'Chinese' banks – banks that are controlled by members of the country's Chinese business community, and suggested that this was the secret rationale. Eight, or 38%, of the existing 21 banks were controlled by Chinese Malaysian interests, compared with two, or 33%, out of six under the plan. An article appeared in the *Asian Wall Street Journal* in mid-1999 that portrayed Daim's merger plan in anti-Chinese terms, which further fuelled criticism. Daim protested that he was not anti-Chinese and that the merger plan had nothing to do with race. If he was anti-Chinese, he told me, he would have gone much further.

Apart from the racial and political connotations, real or perceived, two other aspects of the plan caused considerable consternation. One was that the

---

4   'Cash demands may scuttle Malaysia's bank mergers', *Business Times*, 29 September 1999.

mergers were forced. The second was the speed at which they were to take place. Memoranda of understanding between institutions setting out the broad terms of each merger were required to be signed by 30 September 1999. Due diligence reviews had to be completed by 15 November. Merger contracts had to be signed by 31 December. Approvals from regulatory authorities and shareholders had to be secured by 29 February 2000. And mergers had to be completed by 31 March.

Many analysts argued that the government was attempting to pick winners in advance, rather than allowing the market to determine the shape of things to come. Mahathir conceded the apparent arbitrariness of the plan himself. 'Well, that's an almost arbitrary figure that we've chosen – six banks – but it is not necessary that there will be six ...'[5] Furthermore, even if some of the complementarities between the entities to be merged were obvious, forcing reluctant parties to merge might have guaranteed failure.

Criticism mounted, but Daim remained steadfast. The government's overriding policy concern, he argued, was that Malaysia simply needed fewer and bigger banks to avoid the troubles of the past and to better prepare the sector for the future when they could expect more competition from abroad. As KLSE chairman Azlan Hashim told me, 'Tun is very mindful of the threat of globalisation'.

All financial institutions had to finalise preliminary merger agreements prior to 30 September 1999, a deadline that was actually met, although not without loud complaints from many of the existing owners of the banks and their supporters. Among those who were the most dissatisfied with the plan were three bankers whose banks had not been selected as anchor banks, Quek Leng Chan of the Hong Leong Group (which includes Hong Leong Bank), Azman Hashim who controlled the Arab-Malaysian Banking Group and Rashid Hussain who controlled RHB Bank. All three aggressively lobbied behind the scenes to have the plan modified or overturned. Azman Hashim was even reported to have made a tearful plea to Mahathir asking that he be allowed to retain control of his bank. Rin Khie Mei, a shareholder in Eon Bank and a good friend of Mahathir, was also said to have lobbied the prime minister. Daim remained unmoved. He insisted that there would be no deviation from the plan. He was especially adamant that banks that needed to be rescued by Danamodal should not be made anchor banks.

There was disquiet among bank employees, too, who were fearful of losing their jobs. Goldman Sachs estimated that the bank merger program could slash operating costs in the sector by as much as 20-25% through branch closures and staff reductions.[6] Accordingly, the National Union of Bank Employees opposed the plan, arguing that as many as 70,000 bank employees would be laid off.

---

5   'M'sia may have more than 6 anchor banks: Mahathir', *Business Times*, 4 October 1999.

6   As quoted in East Asia Analytical Unit, *Asia's Financial Markets: Capitalising on Reform*, Commonwealth of Australia, Canberra, 1999, p. 203.

To try to ameliorate such concerns, the government said that involuntary staff reductions would not occur; staff would be shed through voluntary departures and natural attrition.

With national elections due soon, the lobbying and the protests fell on fertile ground. Mahathir announced in October 1999 that the bank merger plan was to be 'reviewed' by the NEAC. Daim remained quiet on the likely softening of the policy. For him, any hint that the government was prepared to be more flexible would set off a round of even more intense lobbying from the owners of the 58 financial institutions.

A week later, it was announced that the forced merger plan had been dropped; instead, institutions would be encouraged to merge voluntarily. Institutions would be allowed to 'choose' their anchor banks instead of being told with which banks they would merge. Also, although the 1 April deadline was still in place, the government would no longer rigidly enforce it. Most importantly, however, the group of anchor banks was expanded from six to ten, with RHB Bank, Hong Leong Bank, Arab-Malaysian Bank and Eon Bank now being included as anchor banks. Rashid Hussain, Quek and Azman Hashim – the three who had so vociferously lobbied Mahathir – controlled the first three, respectively, and the last had Rin Khie Mei, who had also lobbied Mahathir, as a shareholder. Bank Negara's new target date for the consolidation of the sector was the end of December 2000. Ultimately, this date too lapsed, and most banks struggled to contend with the complexities of merging. Nevertheless, the government's plans triumphed in the end and today Malaysia has eight 'anchor' commercial banks: MayBank, Affin Bank, Alliance Bank, RHB Bank, CIMB Bank, Hong Leong Bank, AmBank and Public Bank.

The change of plan was significant given the fanfare with which the original one had been announced and the insistence of the government that it would remain intact. It was difficult to recall any other such prominent policy reversal in recent Malaysian political history. It also showed that there could now be a very direct relationship between lobbying and policy outcomes, with the three main lobbyists getting precisely what they wanted. There was also the inevitable talk of a possible rift between Daim and Mahathir, although both repeatedly rejected this. 'It's a decision made by him and me. The first decision was also made by us. So there's no conflict,' Mahathir was widely quoted as saying.

Stock Market Reform

Another long-held policy preoccupation of Daim's was the reform of Malaysia's stockbroking sector. An avid stock market player himself, he was directly aware of the local stockbroking industry's shortcomings. Corporate governance of listed companies, the behaviour of Malaysian stock investors and the institutional arrangements that underpinned the KLSE had all been the subject of Daim's speeches and policy pronouncements. He warned (not always successfully) Malaysia's listed companies of the perils of asset shuffling and related-party transactions. In a speech delivered at a lunch organised by the Federation of

Public-Listed Companies in May 1990, he said, 'In the past, there had been many cases of company failures due to dishonest management. One of the most common tactics employed by this category of management is the injection of assets belonging to the management into the company, commonly called non-arm's length transaction. Usually the assets to be injected are of low quality. The acquisition prices are also relatively high. In the end, the company concerned is saddled with a huge amount of debt which it could not service and eventually, had to be placed under receivership … This has to stop.' The message was quite blunt, but Daim went on to single out a particular sector. 'This injection of low-quality assets is quite common in property development companies.' He also said that trading should be based on 'fundamentals' rather than 'rumours'. 'There have been a number of instances in the past when rumour mongers have made their presence felt on the local stock market,' he observed.[7]

Daim also regards insider trading as a serious offence. 'It is cheating the public,' he told me, despite the view of some economists that insider trading is not harmful to the economy as it moves share prices closer to where they should be. The practice might be 'efficient' in terms of the functioning of the economy, but, according to Daim, it is not 'fair'.

On occasion, the KLSE has been prone to speculative bubbles, a point not lost on Daim. In January 1994 (by which time he was out of the cabinet), he advised in a media release that the stock market had become way over-heated and was heading for a major correction. 'We have reached a dangerous stage. Everybody is getting into the market. Everybody is busy on the phone. Nobody seems to work. Everybody talks about shares only. It will affect productivity.'[8] He again warned of excessive enthusiasm in the stock market in early 2000. The KLSE had again taken on the hue of a casino. In one week in January, the Composite Index surged by almost 14%. Daim was again quoted in the media advising investors to buy shares based on a company's fundamentals. He conceded that Malaysians were wiser stock market investors than before, but that they needed to be mindful that stocks can fall as well as rise in price.[9]

Of course, the irony in Daim's admonishing stock investors for following rumours and for excessive enthusiasm is that in the past, particularly in the late 1980s and early 1990s, he himself was at the centre of many of the rumours, unwittingly or not. As was mentioned in Chapter 4, suggestions that he was behind this or that stock at once sent its price soaring, something which, as mentioned, he considered 'a nuisance'.

Daim's appraisal of stockbroking in Malaysia was on occasions typically blunt. For example, he said in a speech to a conference of stockbrokers held in Kuala Lumpur in May 1985 that their professional competence left 'much to be

---

7   As reprinted in *Daim Speaks his Mind*, Pelanduk Publications, 1995.

8   Ibid.

9   'Buy shares based on companies' strength: Daim', *The Star*, 21 January 2000.

desired'.[10] It is difficult to imagine the audience leaping to its feet with rousing applause on hearing that appraisal of their abilities. He then went on to say, and it is worth repeating at length, 'The stockbroking industry should rid itself of the general impression as mere dealers in scrips. At present, the professional competence of our securities industry personnel leaves much to be desired. A lot more needs to be done on this front ... stockbroking firms need to enlarge their capital resources ... the capital of some of our broking firms has not grown in line with increased capitalisation and turnover. Larger and stronger firms are needed to provide the professional research and competent advice and to be able to service large institutional clients with confidence. I view the need for stockbroking firms to increase their capital resources as extremely important and urgent.' Daim added in the same speech that '[T]here is substantial volume of trading of Malaysian stocks across the Causeway, a significant portion of which is undertaken by Malaysians. This constitutes not only a loss of commissions to Malaysian stockbrokers but also a loss of foreign exchange. The Malaysian securities industry should therefore seriously think of how it could successfully compete to bring home this business. At the same time, it should also provide incentives and facilities for foreign investors to trade on the KLSE.'

So, for Daim, the problem was not excessive enthusiasm of investors (at least not initially), but the capacity of the local stockbroking industry to service the growing demand for stock market investment. The proof of that was the enormous trade in Malaysian stocks in Singapore. Many investors, including Malaysians, preferred to do their Malaysian equities trading in Singapore because the stockbrokerages there were more efficient, competitive and reliable. Studies on the relative competitiveness of Malaysian stockbrokers were unnecessary. The market had made its judgment. Singaporean brokers had large capital bases and could handle large volumes of trade. Most Malaysian brokers, on the other hand, could not. Some had paid-up capital of as little as M$250,000.

The weaknesses of Malaysia's stockbroking sector became clear during the Pan-El debacle with which Daim had to deal early on. There were too many securities houses and they were too small. The collapse of Pan-El in turn threatened a number of stockbroking firms that did not have the capital reserves to sustain serious losses. Daim advised the brokerage houses to merge and to increase their paid-up capital. In the interim, he also awarded three broking licences to the country's three largest banks. The Pan-El debacle was the perfect justification to order such changes when otherwise the vested interests might have complained too loud and blocked reform. Daim turned the debacle into an opportunity for reform.

The day before his official retirement from cabinet in March 1991, Daim introduced a rule that limited the number of stockbroking firms listed on the

---

10 Speech by Daim to the 'Securities Industry in Malaysia' conference, Kuala Lumpur, 18 May 1985, and reprinted in *Daim Speaks his Mind*, op. cit.

KLSE to ten. Critics charged at the time that the ruling would protect politically connected companies that already included a listed stockbroker from additional competition. To some extent, this might have been one of the effects of the rule. However, it was also one way of ensuring that listed stockbrokers would be able to grow and be sufficiently capitalised to protect their clients, while ensuring, with ten listed brokers, that there would still be sufficient competition among the larger ones. Daim's successor, Anwar, lifted the restriction to just ten listed stockbrokers in 1995, one among a range of measures that had the effect of thwarting Daim's attempts to consolidate the stockbroking sector. By the time of Daim's reappointment as finance minister in 1998, the number of licensed stockbrokerages in Malaysia had mushroomed to an astonishing 64.

By early 2000, Daim again turned his attention to consolidating Malaysia's stockbroking industry, but the timing was not fortuitous. Daim's policy defeat over the bank merger plan was not a good basis upon which to try and force mergers in the stockbroking industry. The plan, which Daim announced in February 2000 as part of the reissued 2000 Budget, called for the consolidation of Malaysia's stockbroking sector to ensure that stockbrokers in future would be large enough and have sufficient capital to meet growing international competition. (The NERP had specifically recommended that, 'The current stockbroking industry should be consolidated through mergers, takeovers and closures'.[11]) The Securities Commission chairman said that within two or three years he expected to see no more than ten stockbroking firms, due to mergers and takeovers among the then existing 64 licensed brokers. Later, the government refined this to mean that the sector should combine into 15 stockbroking companies by the end of 2000. Brokers were required to combine with at least three rivals. The larger, consolidated brokers would be known as 'universal' brokers and be analogous to the anchor banks. Rightly, Daim observed that it was ridiculous for an economy as small as Malaysia's to have 64 brokerages.

However, this plan, like Daim's bank merger plan the previous year, was thwarted. Key players in the stockbroking sector appealed to Daim for more time and greater flexibility in the mergers. After his very public policy defeat on the bank mergers, he elected to pass the issue to the Securities Commission and let it determine whether the stockbroking merger policy should be softened or not. It agreed that it could be. Daim, resigned to the fact that it was now difficult for the government not to cave into other special interests in the wake of the collapse of his original bank merger plan, reluctantly went along with the commission's recommendations. There seemed little point in hanging on to the original policy when he could not be sure that the government and the prime minister would stand firm in the face of lobbying from the owners of the stockbrokerages. The end-of-year deadline for the mergers was removed and a new rule that prohibited owners of banks from also owning a stockbrokerage was cancelled. Instead, a rule

---

11 National Economic Action Council/Economic Planning Unit, *National Economic Recovery Plan: Agenda for Action*, Kuala Lumpur, August 1998, p. 83.

was introduced which banned owners of stockbrokers from also owning property or construction interests.

Quek Leng Chan of Hong Leong Bank, Azman Hashim of Arab-Malaysian Bank and Rashid Hussain of RHB Bank benefited from the backdown, as each had a stockbrokerage (although they also had significant property interests that would be caught by the new rule). It was these three who had been among the fiercest lobbyists to convince Mahathir to overturn Daim's original bank merger plan.

Daim was disappointed with both policy reversals. He felt that the implications of the backdowns went wider than merely the stockbroking and banking sectors, in showing how government in Malaysia was conducted overall. Analysts agreed. One unnamed analyst was quoted in the *International Herald Tribune* as saying, 'It's happening again. The Malaysian authorities do yield to pressures from vested interests and are prone to policy flip flops.'[12] Daim was well aware of the perception. 'The government has now bought itself a huge problem,' he said to me in mid-2000. The backdowns showed that the government could be pressured by special interests. Mahathir, according to Daim, is 'driven' by the private sector because he feels that it is the engine of growth. Daim concurs with this approach but feels that the government also needs to take a lead in pushing and cajoling business, for its interests do not always equate with those of the nation. It was a sentiment shared by the then chairman of the Back Bencher's Club Dato' Jamaludin Jarjis. 'I agree with him', said Dato' Jamaludin. 'A lot of people find it difficult to put the national interest above their own sectional interests'. Then Defence minister Najib explained to me that his view was that, 'We must be accessible to the corporate sector, but of course one must draw the line somewhere so that the individual interests are not too overwhelming.' But Universiti Malaya Professor Mahani Zainal Abidin felt that the line might have been crossed. 'A lot of the policies had to take too much account of pressure from business during the economic crisis,' she told me in late 2000. For his part, Daim exhorted business to help maintain the march for reform. Even though the economy was recovering, it was no excuse to back peddle and to abandon the strong decisions taken by the NEAC during the crisis. 'We should not have second thoughts – all the things were consulted on and argued for, so why change?' said Azlan Hashim to me, paraphrasing Daim's view.

Consolidating the Regulatory Institutions

It was little appreciated that Daim's vision of consolidation in the banking and stock broking sectors was also matched by a desire to see consolidation in the institutions that regulate those sectors, particularly in relation to the equities market. Daim decided that the KLSE should be the principal market support

---

12 'Malaysia scraps merger deadline for brokerages', *International Herald Tribune*, 13 June 2000.

institution and was hoping to encompass more. To this end, by early 2001, the KLSE encompassed eleven separate corporate entities. It owned 100% of the offshore Labuan International Financial Exchange, while the Kuala Lumpur Options and Financial Futures Exchange (KLOFFE) was acquired by the KLSE at the end of 1998. The move enabled the rationalisation of equity and derivatives markets and the resources devoted to servicing those markets. The KLSE also controlled the Securities Clearing Automated Network Services (SCANS), and the Malaysian Central Depository. In 1999, it entered into an agreement with the Malaysian Exchange of Securities Dealing & Automated Quotation Bhd (MESDAQ) to provide clearing settlement and depository services. In March 2000, it signed an MoU with the Commodity and Monetary Exchange of Malaysia (COMMEX) that allowed for the latter to join it via KLOFFE. Included in the plans was the bringing together of SCANS and the Malaysian Derivatives Clearing House to provide more uniform clearing and settlement services. Under the auspices of Daim's National Bond Market Committee, the KLSE was also tasked with developing the trading infrastructure to establish a private bond market in Malaysia.

Under Daim's plans, investors would be able to contact a single universal dealer or broker, who would be able to trade in stocks, options and other derivatives, commodities and bonds via an amalgamated and enhanced KLSE, which in turn would be cleared and settled through an amalgamated clearing house. There would be administrative savings all round. Azlan Hashim told me that 'Tun's view and desire has always been to strive for efficiency'. He saw in consolidation enormous cost efficiencies but also greater security. Bigger institutions have greater capital reserves to withstand trading vicissitudes.

The Clob

Daim's most daring initiative during his first stint as finance minister was to split the Kuala Lumpur Stock Exchange from the Stock Exchange of Singapore. It was a bold move. There had been many hints that Malaysia was considering a split between the two exchanges, but when Daim made the formal announcement in his 1990 Budget speech (delivered in 1989), it was met with widespread media attention. The practical effect of the split was to de-list Malaysian shares from the SES. The Singapore government had been given advance warning, and when the split came the Singaporeans unilaterally introduced the Central Limit Order Book (Clob), which allowed Malaysian shares to continue to be traded in Singapore. The Malaysian cabinet was unhappy about the Singaporeans' move – it never formally recognised the Clob – but accepted an informal assurance from the Singapore leadership that the Clob would be 'temporary'.

What the Malaysian government discovered in 1997 was that Singapore's Central Depository Pte Ltd (CDPL) effectively owned the Clob and that all shares purchased through the Clob went into the CDPL. In turn, the CDPL operated accounts with Malaysia's Central Depository System (CDS) via Malaysian brokers. But the majority of these accounts were with Hwang-DBS Bhd based in Penang. So the beneficial owners of Malaysian shares traded on the Clob in Singapore did not have legal ownership of those shares as far as the Malaysian CDS was concerned. What they had was a statement from the CDPL, which summarised their stockholdings on a monthly basis.

Given that the trustees and the share owners remained the same, transactions on the Clob were not reflected on the CDS. The Singapore-based CDPL was also able to lend the shares for short selling in Clob despite regulations in Malaysia prohibiting short selling there and without the CDS even being aware that short selling was occurring. Malaysian shares could thus be short sold, leading to a fall in their price on the Clob, which would then be reflected in share prices on the KLSE as it usually moved in sympathy with Clob prices. Needless to say, it was a highly unusual arrangement and one which the Malaysian government could not be expected to tolerate indefinitely.

One of the reasons for the SES's reluctance to do away with Clob trading, despite the unhappiness of the Malaysians, was the revenues it generated for the SES. It earned clearing fees from the Clob but took little responsibility for regulating it. The Malaysians rightly claimed, however, that: 'The existence of Clob made surveillance of market manipulation, insider trading, short selling [selling borrowed shares in the hope that their price will decline], share price rigging and other illegal activities difficult and ineffective. Clob was also hampering investor protection efforts by the KLSE against such unfair market practices.'[13]

Many said at the time of the KLSE being delinked from the SES that the KLSE would collapse under mismanagement and amateurism. However, Daim introduced a range of measures to ensure greater professionalism and financial viability among Malaysia's stockbrokers. For Daim, what was important was for the KLSE to be efficient so as to be able to compete fully with the SES. In time, the KLSE did improve its operations. Its market capitalisation soon surpassed that of the SES, and by 1993 it became one of the most robust stock markets in the world, easily surpassing Singapore in terms of volume. In January 2000, volumes of around M$3.6 billion a day were recorded, and by mid-1999, approximately 750 companies were listed on the KLSE.

Daim also argued, back in 1989, that the Clob would be a temporary phenomenon. Once the KLSE introduced scripless trading, those who traded on the Clob would do so at their own risk. On this, he was wrong – the Clob did not go away of its own accord. But his warning was prophetic nonetheless. Daim had to wait until his second time as finance minister to fix the problems of Malaysian stockbroking and the Clob. He wasted no time when he did, though. It was one of the first things he attended to after his appointment in 1998.

Trading in Clob shares was suspended shortly after the Malaysian government imposed its capital controls and then formally ceased on 16 September 1998. At

---

13 From a letter from Mohamad Azam Ali, senior manager, public affairs, KLSE, published in *Asian Wall Street Journal*, 13 July 1999.

the time, there were 112 counters traded on the Clob. Along with the controls, the Malaysian authorities also disallowed the registration of ownership of Malaysian shares through trustees such that beneficial owners would in future be required to register their own names. Shares were not allowed to be traded until their beneficial owners were registered with Malaysia's CDS. Effectively, this destroyed the Clob overnight. The government claimed that its move to ban the trade of Malaysian stocks outside Malaysia was principally to prevent short-selling activities. Shares on the Clob in Singapore could still be borrowed and short sold, thus negating the Malaysian government's intentions to ban such practices on the KLSE. Many Clob investors were caught by surprise by the Malaysian government's ban. Many had not been aware that the Malaysian authorities had never formally recognised Clob trading. There were 172,000 Clob investors, mostly Singaporeans and Malaysians. Mark Mobius, president of the Templeton Emerging Markets Fund, said of the move, 'As long as Clob money is tied up like that, it's not a very good indication of their [the Malaysian government's] attitude to foreign investors.'[14] But this was not completely accurate. Many Clob investors were actually Malaysians.

The Clob shares remained frozen for more than a year, as Malaysia and Singapore could not agree on how the shares should be treated. Daim insisted that the private sector should resolve the problem, as it was essentially a private sector issue. Various proposals were submitted by companies to the KLSE, but the SES could not agree with the terms. Some of the proposals featured Malaysian companies acquiring the Clob shares at substantial discounts to their then trading price – which would have led to hefty windfall profits for those Malaysian companies had their proposals been accepted. Not surprisingly, such proposals were met with howls of outrage in Singapore. Daim, however, contends that one proposal mooted at the time originated not from Malaysia but from Singapore, from none other than the stockbrokerage Vickers Ballas, which was at the time 40% owned by the Singapore government-linked Singapore Technologies. (The CEO of Singapore Technologies at the time was Ho Ching, a daughter-in-law of Lee Kuan Yew.) Daim says that the Vickers Ballas proposal, which was never formally submitted, allowed for the brokerage to acquire the Clob shares from shareholders at discounts of up to 40% of the prevailing market price.

The impasse was not broken until April 2000. Lee Kuan Yew telephoned Daim and said that he was about to travel to the United States and he was keen to have the Clob issue resolved by the time he returned to Singapore. The lack of resolution had gone on long enough and Lee was worried it might affect Singaporeans' perceptions of their government's handling of the issue. Would Daim help? Lee offered greater cooperation from the Singapore side if Daim could oversee the Malaysian side. According to Daim, Lee explained that as many as 150,000 of the frozen Clob accounts belonged to Singaporeans and

---

14 'Templeton's Mobius still bearish on M'sia', *Business Times*, 25 September 1999.

that if each of those Singaporeans lived in a house of three voting adults, then as many as 450,000 voters would be affected by the Clob issue – and that was a huge part of the Singapore electorate. Lee felt there would be serious consequences for the ruling People's Action Party at the next elections if the Clob issue was unresolved. Singaporean officials were dispatched to Kuala Lumpur to negotiate with Daim, and over the course of a weekend a resolution was arrived at. A Malaysian-controlled company would be allowed to facilitate the transfer of the Clob shares from Singapore's CDPL, to their beneficial owners. After this, the shares would then be made tradeable on the KLSE on a staggered basis so as not to unduly disrupt the KL market. For this, the company was to receive a management fee. The plan ultimately proved popular and almost all former Clob shareholders elected to participate in it.

On Reflection

I asked Daim what had been his main failures in public life. In typical, self-effacing Malay style, he shrugged and said that there were many – too many for him to identify any one in particular. However, when pressed, he eventually said that perhaps the banking and stockbroking mergers should have been forced at the height of the economic crisis. This, he felt at least in mid-2000, had been his most significant failing. Had he sought to do it then, he would have achieved all that he wanted in these two areas. Instead, it had been left until Malaysia was in recovery and the interests that opposed such moves were in a stronger position. The irony that he had bailed out the banks and their owners, particularly during the economic crisis, and that this had allowed them to turn around and undermine his policies in the area, was not lost on him. As mentioned in Chapter 11, Daim observed that, 'If there is a failure with Malaysia Inc, it's that the private sector uses its influence with the government too much.'

I asked Daim again, in early 2015, what he considered his successes and failures in public life had been, hoping that with the passage of more than ten years his thinking might have evolved and he might have new perspectives. He seemed more sanguine and perhaps more realistic about what could have been achieved. He now seemed to have a clearer view of what his successes had been and what he reasonably could have expected to achieve. He is credited with 'saving' the Malaysian economy not once but twice, but perhaps the more enduring legacy of Daim's efforts in government are more to do with the reforms he introduced to business and the finance sector to make the economy stronger and better able to serve Malaysia's interests in a more sustained way. Daim didn't just pull Malaysia out of crisis. He put it on a far better footing compared with when it entered each crisis. He did not achieve all that he wanted but he seems to better appreciate that perhaps he was hoping for too much. Contrast his achievements with what was humanly possible by way of reform and his achievements are very great indeed.

He also feels that his efforts to propel young Malays on a business path was also a success, particularly because there are now so many more Malays in business. Daim certainly engineered a cultural change in Malaysia. In the past, said Daim, well-qualified Malays headed straight to the civil service but now, they 'want' to go into business. For Daim, that is a big change. But he is quick to offer that there have been many 'disappointments' in this regard as well. Malay culture seems to dictate that once you are successful, you tend to sit back and relax. 'Malays don't want to carry on with their success. If they make it then they withdraw – they retire – they don't carry on building and developing,' he says. He adds that 'the biggest problem with the Malays is the get-rich-quick attitude – on that nothing has changed.'

XIX

POLITICAL CUT & THRUST

Shortly before the November 1999 national elections, Daim told journalists that he would like to retire from politics at the election, although he would leave it up to Mahathir to decide if he should run again. 'With the economic revival, I actually plan to retire. Whether the time is right or not, it is the top leadership that makes the final decision.'[1] He said that he had asked not to be nominated as a candidate in the 1995 elections after his retirement from the cabinet in 1991 but had been 'directed' to stand. Ultimately, Daim didn't retire at the 1999 elections either. It was just as well. Despite the government's win, it lost 14 seats to the opposition. The minister most likely to replace Daim as finance minister, Second Finance Minister Mustapa Mohamed, lost his seat. Among the other casualties were the domestic trade and consumer affairs minister, the rural development minister, the deputy science, technology and environment minister, and a deputy minister and minister in the Prime Minister's Department. High-profile minister and later prime minister Najib Tun Razak was lucky to retain his seat. He did so by just 241 votes. It was not the sort of result one might expect from a dictatorship, as Malaysia has sometimes been simplistically portrayed overseas.

Daim was challenged in Merbok by the Keadilan party's Mochtar bin Mansor. Forces linked to the opposition sought to play up the many unproven allegations about Daim. Prior to the election, Daim's political secretary, Arzmi Hamid, was quoted as saying that everybody knew that the allegations of Daim's malpractice, cronyism and corruption which had been widely circulated on the Internet were untrue.[2] Daim went on to win his seat with a clear majority. At 30,285 votes, his support was more than twice the 14,909 votes that Mochtar received. And on 10 December 1999, Daim was reappointed finance minister.

At the national level, the opposition Islamic PAS party sought to demonstrate its relative Islamic credentials and accused Daim during the campaign of approving gambling licences for Sabah during his first stint as finance minister. Daim was able to respond that it was Anwar, and not him, who had approved the licences, as they had been granted in May 1996. The licences had been approved for slot machine outlets, Sandakan Turf Club and Diriwan Corporation. Daim claimed that he had never approved any gambling licences in his political career, and had actually closed the Social Welfare Lottery when he was finance minister the first time around.[3]

---

1 'Mustapa, Razaleigh likely Daim successors?', *Business Times*, 16 November 1999.
2 'Daim difficult to topple in Merbok', *The Sun*, 27 November 1999.
3 'Anwar approved gambling licenses', *The Star*, 27 November 1999.

Malaysia's version of democracy is frequently criticised both abroad and by some academics and non-government organisations within Malaysia. 'Elections in Malaysia don't mean as much as they should in a former British colony. Institutions still exist, but they are weak, partisan or hollow,' wrote Barry Wain in the *Asian Wall Street Journal* ahead of the 1999 national elections.[4] (Most of Malaysia's popular media are either government-controlled or highly sympathetic to the government and are particularly shameless at election time in pushing the government's case. As has been mentioned, Daim readily labelled the newspapers in the New Straits Times Group in 2000 as 'party newspapers', even though they no longer were controlled by UMNO.) Nonetheless, the casualty list of ministers and other senior government figures from the 1999 elections demonstrated that democracy in Malaysia isn't quite as blunt as some might suggest. (The 2013 general elections similarly produced an upset whereby the government won a relatively slim parliamentary majority despite winning just under half of all votes cast. Similar outcomes have on occasion occurred in the United Kingdom and Australia for example, but the Malaysia result was a direct result of quite egregious malapportionment of voters among electorates.)

The 1999 elections had given Mahathir's government a very sharp message. And the government took notice, too, as evidenced in Daim's own case by his renewed interest in making regular 'grassroots' visits to his electorate in the wake of the election result. So, the electorate had voted, delivered a message and the government was responding. Elections are yet to bring about a change of government in Malaysia, but the 1999 elections for one showed that they can bring changing government.

PAS was a big winner in the 1999 election. It retained the state government in Kelantan state and seized the state government from Mahathir's coalition in Terengganu state. It won 13 of the 14 federal seats in Kelantan and all eight federal seats in Terengganu. It also took more than half the federal seats in Kedah, Daim and Mahathir's home state. PAS's strong showing meant that it was able to replace the DAP in the federal parliament as the official opposition. The elections showed that PAS was simply not going to go away. Prior to the 1986 election, it was discovered that the financial position of the state government of Kelantan had been allowed to significantly deteriorate. The UMNO leadership resisted the temptation to find a new candidate for the post of Menteri Besar (chief minister) of Kelantan. The incumbent was re-elected and the problems in Kelantan dragged on. Rather than being nipped in the bud, they became more intractable and in 1990, the state government fell to the opposition PAS.[5] From there, PAS's strength grew.

The new PAS chief minister of Terengganu announced within two days of the 1999 elections that his government would immediately restrict the sale of alcohol

---

4   B. Wain, 'Malaysia's mock democracy', *Asian Wall Street Journal*, 26 November 1999.

5   M.S. Cheong and Adibah Amin, *Daim: The Man Behind the Enigma*, Pelanduk Publications, 1995, p. 92.

and ban gambling in the state. It also intended to make Friday and Saturday the weekend, with Sunday being a workday, similar to what had already occurred in Kelantan. A new tax of between 5% and 10% was also to be imposed on non-Muslim businesses to match the 'zakat' (tithe) taxes that Muslims already paid in that state. Accordingly, investors delivered a swift verdict on the election outcome. Despite Mahathir's apparently resounding victory, the KLSE's Composite Index fell almost 1.5% the next day, and then kept falling for the rest of the week.

Some were quick to sound the death-knell for UMNO. Academic Khoo Boo Teik wrote in an essay, 'The truth is, [Mahathir's] UMNO party no longer has a "politics as usual". Beyond the accumulated problems of chronic factionalism – policy differences, personality clashes and power struggles – UMNO is breaking down irrevocably.'[6] But party infighting is par for the course with UMNO. If politics at the national level are stultified, politics within UMNO are anything but. In the mid-1970s, Prime Minister Hussein Onn prosecuted rival Harun Idris, despite pleas from Mahathir and Daim for clemency. In the 1980s, there were the protracted bitter battles between Musa Hitam and Tunku Razaleigh Hamzah in 1981 and 1984, plus the all-out war between Mahathir's 'Team A' and Razaleigh's 'Team B' which split UMNO and led to its deregistration in 1988. The factionalism continued between 1990 and 1995 under the guises of New UMNO and Semangat '46. In 1993, Anwar Ibrahim led his 'Vision Team' to oust Ghafar Baba and Abdullah Badawi from senior positions. Khoo needn't worry. Internal fighting and manoeuvring is politics as usual for UMNO.

More disputation seemed likely in the lead-up to the May 2000 UMNO General Assembly. Tunku Razaleigh seemed likely to threaten to challenge Mahathir for the presidency of UMNO. He had little declared support and ultimately was not allowed to stand, on the grounds of a technical problem with his nomination. Possibly, this was a political misstep on the part of the UMNO leadership. Had Razaleigh been allowed to stand, almost certainly he would have been comprehensively defeated and thus politically finished. With his support level not formally tested after the UMNO elections, Razaleigh was politically alive to fight another round. He might still fight on, but what were his chances now? Was his political career over, I asked Daim. 'Who knows in politics?' he replied. Why had Razaleigh not picked up support from those UMNO branches most disaffected by the treatment of Anwar? According to Daim, Malay culture dictates that the position of leader is respected and so the person holding that position tends to be supported and this is what happened.

I asked Daim if Razaleigh would make a good prime minister. 'Razaleigh is a prince,' Daim explained, 'from a royal family. Royalty has different values.' Razaleigh as prime minister would be 'very lavish, and he would be a populist. The people would like him but he would spend a lot of money.' Daim was merely acknowledging a propensity for something that Razaleigh had shown

---

6   B.T. Khoo, 'Malaysia's political meltdown', *Asian Wall Street Journal*, 19 November 1999.

before, when he was minister for finance. Later Daim said to me that age can change people. 'I think it applies to politics too. Hopefully, politicians learn from past mistakes.'

Policy Debate

Shortly before the 1999 elections and into 2000, apparent policy differences emerged between Mahathir and Daim. The most obvious difference related to banking mergers as highlighted in the last chapter. The differences between Daim and Mahathir over the reforms were questions more of degree than substance, to be fair. One wanted to move more quickly than the other, but broadly both agreed on the destination. It was not the first such policy disagreement between the two and almost certainly would not be the last.

Daim told me in mid-2000 that since becoming finance minister a second time, he saw Mahathir often, although not always on a one-to-one basis. There were three regular meetings each week where the two met up. Tuesday was the weekly NEAC meeting at which both Daim and Mahathir were present, Wednesday was the day the cabinet had its weekly meeting, and Thursday was when a small group of key government figures, including Daim and Mahathir, held their political strategy meetings. In Daim's words, there was a weekly meeting to deal with each aspect of 'economy, cabinet and politics'.

During Daim's first period as finance minister, he unsuccessfully sought to implement a value added tax (VAT). He has been quoted as saying that his main disappointment from his first stint as finance minister was the cabinet's rejection of his VAT proposal. He had proposed that Malaysia start with a 5% broad-based tax that would be imposed on services as well as goods. He felt that the government should then see the reaction to its introduction with a view to then raising the tax. According to Daim, the then existing system of sales tax was distortionary, full of loopholes and easily evaded. VAT would eliminate a lot of the problems and force businesses to keep good books, something that would actually benefit them. Daim felt that a VAT would encourage investment, as it would reduce the government's reliance on corporate and personal taxes. He also felt that relying on these other taxes would not lead to the tax pool required to run the government. Daim pointed to the experience of the Indonesian government which saw a 30% increase in tax revenues from its introduction of a VAT. But the main opponent in cabinet to the whole proposal was none other than Mahathir. He rejected it on political grounds. He had noted the trouble such moves had caused governments in Japan and elsewhere. VAT-like taxes made economic sense but were not popular with voters. Ultimately, the government introduced the Sales and Service Tax (SST), which could be a forerunner of a VAT. Daim says he still supports VAT but not in the way it is being implemented by this Government as it has caused hardship to some groups within society.

But in 1999, the relationship had to endure a significant test. Daim's desire to force consolidation in Malaysia's banking sector was met with a subsequent backdown on the policy by the government after lobbying pressure from bank owners. The resulting policy defeat was made all the more difficult for Daim because he had insisted publicly that the policy would not be changed. Daim accepted the decision, but clearly he did not like it. In my discussions with him, he pointed out that the caving in to lobbying would make the job of government in Malaysia all the more difficult in future, but at no stage did he directly criticise Mahathir. Instead, he said of Mahathir, 'He knows that I am loyal to him and that I serve him.' And when it came to disagreements over policy matters, which Daim said were 'regular', it was he that ultimately backed down. 'He, after all, is the prime minister,' said Daim of Mahathir. Defence Minister Najib Tun Razak also spoke to me of Daim and Mahathir's relationship: 'They have a very deep and personal relationship. Like two brothers there will be disagreements from time to time. But ultimately the younger brother will defer to the older brother. It is not the disagreements that are important but how they are resolved; how they are handled.' Flexibility can be added to loyalty as reasons for why Daim stayed in favour with Mahathir for as long as he did.

Nonetheless, the now-defunct *Far Eastern Economic Review* reported in its 25 May 2000 issue that Daim had twice offered his resignation to Mahathir over the bank merger issue.[7] In our conversations, Daim was adamant that at no stage had he offered his resignation, either in writing or verbally. Nevertheless the rumours of a rift between Daim and Mahathir continued for the rest of the year and into 2000, despite denials by both men. Following the government's win at the November 1999 general election, Daim told Mahathir that he did not want to serve in the cabinet again, but Daim's obvious successor, Second Finance Minister Mustapa Mohamad, lost his seat in the elections, so Mahathir asked Daim to stay on. Daim agreed. Speaking about rumours of a rift between him and Mahathir in late 1999, Daim said, 'If there was any problem between us, I wouldn't have stood for the elections ... there is no problem between us.'[8] However, another series of events occurred which did suggest a possible rift between the two men, particularly to those intent on finding it. Daim though has his own explanations for each event.

In early 2000, Daim and Mahathir appeared to support different candidates to become the new head of Bank Negara. Daim backed Mustapa Mohamad, although, as he later told me, Mustapa hurt his own chances for the post by continuing to make partisan political comments. He had advised Mustapa to refrain from making such overt comments in the media, but Mustapa continued to do so. Civil servants, particularly senior ones in Malaysia, should at least give the appearance of being non-partisan. Mahathir backed the then deputy governor, Zeti Akhtar Aziz. It was she who was ultimately appointed. (Mahathir named Mustapa as UMNO's information chief soon after.) Daim said to me later that the portrayal of him backing Mustapa and Mahathir backing Zeti was too

7   'Parting ways?', *Far Eastern Economic Review*, 25 May 2000.

8   'No rift with PM, says Daim', *The Sun*, 7 December 1999.

229

stark. Ultimately, it was a joint decision and Mustapa's political comments had made the choice easier, though it was true that he had been Daim's initial choice.

Another event that was portrayed as evidence of a rift between Daim and Mahathir was Mahathir's appointment in mid-2000 of Nor Mohamad Yakcop as his special adviser on economic affairs – a post that had not existed before. I asked Daim how he felt about the appointment. He said that Yakcop was one of the few government officials with a good understanding of foreign exchange markets and that Mahathir brought him in to attend NEAC meetings to advise on forex issues. But was Yakcop's appointment to Mahathir's office a slight to Daim as implied by some sections of the foreign media? 'No!' replied Daim emphatically. After Yakcop resigned from the central bank, 'Mahathir had to put him somewhere,' Daim joked. Upon the retirement of bank government Ali Abul Hassan bin Sulaiman and the appointment in that role of Zeti Akhtar Aziz, Mahathir had considered appointing Yakcop as deputy governor. Daim told me that he wrote to Mahathir setting out his objections to such an appointment given the problems Daim felt had arisen during Yakcop's time at the central bank and also during his time in the private sector. Subsequently, and in light of these objections, Mahathir made Yakcop an advisor in the Prime Minister's Office and appointed him to the NEAC's Executive Committee. Daim felt that this was Mahathir's prerogative as prime minister and had no objections to these appointments, but he did not agree that Nor Yakcop should be made Deputy Governor. Mahathir could not insist as Daim said that the appointments of Governors and Deputy Governors were within his powers as Minister of Finance.

The *Far Eastern Economic Review* also reported that Abdullah Ahmad, who had taken editorial control of the New Straits Times Group, was a 'Mahathir man' and that this was yet more evidence that Daim was being squeezed out. Daim scoffed at this when I put it to him. 'I've known him longer than has Mahathir. I was the one who recommended that he be released from ISA detention, I recommended that his wife go to London even though she was not in the foreign service but in the home service [this meant that Abdullah could go to London as well – he wanted to shift there temporarily for his own reasons] and I recommended him for a Tan Sri. He reports to us both.' If Abdullah was a 'Mahathir man', then in Daim's eyes there was no reason why he was not also a 'Daim man'. (Abdullah died of cancer in 2015.)

At around the same time, Mahathir rejected a bid by Singapore Telecom to buy 20% of Renong subsidiary Time dotCom. The *Review* also offered the reversal as further evidence of differences between Mahathir and Daim. Daim had backed the deal and Mahathir had reversed it, claimed the *Review*. Daim offered a different explanation to me. Approval for the deal in the first place was not granted by Daim but by Mahathir. Daim claims he was neither happy nor unhappy with the offer, as it was purely a private sector deal and he could therefore see no reason to intervene. In such a situation he would grant approval automatically, which he says should not be taken as a sign that he backed any particular proposal but rather that he did not want to stand in its way. Nonetheless, he did remark that once a decision is made, it is usually best if it is stuck to. Generally, policy reversals do not make for good government, although Daim concedes that it is the government's right to change its mind, particularly in the light of new information. He felt that, perhaps initially, insufficient thought had been given to the Singapore Telecom deal, which then meant the government had to reverse its approval. For a time, government in Malaysia appeared to have become more uncertain. Partly, a consequence of this was the slide in the KLSE's Composite Index around June 2000, when most other bourses in the region were experiencing gains. Investors do not like policy uncertainty.

The Singtel deal would have meant a substantial cash injection for the heavily indebted Renong subsidiary, as well as valuable skills transfer for the company. However, key to Mahathir's objections was the fact that Singapore Telecom is a Singapore government-linked company. As if to underscore its government connections, it was headed by a son of Lee Kuan Yew. Mahathir was understandably concerned that a foreign government would end up with close ties to what he considered an important Malaysian company. His concerns received added legitimacy little more than a month later in early July 2000 when the US Federal Bureau of Investigation (FBI) registered its security-related concerns with the Treasury Department about a plan by Japan's Nippon Telegraph & Telephone (NTT) to take over US Internet service provider Verio Inc. Whereas Mahathir's concerns were portrayed by some as further evidence of his xenophobic and nationalistic tendencies, the FBI's concerns were simply reported as a straight news story.[9] To portray the reversal of the approval for Singtel to buy 20% of Time dotCom in terms of a possible rift between Daim and Mahathir seemed simplistic. (In any event, the shares were sold to a Singapore company, during the premiership of Abdullah Badawi.)

Nevertheless, the rumours of a rift did not abate and the two men tried all manner of ways to reassure the media that they were working together as usual despite their occasional policy differences. Mahathir told reporters at the UMNO General Assembly in May 2000 that 'there have been many reports about rifts between me and Daim for ages. Ever since Tun joined the Government they have been saying he doesn't get along with me ... Yet in times of crisis, he joined the Government and helped solve some of our problems. Before this there was also talk, but somehow or other we still smile at and hug each other, and we still run the Government, I think quite successfully.'[10] Mahathir also announced that he had reappointed Daim as UMNO's treasurer.

Daim told a Malaysian newspaper, 'I agreed to join the government for one purpose and that is to help revive the economy and then be allowed to leave.

---

9 See 'NTT plan triggers US security fears', *Asian Wall Street Journal*, 7 July 2000.

10 'Talk of rift with Daim not new says Dr Mahathir', *Business Times*, 12 May 2000.

11 As reported in 'Daim says he's "absolutely loyal" to Mahathir', *Business Times*, 12 June 2000.

The PM agreed and when that happens is between me and him.'[11] He said in the same interview, 'Why did you think I returned to the Government if not to help Mahathir? The premier has done a lot for the country. I feel at ease working for him.' Deputy Prime Minister Abdullah Badawi also chipped in and said in a television interview, 'He [Daim] works well with the PM. I think the two men understand each other very well. They may have some differences of opinion in certain things but the most important thing is that when a decision is made, both of them are fully behind the decision made.'[12] Daim did finally resign in 2001. By then he had felt that he had contributed as much as he could, and it was time to return to his other interests.

Daim became bored with his work, which had become routine, during the last few years of his first stint as finance minister. As has been mentioned, he considers that he stayed on too long and should have resigned much earlier than he did. Daim enjoys a challenge. He likes to get things done. Unless there are reforms to be made, a healthy economy is not something that holds his interest as finance minister. He told me that he had started to reread the letters that he had sent to Mahathir during his first stint as finance minister in the 1980s. He remarked how repetitive things seemed. The issues then were still the issues that dominated public policy in Malaysia towards his second stint at the finance ministry. He said with a hint of exasperation that, on reading the letters, he was surprised at how little things had changed. Some of the letters produced interesting revelations. Daim was already talking about corporate governance back then and had also written to the prime minister about issues such as the need for stock broking mergers and the promotion of venture capital. These things had not been taken care of, so it seemed there was still work to be done. Quite possibly, the policy challenges and debates of Daim's second time as finance minister ensured that he would not grow bored in the job, at least not too soon, and that paradoxically, he would prefer to leave later rather than sooner.

12 CNBC Asia broadcast, 12 June 2000.

XX

THE LATER YEARS

Daim's final, formal departure from politics occurred in 2001. Did he leave under his own steam? Was he pushed? Did Mahathir want him to go? Had they fallen out? The Kuala Lumpur rumour mill was working overtime. But as is so often the case, the truth was not nearly as exciting as the speculation. Daim had simply had enough. He was tired of government and tired of politics. For years, so much of his focus had been on Malaysia's domestic problems. The economic crisis in which Malaysia had found itself the second time had largely been worked through and Daim could see no more major mountains to climb, and no more complex policy riddles to be worked through that couldn't be handled by others. He was restless and as intellectually curious as ever. It was time for Malaysia's Ibn Battuta to again turn his focus to his own interests and to abroad.

In 2004, Daim did not seek re-election to Parliament and retired from politics. Instead, he turned his mind to business and building up his network of foreign banks. His ICB Group had been founded between his stints as finance minister, and his final departure from politics allowed him more time to spend on the Group.

ICB first opened banks in Prague in the Czech Republic, and Budapest in Hungary in 1993. Thereafter, the group expanded with banking licenses in Africa and elsewhere and grew to also encompass banks in Djibouti, Sierra Leone, Gambia, Mozambique, Ghana, Guinea, Malawi, Tanzania, Senegal, Zambia, Indonesia, Laos, Bangladesh and Albania. Typically, each bank was small, and the total assets of the group generally were under $2 billion. The banks were niche operators in small economies, but Daim figured economies of scale could be generated by opening a chain of banks across borders.

In 2007, the holding company for the banking group, ICB Financial Group Holdings, was listed on the London Alternative Investment Market (AIM), a part of the London Stock Exchange, with Daim retaining a majority shareholding. The main purpose of the listing was to achieve a market valuation for the group to allow it to better raise finance. But there was also a prestige element. Daim wanted to prove that his bank – his creation – was successful and accepted by independent investors. He told me that he wanted to prove that Malaysians and most particularly Malays can succeed anywhere in the world and have the capacity to compete globally instead of looking inward and waiting for government handouts.

ICB delisted from AIM in 2012. Daim felt that he had grown ICB's international network as far as he could. The growing need for banks everywhere to have a stronger capital base meant that it was difficult to expand the banks further without taking on new and substantial investors. By now in his seventies, Daim decided it was preferable to sell up. Little by little, operations in the various countries were sold off. In 2013, for example, the banks in Sierra Leone, Gambia, Guinea, and Ghana were sold to a Nigerian bank, and its banks in Malawi, Mozambique and Zambia were sold to a Malawi bank. Before Daim sold these interests, he wrote to Prime Minister Najib to inform him of his intent and to let the prime minister know that he would be very happy to sell the interests to a Malaysian bank should it want to access the African market, but Najib replied that he was unable to get any Malaysian banks interested.

As mentioned, putting together a group of banks in some of the world's most difficult economies was an enormous achievement. Few business people anywhere have achieved such a thing and very few Malaysians have. But not everyone saw it that way. Daim's achievements continued to attract innuendo from those who felt there could be some gain in propagating it. Anwar Ibrahim, who was by now Malaysia's opposition leader, asked in a meeting in early 2014 with the Tanzanian president, finance minister and central bank governor, to confirm that Daim had established a bank in Tanzania. He also asked where the money had come from. Anwar claimed that Daim was 'stashing' Malaysian money overseas. Take away the political hyperbole and Daim's efforts would simply have been defined as a straightforward act of foreign investment. No-one, for example, would describe the Malaysian-Chinese Hong Leong Group's acquisition of a new hotel in London as 'stashing' Malaysian money in the UK, or, indeed, Dell's opening of a new facility in Penang as 'stashing' American money in Malaysia.

Anwar claimed to have subsequently brought Daim's control of a Tanzanian bank to the attention of Malaysia's Anti-Corruption Commission and Daim was investigated. Once again, Anwar produced no evidence of any wrongdoing. Daim jokingly suggested that maybe Anwar was not aware of the Money Laundering Act which was passed after his dismissal. The reality of Daim's action was that he had founded a bank and was now earning investment income for Malaysia. In other countries he would be given a business award. But not in Malaysia, which seemed to be becoming increasingly inward-looking. In 2006, Daim was named by *African Investor* magazine as its 'International Business Leader' for that year. Previous winners of the award are Microsoft Founder Bill Gates, and Virgin Atlantic founder Richard Branson. Daim's efforts were recognised in Africa at least.

Property still remains one of his interests. Indeed, some of the funds from the ICB sales were re-invested into property. An apartment block in Kuala Lumpur was developed and sold off, and other real estate forays were made. But in 2011, Daim commenced something on an entirely different scale.

Construction started on the Ilham Tower, a 274-metre, sixty-storey office and apartment tower on Jalan Binjai in Kuala Lumpur's so-called 'Golden Triangle' office district. Entirely privately owned and half-funded by Daim's own reserves, with the other half coming from borrowings, it certainly puts the lie to claims that Daim was sending money overseas. In truth, the project was one of the largest single, private investments in Malaysia ever undertaken by a Malay. It is a big statement – a beacon perhaps – at a time when Daim still decries the lack of commercial land in Malaysia's towns and cities in private Malay hands. 'Less than one percent' is in private Malay hands he claims. He said that he wants it to be a reminder to other Malays of what is possible.

Daim had the tower designed by the London-based architects Foster+ Partners, one of the world's best known, top-end architectural firms. As Daim says, they engaged the firm to design the tower in the midst of the 2009 recession in Europe and the US when little new buildings were being commenced, and so he was able to drive a hard bargain with the London-based firm.

The tower is not as tall as the nearby Petronas Towers which come in at just under 452 metres high, but is almost as tall as London's Shard Tower which is 284 metres tall without the architectural spire that was added to the tower's top. The Shard is the tallest building in Western Europe.

The building was commenced when there was no shortage or even a forecast shortage in the premium commercial property market in Kuala Lumpur. 'Isn't this very risky?' I asked Daim in 2014 just as the building was 'topped off'. 'Yes!' he said with a slight giggle and a glint in his eye. 'But that's what I like. I've always taken risks.' He conceded that the project was taking up all the available cash he had, and for the first time in a while, he was having to be careful with how he spent his money.

Daim has done very well in business, but how does he feel about the state of Malay business today? Despite the NEP and despite the government's policy of targeting particular Malay entrepreneurs for selective advancement, Daim still feels that Malays are inadequately represented in business. The Malays themselves are partly to blame according to Daim. In London in 2015, he told me that too many Malays still want immediately to be the managing director of whatever enterprise they enter. They need to be prepared to start from the bottom and work their way up, he said. They need to learn and to copy.

But even for capable Malays, the biggest problem still was their relative inability to get finance. And when they can, too often the banks are very quick to foreclose. Daim recommends that many young Malays work with local Chinese businesses first. 'Go and work for them and learn from them', he told me. 'Learn not just how they do business but about their culture and particularly their business culture – how they control costs and so on. Learn the language, and even better if you marry them!' Many Malays work for the local offices of multi-nationals and whilst this provided good training according to Daim, it still is not enough. The multi-nationals, according to Daim, teach you about management rather than business. They have not proven to be good incubators for successful Malay entrepreneurs.

For Daim, the Malays have learned a little but not enough. In 2014, he said at a forum hosted by the Malay Entrepreneurs and Merchants Association that the assets held by Malays in Malaysia's cities was still too low. 'Basic business knowledge, mathematical skills, foreign languages, and the concept of profit and loss should also be inculcated since young, so that business culture could grow in Malay society', he was quoted as saying.[1] He also criticised the apparent ineffectiveness of government agencies aimed at helping the Malays – even though there was a big number of such agencies, there seemed to be little improvement of Malay business involvement in the towns and cities.

What advice does Daim have today for Malays wanting to go into business? His advice has changed little over the years, largely because it is based on his own success. As he says, he is not an expert on how to achieve in business, he can only offer advice based on his own experiences. In a speech to business students at Universiti Utara Malaysia (UUM) in March 1995, he advised students that they should ask themselves if they really wanted to succeed before they embarked on business. And if they did want to succeed, did they have the strength, stamina and discipline to match that desire?

They also had to choose the right business: '…there is absolutely no point in going into a business that you have absolutely no interest in…Work should be satisfying, something you look forward to, otherwise you will give up at the slightest hint of a problem.'

He nominated hard work and more hard work as a key determinant for success. Controlling costs was another. '…it is not, I repeat, not necessary to ensure success that you must have a big office, many staff and a Mercedes-Benz. These are burdens that you don't need when you are starting.' For Daim, too many young Malay entrepreneurs wanted the trappings of success before they had the success itself. Too little has changed in this regard in his view. Says Daim in relation to his Taman Maluri project, 'I was at the site day and night to solve problems. I never put off tomorrow what I could do today. Every day of delay costs money. Interest accumulates even when you are sleeping.' Nor did he surround himself with unnecessary staff. He took on as few as was needed to keep costs down. 'I was also everything from manager to office boy.' And when he did need outside help, he did not take people on as employees but as consultants so that he could avoid all the employee on-costs that employees bring. He advised that those staff that are taken on must be good. 'Be firm but fair', he exhorted. But he is not sentimental. 'Take good care of your staff and they will take good care of your business. But the lazy ones must be sacked. Don't allow them to destroy the good ones.'

Later in the speech, he advised, 'Do not be greedy. Greed destroys your self-respect. Do not worship money that you would lose your morals and lose your religion for money.' And when success comes: 'Just because you have made lots of money, do not then think that you are superior to or better than the next person. The small courtesies in life are still important – return phone calls, answer letters, show up on time, be polite, diplomatic, considerate. Money in the bank is not a license to be rude or arrogant. Neither does it mean that you have to flaunt your

---

1   Bernama, 'Daim urges Bumiputera to venture into business', April 22, 2014.

wealth.' This is certainly advice that Daim has himself always followed. In my interviews with business and political leaders who have interacted with Daim, the one word they all used to describe him was 'humble'.

The growing insularity of some Malays in an increasingly global and integrated world worries Daim. As has been mentioned, even back in 1995, he said in the speech that, 'Some Muslims believe this world is for the non-Muslims, that Muslims should only pray and think of the hereafter. So why go into business and make money? ... For the Malays and Muslims, we have to change that belief. It is a wrong interpretation of the Islamic faith. I have yet to come across any religion that discourages its followers from doing business. As long as it is not haram (forbidden) and your business practices are not immoral, I cannot see any reason why Muslims cannot pursue a career in business.'[2] If anything, Daim's concerns in this regard have grown since then. Religious debates of a type that had never or rarely occurred among the Malays seem to have been imported from the Middle East, and rather than promote Malay development, they are tending to undermine it.

Corruption in Malaysia is another concern. 'Corruption has got worse,' he told me in London in 2015. He felt that Mahathir had been too soft in dealing with corruption and that Najib as prime minister (he was appointed in 2009) had said the right things about dealing with corruption but had not done them. By early 2015, the current Malaysian government under Najib seemed beset by allegations of corruption, infighting and scandal. The malaise of the government under Najib reached a new low in mid-2016 when the US government moved to confiscate assets in the US which it believed had been stolen from a Malaysian government development fund, 1MDB.

Daim said to me that he wondered if it might be best if Tunku Razaleigh or some other candidate acceptable to both sides of the political divide be installed instead as a compromise prime minister to allow UMNO time to heal its divisions and prepare for the next election. Politically, this would be preferable to holding an early election which would bad for UMNO and perhaps more particularly, risky for the broader community with the potential for unrest.

I asked Daim, when looking back, what roles in public life he regrets not having had. His answer is immediate. 'Mayor of Kuala Lumpur!' he said. 'Why?' I asked. 'Because development in Kuala Lumpur has become so ugly, and corrupted.' He feels that more could have been done to plan new areas and buildings better. But after more thought he also nominated another role: 'Attorney general – to clean up the mess and to charge with corruption all those who should be charged.'

Some of Daim's most strident criticism is reserved for Malaysia's judiciary. It is an area in which he takes a keen interest as a former lawyer. At the time of his resignation from his first stint as finance minister, he wrote to Mahathir to say that Malaysia was producing too many lawyers and that those resources

---

2   Daim, Z., 'Managing business: My personal experience', speech to business students at Universiti Utara Malaysia (UUM), published in March 1995.

should be directed to educating students in other disciplines. Too many lawyers would make Malaysia excessively litigious. 'Business cannot afford it,' said Daim of what he had written to Mahathir. 'America can because it is a rich country. It can afford lots of lengthy court cases and litigation, but Malaysia cannot.' For all the resources put into the legal and judicial system in Malaysia, Daim still has concerns over the quality of the outcomes that it produces.

He said to me that there is a perception in Malaysia that some judges and prosecutors 'are not clean'. But that is not the only concern. Both he and Mahathir were 'very disappointed' with the quality of judicial decisions. 'I get the impression that when they are appointed, they try to please the government. That is not their role ... They should not be pro-government – but pro-justice ... The judges are independent, so why do they behave as they do?' According to Daim, some members of the judiciary feel that they should do the government's bidding, but then had gone overboard to the point of embarrassing the government. Back in 2000 when he and I discussed this Daim cited by way of example the fact that every single petition against a successful UMNO candidate arising from the 1999 general elections that had been lodged with the election judges had been dismissed for technical reasons. To Daim, such a situation was clearly ridiculous. Electoral laws allowed a candidate to seek a recount if the majority in the seat is 2% or less. Those candidates that sought recounts on this basis usually did so after the final count has been announced. But, according to Daim, the election judges had invariably dismissed the petitions by saying that the candidates should have lodged the petition earlier on in the count, but as Daim says, how can a candidate know that he or she is entitled to a recount under the 2% margin rule until the count has been finalised and the final winning margin is revealed? On top of that, no appeals were allowed, although Daim had less trouble with this, as each constituency had a right to representation and lengthy appeals would have left some without representation.

Post-politics also allowed Daim to spend more time with his younger children. He admits that for most of his life in business and politics, his family had to take a backseat, and that too often he was an absent father. Certainly, one does get a sense that Daim was a late developer when it came to parenting skills. In this regard, Daim is very much a product of his own upbringing. The youngest of thirteen children, Daim got to spend little time with his father – there was simply too much competition for his father's time and so consequently, he was a remote figure.

But since leaving politics, Daim has spent more time with his two youngest sons and actually seems to have enjoyed parental responsibilities. He has tried to make up for his lack of hands-on parenting with his other children by ensuring that they and their mothers are all looked after financially. The trusts that Daim has established for his children and their mothers means that there has been a clean and even distribution of his wealth. Inheritance issues have been settled and there should be no need for infighting over assets. His daughter continues to run Taman Maluri, the main real estate venture in Kuala Lumpur that was the primary, initial source of his wealth, essentially as her own venture, with little input from Daim. His oldest son has various business involvements but again, these are quite apart from Daim's involvements. Daim's two youngest sons are still in school and university. They are doing very well, having studied hard and gained entry to some of the UK's most prestigious academic institutions under their own steam. Will they go into business? Daim doesn't know. He has no plans to push them. His maxim to the Malay business students that you should only go into business if it really interest you and you are prepared to work hard at it holds even for his sons. But Daim seems to be satisfied. A well-deserved place in Malay and Malaysian history, an extraordinary political career, stellar business achievements, and now some clever sons. Daim can rest easy – his legacy is assured, although resting is not something he is accustomed to.

BIBLIOGRAPHY

Abidin, Mahana Zainal, *Rewriting the Rules: The Malaysian Crisis Management Model*, Prentice Hall, 2002.

Backman, Michael, *Asian Eclipse: Exposing the Dark Side of Business in Asia*, John Wiley & Sons, 1999; 2001.

Cheong Mei Sui and Adibah Amin, *Daim: The Man Behind the Enigma*, Pelanduk Publications, 1995.

Cheong, Sally, *Bumiputera Entrepreneurs in the KLSE*, CRS, 1996.

Daim Speaks his Mind, Pelanduk Publications, 1995.

East Asia Analytical Unit, *Asia's Financial Markets: Capitalising on Reform*, Commonwealth of Australia, Canberra, 1999.

Finance Committee on Corporate Governance, *Report on Corporate Governance*, Kuala Lumpur, February 1999.

Gomez, Edmund Terrence, *Political Business: Corporate Involvement of Malaysian Political Parties*, James Cook University, 1994.

Gomez, Edmund Terrence, *Chinese Business in Malaysia*, Curzon, 1999.

Ismail Noor and Muhammad Azaham, *The Malays: Par Excelence...Warts and all*, Pelanduk Publications, 2000.

Jomo, K.S. (ed.), *Malaysian Eclipse: Economic Crisis and Recovery*, Zed Books, 2001

Khoo, Boo Teik, *Paradoxes of Mahathirism*, Oxford University Press, 1995.

Lee, Kuan Yew, *From Third World to First: Singapore and the Asian Economic Boom*, Harper Collins, 2011.

Mahathir Mohamad, *The Malay Dilemma*, Times Books International, 1970.

Mahathir Mohamad, *The Malaysian Currency Crisis: How and Why it Happened*, Pelanduk Publications, 2000.

National Economic Action Council/ Economic Planning Unit, *National Economic Recovery Plan: Agenda for Action*, Kuala Lumpur, August 1998.

Searle, Peter, *The Riddle of Malaysian Capitalism*, Allen & Unwin, Sydney, 1999.

World Bank, *The East Asian Miracle*, Oxford University Press, 1993.

INDEX